Vital Records of Pittsburg New Hampshire 1904-2008

Richard P. Roberts

HERITAGE BOOKS
2009

HERITAGE BOOKS
AN IMPRINT OF HERITAGE BOOKS, INC.

Books, CDs, and more—Worldwide

For our listing of thousands of titles see our website
at
www.HeritageBooks.com

Published 2009 by
HERITAGE BOOKS, INC.
Publishing Division
100 Railroad Ave. #104
Westminster, Maryland 21157

Copyright © 2009 Richard P. Roberts

All rights reserved. No part of this book may be reproduced or transmitted in any form or by any means, electronic or mechanical, including photocopying, recording or by any information storage and retrieval system without written permission from the author, except for the inclusion of brief quotations in a review.

International Standard Book Numbers
Paperbound: 978-0-7884-5027-3
Clothbound: 978-0-7884-8248-9

TABLE OF CONTENTS

Introduction 1

Births 5

Marriages 77

Deaths 175

INTRODUCTION

Early vital records of many New Hampshire towns can be located either through the State's Vital Records Department or on microfilms made available through LDS Family History Centers. Some, however, have been lost or are inaccessible for various reasons. A valuable, but labor intensive, source of information for events occurring in 1887 and thereafter is the vital statistics which are provided in a section of the Annual Town Reports of many New Hampshire towns. Many of these town reports have been collected at the New Hampshire State Library in Concord, as well as more local repositories.

The amount of information published in these Annual Town Reports varies tremendously over time. Early records are far more detailed and comprehensive. Recent records are rather cursory, but issues of confidentiality amd sensitivity to the privacy of those residents still living offsets the lack of information of genealogical value.

While the information provided is often very helpful, one must keep in mind that it is not fool-proof or universally accurate, nor is it the primary source or the actual vital record itself. The fact that much of the data is self-reported suggests that it is reliable. However, errors in transcription, spelling (particularly with respect to French-Canadian and European families), and printing are often obvious. In addition, there may be, for example, two children listed as the third child of a particular couple, or the mother's maiden name, age or place of birth differs or is inconsistent from one entry to another. It is also important to note that a birth, marriage or death may have been reported in another town although the subject resided in Pittsburg, or the entry may not have been made in the first place.

Despite these shortcomings, the information contained in the Annual Town Reports can be a valuable tool for the genealogist. Marriage and death records from the late 1800's iften identify parents who were married nearly a century before. Finally, those families that have remained in Pittsburg or adjacent towns for several generations can be traced and connected to the present. Unfortunately, Pittsburg failed to report the vital statistics in its annual reports until 1904, so the information from prior years is not readily available.

Births – To the extent that the information is available, the entries in the list of births are given as follows: child's name; date of birth; place of birth (where provided); the number of children in the family; father's name, place of birth, age and occupation; and the mother's maiden name, age and place of birth. As noted above, the amount of information in earlier records is substantially greater than in more recent years.

At times, the given names of many children are missing from the early records. In this case, the sex of the child is given and they are listed chronologically at the beginning of the surname heading. On occasion, the child's name can be determined from marriage or death records, as well as secondary sources.

Marriages – To the extent that the information is available, the entries in the list of marriages follow this format: groom's name; groom's residence; bride's name; bride's residence; date of marriage; place of marriage (where provided); H, signifying husband's information and W, signifying wife's information, each in the following order – age, occupation, number of the marriage (if other than the first), father's name, father's place of birth, father's occupation, mother's name, mother's place of birth, and mother's occupation. The name of the official conducting the marriage has been omitted but is generally provided in the original document. A separate listing of brides in alphabetical order follows this section in order to allow for cross-referencing.

Deaths – To the extent available, the entries in the list of deaths contain the following information: name of decedent; date of death; place of death; age at death; cause of death; marital status; birthplace; father's name; father's place of birth; mother's name; and mother's place of birth.

BIRTHS

AHEARN,
Nicholas Brian, b. 6/22/1991; Nicholas Eugene Ahearn and Deborah Ann Defeo

ALDRICH,
son, b. 8/3/1908; M/M Willie Aldrich
daughter, b. --/--/1914; M/M Fred Aldrich
daughter, b. 6/15/1925; M/M Henry Aldrich

ALLARD,
Jean Pierre, b. 12/18/1999 in Lebanon; Jean Pierre Allard and Arlene Allard

ALLEN,
daughter, b. 3/17/1915; M/M Harry S. Allen

AMEY,
son, b. 10/14/1924; M/M Holman Amey
daughter, b. 9/20/1928; M/M Holman J. Amey
daughter, b. 5/16/1931; M/M Holman Amey
Alicia Jane, b. 8/5/1988; Paul Roger Amey and Arcia Ann French
Brian Roy, b. 4/30/1972; Roy Edward Amey and Laurel Joyce Gray
Dianna Marie, b. 8/4/1976; Roy Edward Amey and Laurel Joyce Gray
Dottie Jane, b. 9/14/1953 in W. Stewartstown; Holman J. Amey and Dorothy Sprague
Emily Cayenne, b. 4/15/1988; John Holman Amey and Nancee French
Eric John, b. 12/27/1978; John Holman Amey and Deborah Arline Locke
Janeen Louise, b. 5/19/1976; John Holman Amey and Deborah Arline Locke
John Holman, b. 12/25/1949 in W. Stewartstown; Holman J. Amey and Dorothy Sprague

Kassandra Donna, b. 7/9/2001 in Colebrook; Brian Amey and
   Martine Amey
Kristina Diane, b. 10/29/1970; Roy Edward Amey and Laurel
   Joyce Gray
Mark Everett, b. 6/30/1952 in W. Stewartstown; Holman J. Amey
   and Dorothy M. Sprague
Micah Patrick Joseph, b. 2/27/1991; John Holman Amey and
   Nancee French
Nathaniel French, b. 5/14/1985; John Holman Amey and Nancee
   French
Paul Roger, b. 11/23/1956; Holman Josiah Amey and Dorothy
   Myrtle Sprague
Roy Edward, b. 2/26/1951 in W. Stewartstown; Holman J. Amey
   and Dorothy Sprague

ANDERSON,
Donald George, b. 7/6/1949 in W. Stewartstown; Mallet
   Anderson and Dorothy Hawes
Kristina Gale, b. 1/24/1947 in W. Stewartstown; Mallet Anderson
   and Dorothy Hawes
Michael Brian, b. 7/8/1943 in W. Stewartstown; Mallet A.
   Anderson and Dorothy F. Hawes
Yasmin Lee, b. 3/25/1998 in Colebrook; Ryan Anderson and
   Dallas Eileen Anderson

AUDETTE,
Adria Lenore, b. 4/6/1961; Rene Girard Audette and Marion
   Helen Wess
Armand Gerard, b. 10/5/1963; Rene Gerard Audette and Marion
   Helen Wess

BACON,
son, b. 11/26/1908; M/M Willie H. Bacon
son, b. 2/1/1910; M/M W. H. Bacon

daughter, b. 12/13/1911; M/M W. H. Bacon
son, b. 12/29/1927; M/M Gladstone Bacon
daughter, b. 4/3/1930; M/M Gladstone Bacon
Florence L., b. 12/19/1900; William H. Bacon and Nellie Sanborn (1962)
John Henry, b. 11/25/1947 in W. Stewartstown; James H. Bacon and Thelma B. Fogg
Robert Claude, b. 8/21/1935; Claude S. Bacon and Irma Philbrook
Walter Guy, b. 1/16/1905; James Henry Bacon and Archmese Favreau (1963)
William Austin, b. 8/26/1939 in W. Stewartstown; James H. Bacon and Thelma B. Fogg

BALDUCE,
son, b. 1/12/1924; M/M Paul Balduce

BALDWIN,
son, b. 5/30/1908; M/M Frank W. Baldwin
son, b. 4/8/1911; M/M F. W. Baldwin

BALL,
Crystal Kay, b. 7/12/1948 in W. Stewartstown; William Ball and Julia Jordan

BARNES,
Ronald Douglas, b. 12/9/1968; Ralph Douglas Barnes and Priscilla June Smith

BARRY,
Dayna Hamilton, b. 7/24/1971; Alan Richard Barry and Eleanor Gay Hart

BEARMIS,
daughter, b. 3/26/1917; M/M Pete Bearmis

BEAUCHEMIN,
Christina Speros, b. 10/18/1969; Gene Leonard Beauchemin and Virginia Alice Lagoulis
Colleen E., b. 8/21/1962; Gene Leonard Beauchemin and Virginia Alice Lagoulis
Marie Louise, b. 5/19/1971; Gene Leonard Beauchemin and Virginia Alice Lagoulis
Pearl Alice, b. 8/2/1932; M/M Eddie Beauchemin
Victor F., b. 10/16/1964; Gene Leonard Beauchemin and Virginia Alice Lagoulis

BEAUDOIN,
Carol Marguerite, b. 12/12/1952 in W. Stewartstown; Marcel Beaudoin and Aline L. Cusson

BEGIN,
daughter, b. 7/30/1921; M/M Octave Begin
Timmy Joe, b. 8/17/1982; Richard Louis Begin and Judy Ann Jameson

BELOIN,
son, b. 11/1/1912; M/M Nelson Beloin
Colette Monique Marie, b. 3/4/1958; Alcide Ernest Beloin and Yvette Leona Maurais
Jessica Mei-Ling, b. 11/14/1981; Pierre Alcide Beloin and Tracy Hong Lu
Joseph Guy L., b. 5/20/1955; Alcide Ernest Beloin and Yvette Leona Maurais
Leona Louisa, b. 5/19/1959; Alcide Ernest Beloin and Yvette Leona Maurais
Nicol M. S., b. 4/1/1943 in W. Stewartstown; Germain Beloin and Martha Gagnon
Susanne Mary Ann, b. 3/12/1952 in W. Stewartstown; Alcide Beloin and Yvetta L. Maurais

BELOIS,
son, b. 5/7/1919; M/M Nelson Belois

BENNETT,
Luke Anthony, b. 9/15/1981; Anthony Frank Bennett and Holly Ann Firda

BERGERON,
Marie Pauline Lilane, b. 9/6/1933; Zephir Bergeron and Virginia Minard

BERMAN,
Sonya Jeanne, b. 4/13/1963; Wesley Richard Berman and Doris Pauline Abrahamson

BERNHARDT,
William Douglas, b. 1/16/2008 in Lancaster; William Bernhardt and Emily Bernhardt

BERRY,
son, b. 2/19/1904; M/M Fred Berry
Arthur Merle, b. 1/28/1934; Arthur Merton Berry and Lena Mae Wheeler
Randall Carl, b. 5/9/1945 in Pittsburg; Arthur Berry and Lena Wheeler
Richard C., b. 12/7/1941 in Pittsburg; Arthur M. Berry and Lena Mae Wheeler

BERRYMAN,
James Edward, Jr., b. 2/27/1951 in W. Stewartstown; James E. Berryman, Sr. and Thelma Woodsworth

BIBBO,
James Vincent, IV, b. 10/27/1970; James Vincent Bibbo, III and Donna Lee Lindsay
Jeffrey Lindsey, b. 11/27/1972; James Vincent Bibbo, III and Donna Lee Lindsay

BILODEAU,
Lucile Irene, b. 11/4/1940 in W. Stewartstown; Harvey Bilodeau and Yvonne Fillion

BIRON,
Michael Albert, b. 12/8/1959; Roland Romeo Biron and Monica Claudette Giguere

BISSONNETTE,
Marie C. R., b. 1/14/1948 in W. Stewartstown; Alphonse Bissonnette and Georgette Blouin
Raymond B., b. 10/27/1951 in W. Stewartstown; Alfonse Bissonnette and Georgette Blouin

BLAIS,
son, b. 12/20/1920; M/M Gideon Blais
son, b. 5/1/1922; M/M Roy Blais
son, b. 2/8/1924; M/M Roy L. Blais
son, b. 12/16/1925; M/M Roy L. Blais
Brenda Lee, b. 7/10/1957; Roland Roy Blais and Leona Effie Edes
Dennis George, b. 5/22/1951 in W. Stewartstown; Howard W. Blais and Madeline Tenny
Donald Ray, b. 7/25/1947 in W. Stewartstown; Howard W. Blais and Madeline Tenny
Howard Wayne, b. 4/10/1950 in W. Stewartstown; Howard W. Blais and Madeline Tenny

BLANCHARD,
Dennis Roy, b. 2/23/1947 in W. Stewartstown; Roy Blanchard and Bernadine Hicks
Elaine Clair, b. 9/17/1972; Eric Guy Blanchard and Suzanne Elaine Leigh
James Talbot, b. 2/17/1962; William Guy Blanchard and Beverly Irma Jeffers
Michael Eric, b. 8/19/1975; Eric Guy Blanchard and Suzanne Elaine Leigh
Peter Gerald, b. 6/28/1978; Eric Guy Blanchard and Suzanne Elaine Leigh

BLODGETT,
daughter, b. 6/7/1912; M/M Arthur Blodgett
daughter, b. 1/9/1915; M/M Arthur Blodgett
daughter, b. 8/24/1918; M/M Arthur Blodgett

BOLDUC,
Brianna Lynne, b. 1/9/1989; Michael Leslie Bolduc and Katherine Ann Marie Bourassa
Joseph Peter, b. 3/15/1943 in Pittsburg; Royal J. Bolduc and Yvonne Facteau

BOLTON,
Angela Mae, b. 8/23/1983; William Ernest Bolton and Florence Lorene Cunningham
Ashley Lorene, b. 4/9/2003 in Littleton; Daniel Bolton and Julie Bolton
Jennifer Augusta, b. 2/19/2005 in Lancaster; Daniel Bolton and Julie Bolton

BOURASSA,
Marie Lynn, b. 5/25/1957; George Joseph Bourassa and Nellie Leonida Cayouette

Rose Anne, b. 10/28/1952 in Berlin; George J. Bourassa and Nellie Cayonette

BOUTIN,
Matthew Scott, b. 11/16/1995 in Colebrook; Ronald Matthew Boutin and Shannan Marie Boutin
Saralyn Jeannine, b. 8/19/1981; Gerald Gilles Boutin and Kelly Lynn Gould
Seth Michael, b. 2/24/1984; Gerard Gill Boutin and Kelley Lynn Gould

BOYCE,
Jessica Frances, b. 1/12/1981; Richard Stillman Boyce and Andrea Alexis Spiewak

BRIAN,
son, b. 2/26/1919; M/M Robert H. Brian

BROOKS,
son, b. 10/28/1905; M/M Fred Brook
daughter, b. 9/27/1908; M/M Walter E. Brooks
daughter, b. 9/15/1923; M/M Francis Brooks
daughter, b. 8/26/1924; M/M Francis Brooks
Lillian Mae, b. 9/1/1938 in W. Stewartstown; Charlie Brown and Reva Brooks
Martha Ann, b. 3/10/1954; Lester Melrose Brooks and Theresa Claire Cote
Russell Edward, b. 9/10/1937 in Pittsburg; Leo M. Brooks and Margaret N. Allen
William Francis, b. 2/23/1941 in W. Stewartstown; Reva Brooks

BROWN,
son, b. 12/8/1904; M/M George C. Brown
daughter, b. 12/26/1904; M/M Isaac Brown
son, b. 1/16/1905; Annie Brown

son, b. 9/26/1905; M/M Elwin Brown
son, b. 2/23/1917; M/M Elwin Brown
son, b. 1/10/1919; M/M Herbert L. Brown
daughter, b. 6/6/1920; M/M Herbert Brown
daughter, b. 7/1/1924; M/M Herbert Brown
daughter, b. 4/21/1927; M/M Isaac Brown
child, b. 11/18/1928; M/M Herbert Brown
daughter, b. 10/16/1930; M/M Isaac Brown
Bruce Elwin, b. 4/4/1949 in W. Stewartstown; Allen W. Brown
    and Harriet Fuller
Carroll Sue, b. 7/8/1947 in W. Stewartstown; Alfred Brown and
    Virginia Clogston
Danny Lyle, b. 12/23/1949 in W. Stewartstown; Alfred P. Brown
    and Virginia Clogston
Hilda Francis, b. 4/1941 in W. Stewartstown; Otis J. Brown and
    Barbara Lapoint
Jennifer Lee, b. 7/4/1947 in W. Stewartstown; Isaac Brown and
    Leitha Young
Kelly Clogston, b. 11/2/1953 in W. Stewartstown; Alfred P.
    Brown and Virginia Clogston
Lance Harry, b. 6/1/1951 in W. Stewartstown; Floyd H. Brown
    and Shirley Woodsworth
Larry Miles, b. 6/16/1950 in W. Stewartstown; Floyd H. Brown
    and Shirley Woodworth
Leslie Herbert, b. 12/16/1946 in W. Stewartstown; Floyd Brown
    and Shirley Woodworth
Margaret Susan, b. 12/24/2007 in Lancaster; Jeremy Brown and
    Karrie Brown
Merry Lee, b. 6/17/1955; Floyd Harry Brown and Shirley Alice
    Woodworth
Wallace Merrill, b. 2/8/1935; Isaac Brown and Mable Merrill
William Dean, b. 12/8/1938 in W. Stewartstown; Allen Brown and
    Harriet F. Fuller

BRUNELLE,
David A., b. 7/15/1941 in W. Stewartstown; Clark Brunelle and Hazel Anderson

BRUNGOT,
Joanne, b. 6/19/1966; Norman Stanley Brungot, Jr. and Jacqueline Margaret Covey
Kimberly Anne, b. 9/12/1972; Norman Stanley Brungot, Jr. and Jacqueline Margaret Covey
Norman Stanley, 3rd, b. 4/4/1969; Norman Stanley Brungot, Jr. and Jacqueline Margaret Covey
Sharon Sophia, b. 5/31/1967; Norman Stanley Brungot, Jr. and Jacqueline Margaret Covey

BRYANT,
Raelene Marie, b. 7/15/1961; Ray Allen Bryant and Jean Crawford
Rozanne Lee, b. 8/2/1956; Ray Allen Bryant and Jean Crawford

BUFFINGTON,
Robert E., b. 5/27/1940 in Pittsburg; Elmer Buffington and Leora Marsh

BUMFORD,
Cheryl, b. 3/18/1948 in W. Stewartstown; Albert Lestage and Donna Bumford
Frederick Schoff, b. 1/5/1938 in Pittsburg; Edson Bumford and Viola D. Schoff
Jill, b. 3/27/1941 in Pittsburg; Edson Bumford and Viola Schoff

BURGESS,
daughter, b. 11/14/1922; M/M Neil Burgess
daughter, b. 11/17/1924; M/M Neal Burgess
daughter, b. 12/26/1926; M/M Neal Burgess

BURRILL,
Marrisa June, b. 5/29/1990; Paul Kingman Burrill and Wanda June White
Matthew Kingman, b. 6/16/1993 in Colebrook; Paul Kingman Burrill and Wanda June Burrill

BUTEAU,
Gerard Emile, b. 9/3/1964; Andre Joseph Emile Buteau and Edith Elizabeth Lord

CAMERON,
Deanna Lea, b. 9/2/1975; George Allen Cameron and Corinne Brown

CAMPBELL,
Ashley Marie, b. 8/25/1993 in Lebanon; John Joseph Campbell and Marivic Ortega Campbell

CARLSON,
Carl Timothy, b. 3/4/1963; Carl Thomas Carlson and Beverly Jean Bishop
Heather Lea, b. 7/19/1965; Carl Thomas Carlson and Joanne Ila Jackson
Jodi Elizabeth, b. 9/5/2007 in Berlin; Glenn Carlson and Sondra Carlson
Karen Marie, b. 2/18/1967; Carl Thomas Carlson and Joanne Ila Jackson
Tammy Jean, b. 12/28/1959; Carl Thomas Carlson and Beverly Jean Bishop
Thomas Charles, b. 5/27/1971; Carl Thomas Carlson and Joanne Ila Jackson

CATURIER,
son, b. 11/9/1917; M/M Archie Caturier

CHALOUX,
son, b. 4/28/1914; M/M George Chalaux
daughter, b. 3/2/1916; M/M Charles Chaloux
daughter, b. --/11/1917; M/M Charles Chaloux
daughter, b. 12/21/1918; M/M Charles Chaloux
son, b. 3/23/1920; M/M Charles Chaloux
daughter, b. 5/28/1923; M/M Albert Chaloux
daughter, b. 7/7/1927; M/M Albert Chaloux
son, b. 11/7/1927; M/M Joseph Chaloux
son, b. 4/5/1929; M/M Joseph Chaloux
son, b. 7/8/1931; M/M Joseph Chaloux
Brigitte Marie, b. 4/3/1961; Raymond Leo Chaloux and Celine Jeannine Tetreault
Joseph Leo Raymond, b. 1/3/1936; Joseph Chaloux and Cealere Benoit
Joseph Lionel, b. 2/27/1934; Joseph Chaloux and Celanese Benoit
Joseph William, b. 3/16/1943 in Pittsburg; Joseph Chaloux and Celanese Benoit
Leo Napoleon, b. 6/5/1943 in Pittsburg; Leon Chaloux and Jennett Moulleur
Marie Claire, b. 7/14/1942 in Pittsburg; Leon Chaloux and Jeanette Molleur
Mary Cecile Aline, b. 8/30/1937 in Pittsburg; Joseph Chaloux and Celanise Benoit

CHAMBERLAIN,
Stacy Lynn, b. 10/7/1974; William Arthur Chamberlain and Ramona Jean Lewis

CHAPPELL,
son, b. 12/30/1918; M/M Ernest Chappell
daughter, b. 6/16/1924; M/M Pearl Chappell
Susan Adella, b. 2/29/1948 in W. Stewartstown; Colon Chappell and Doris Prescott

CHASE,
Logan William Judd, b. 5/24/1993 in Colebrook; Warren Eric Chase and Kim Rae Judd Chase
Marcus Warren Judd, b. 3/26/1992; Warren Eric Chase and Kim Rae Judd
Mitchell Adam, b. 2/16/2000 in Colebrook; Troy Chase and Nancy Chase
Travis Joseph Judd, b. 6/7/1995 in Colebrook; Warren Eric Chase and Kim Rae Judd Chase

CHICONIE,
daughter, b. 9/9/1908; M/M Peter Chiconie

CLARK,
daughter, b. 8/17/1910; M/M Willie Clark
Robert Covill, b. 8/6/1935; Kenneth R. Clark and Ruth M. Covill

CLOGSTON,
son, b. 1/8/1908; M/M William H. Clogston
son, b. 10/27/1928; M/M Clifton Clogston
son, b. 1/19/1929; M/M Paul Clogston
daughter, b. 7/9/1930; M/M Clifton Clogston
son, b. 8/27/1931; M/M Clifton Clogston
Bruce Wayne, b. 1/12/1951 in W. Stewartstown; Clifton Clogston, Jr. and Irma F. Lord
Cindy Joy, b. 5/31/1953 in W. Stewartstown; Clifton W. Clogston, Jr. and Irma F. Lord
Crystal Ann, b. 4/13/1947 in W. Stewartstown; Keith Clogston and Dorothy Dalton
Dale Clifton, b. 1/21/1953 in W. Stewartstown; Edmund L. Clogston and Geneva M. Covell
Donna Lee, b. 11/28/1949 in W. Stewartstown; Clifton Clogston, Jr. and Irma Lord
Edmund Linden, b. 7/25/1934; Clifton Clogston and Evelyn Day

Janice Hope, b. 6/16/1949 in W. Stewartstown; Keith W. Clogston and Dorothy Dalton
Jennifer Suzanne, b. 3/21/1984; Ricky Clifton Clogston and Helen Camille Madore
Lorna Jean, b. 12/19/1963; Edmund Lyndon Clogston and Linda Jean Washburn
Marc Roger, b. 12/11/1959; Edmund Linden Clogston and Barbara Ann Bennett
Michael Linden, b. 12/11/1959; Edmund Linden Clogston and Barbara Ann Bennett
Ricky Clifton, b. 7/24/1959; Clifton Wood Clogston, Jr. and Irma Francese Lord
Sarah Lee, b. 4/21/1981; Bruce Wayne Clogston and Cheryl Elaine Owen
Sheree Dawn, b. 8/20/1979; Bruce Wayne Clogston and Cheryl Elaine Owen
Steven Thomas, b. 8/10/1982; Ricky Clifton Clogston and Helen Camille-Marie Madore
Vicki Ann, b. 9/18/1967; Edmund Lyndon Clogston and Linda Jean Washburn

CONROY,
Kara Lee, b. 12/28/1968; Robert Edward Conroy and Marie Leona Roppel
Kimberlee Sue, b. 8/24/1964; Robert Edward Conroy and Marie Leona Roppel

COUTURE,
son, b. 6/1/1929; M/M Archie Couture
Natasha Lynn, b. 3/16/1995 in Colebrook; Ricky Paul Couture and Shelley Lynn Couture

COVELL,
son, b. --/--/1906; M/M Grant Covell
son, b. 6/6/1909; M/M Grant Covell

daughter, b. 12/19/1910; M/M Everett Covell
son, b. 6/4/1923; Sadie Covell
son, b. 11/8/1923; M/M Everett Covell
daughter, b. 12/10/1927; M/M Shirley Covell
Darrel Frederick, b. 12/10/1966; Lesley Lafe Covell and Ruth Helen Foote
Diane Ruth, b. 8/30/1959; Leslie Lafe Covell and Ruth Helen Foote
Earl William, b. 6/19/1933; Wilbur Covell and Ledora Philbrook
Gary Winston, b. 11/24/1940 in Pittsburg; Forrest Covell and Hilda A. Dearth
Gregory Earle, b. 3/4/1953 in W. Stewartstown; Earle W. Covell and Nancy A. Young
Julieanne Hilda, b. 3/23/1960; Gordon Leonard Covell and Noma Elizabeth Lynch
June, b. 4/17/1933; Reginald Covell and Josephine Gilbert
Mark Lesley, b. 9/3/1960; Lesley Lafe Covell and Ruth Helen Foote
Matthew Edwin, b. 7/9/1975; Lesley Lafe Covell and Ruth Helen Foote

COVEY,
Lori Irene, b. 4/13/1969; Ernest Victor Covey and Sharon Lee Patterson
Scott Ernest, b. 6/4/1972; Ernest Victor Covey and Sharon Lee Patterson

COVILL,
son, b. 9/9/1905; M/M Everett Covill
son, b. 9/12/1927; M/M Forest Covill
son, b. 10/21/1928; M/M Forrest Covill
son, b. 12/12/1929; M/M Forrest Covill
son, b. 11/7/1930; M/M Forest Covill
daughter, b. 9/8/1931; M/M Reginald Covill

Cindy Lynn, b. 2/8/1963; Gordon Leonard Covill and Norma Elizabeth Lynch
Craig Robert, b. 1/31/1961; Robert Dearth Covill and Margaret Crawford
Danielle Lee, b. 7/14/1984; Roger Gordon Covill and Deborah Marie Slack
David Gerald, b. 4/13/1955; Lindsey Leroy Covill and Roberta June Merrill
Deborah Margaret, b. 2/24/1951 in W. Stewartstown; Lindsey L. Covill and Roberta J. Covill
Dennis Lindsey, b. 3/3/1950 in W. Stewartstown; Lindsey L. Covill and Roberta Merrill
Dwayne Otis, b. 1/31/1965; Gary Winston Covill and Hilda Francene Brown
Forrest Alfred, b. 8/3/1948 in W. Stewartstown; Bernard Covill and Katherine Banks
Forrest Alfred, II, b. 7/21/1968; Forrest Alfred Covill and Linda Ellen Keezer
Gail Hope, b. 5/23/1944 in W. Stewartstown; Clesson Covill and Alice Chappell
Geneva Maude, b. 7/27/1934; Forest Alfred Covill and Hilda Addie Dearth
Joanne Elaine, b. 5/22/1936; Forest Covill and Hilda Dearth
Keith Warren, b. 7/6/1935; Reginald Covill and Josephine Gilbert
Lafe Stephen, b. 8/28/1968; Gordon Leonard Covill and Norma Elizabeth Lynch
Larry Gene, b. 11/13/1941 in Pittsburg; Reginald Covill and Josephine Gilbert
Leslie Lafe, b. 6/15/1940 in Pittsburg; Forest A. Covill and Hilda A. Dearth
Linda Lou, b. 6/15/1939 in Pittsburg; Forest A. Covill and Hilda A. Dearth
Lori Ellen, b. 8/26/1969; Forrest Alfred Covill and Linda Ellen Keezer

Mandi Marie, b. 4/5/1981; Roger Gordon Covill and Deborah Marie Slack
Mark David, b. 10/11/1954; Earl Wilbur Covill and Nancy Arleta Young
Michael Everett, b. 6/29/1958; Robert Dearth Covill and Margaret Crawford
Myrna Ray, b. 4/4/1944 in W. Stewartstown; Reginald Covill and Josephine Gilbert
Robin Lee, b. 8/25/1965; Gordon Leonard Covill and Norma Elizabeth Lynch
Roger Gordon, b. 5/4/1958; Gordon Leonard Covill and Norma Elizabeth Lynch
Shawn Ray, b. 10/7/1963; Robert Dearth Covill and Margaret Crawford
Sheridan James, b. 12/4/1948 in W. Stewartstown; Paul Raynolds and Madeline Covill
Sherwood G., b. 7/14/1939 in Pittsburg; Clesson Covill and Alice Chappell
Whitney David, b. 12/2/1992; David Gerald Covill and Cheryl Ann Mackey
Zacharie Roger, b. 12/25/1988; Roger Gordon Covill and Deborah Marie Slack

CRAWFORD,
daughter, b. 4/18/1904; M/M Almon F. Crawford
daughter, b. 10/18/1914; M/M A. J. Crawford
daughter, b. 1/6/1931; M/M Carroll Crawford
son, b. 5/31/1934; Orrie Crawford and Doris Cook
Edwin Lee, b. 3/25/1936; Orrie Crawford and Doris Cook
Ellen, b. 11/8/1937 in W. Stewartstown; Orrie Crawford and Doris Cook
Ethel Caroline, b. 7/7/1937 in W. Stewartstown; Carroll Crawford and Caroline Dorman
Nancy E., b. 7/18/1942 in W. Stewartstown; Carroll E. Crawford and Caroline Dorman

Robert, b. 4/27/1939 in W. Stewartstown; Orrie L. Crawford and Doris Cook

CRETE,
Yolande, b. 3/30/1946 in W. Stewartstown; France Crete and Blanche Hebert

CROSS,
Rachel Marie, b. 6/20/1984; Ricky Dale Cross and Penny Lea McKeage

CURRIER,
daughter, b. 8/4/1919; M/M Harold Currier
son, b. 10/14/1924; M/M Harold Currier

CUSHMAN,
Martha, b. 6/8/1941 in W. Stewartstown; James A. Cushman and Leola B. Butler

DAIGNAULT,
Helen Constance, b. 11/2/1947 in W. Stewartstown; Ulde Daignault and Ida Parriseau

DALTON,
Merrill Albert, b. 1/27/1940 in Pittsburg; Albert Dalton and Lois Gray

DANFORTH,
daughter, b. 3/8/1904; M/M Willis J. Danforth
daughter, b. 2/19/1908; M/M Willie J. Danforth
son, b. 3/25/1914; M/M Addison B. Danforth

DANIELS,
Delaney Crystal, b. 3/10/2003 in Littleton; Stephen Daniels and Michele Daniels

DANIS,
daughter, b. 10/20/1924; M/M James Danis

DAVIS,
daughter, b. 8/19/1921; M/M Frank Davis
Paris Hannah Florance, b. 7/14/2004 in Lebanon; Peter Davis and Tracy Davis
Savannah Rayn, b. 11/21/2006 in Littleton; Peter Davis and Tracy Davis

DAY,
son, b. 4/29/1907; M/M Orie L. Day
daughter, b. 10/1/1907; M/M Lyle Day
daughter, b. 6/27/1910; M/M Lyle Day
son, b. 8/27/1910; M/M Irving Day
daughter, b. 2/23/1916; M/M Rufus Day
son, b. 7/20/1931; M/M Harry Lee Day
Gerald Alfred, b. 3/11/1947 in W. Stewartstown; Alfred Day and Geraldine Forbes
Heather Ann, b. 9/3/1978; Gerald Alfred Day and Anna Marie Bruno
Helen Marvis, b. 2/28/1948 in W. Stewartstown; Alfred E. Day and Geraldine Forbes
Howard Edwin, b. 2/28/1948 in W. Stewartstown; Alfred E. Day and Geraldine Forbes
Jacob Michael, b. 1/22/2005 in Lancaster; Michael Day and Darlene Demont
Jean Muriel, b. 10/21/1936; Holman Day and Ramona Haynes
Joane May, b. 6/12/1935; Holman H. Day and Romona Haynes
Kenneth Edward, b. 4/2/1934; Wendall Day and Hallie Clark
Lizzie Belle, b. 9/3/1886 in Pittsburg; Parker T. Day and Mary A. Day (1953)
Michael Lyle, b. 9/23/1976; Gerald Alfred Day and Anna Marie Bruno

Robert Wilman, b. 7/15/1945 in Pittsfield; John W. Day and Helen P. Hurd
Shauna Jane, b. 10/8/1972; Howard Edwin Day and Terry Mae Scott

DEARTH,
son, b. 3/22/1927; M/M Israel Dearth
Betty Ann, b. 11/9/1955; Warren William Dearth and Rebeccah Hall
Juanita Irene, b. 10/8/1949 in W. Stewartstown; Warren W. Dearth and Rebecca Hall
Melinda Jean, b. 1/11/1953 in W. Stewartstown; Warren W. Dearth and Rebecca H. Hall
Robert Warren, b. 12/5/1950 in W. Stewartstown; Warren W. Dearth and Rebecca Hall

DECATO,
Mackrissa Mildred, b. 1/9/2008 in Berlin; Christopher Decato and Jodie Decato

DEGRAY,
Madison Clare, b. 3/8/2006 in Lancaster; Charles DeGray and Aimee DeGray

DELABURE,
son, b. 7/31/1921; M/M Hector Delabure

DELMARES,
son, b. 10/4/1915; M/M Esclear Delmares

DENT,
Eric James, b. 9/23/1964; Brian Lee Dent and Margaret Elaine Jacobson

DESCHENE,
Martha A., b. 4/4/1941 in W. Stewartstown; George O. Deschene and Florence Shatney

DESROCHERS,
Ashley Chantale, b. 7/19/1992; Michael Alan Desrochers and Nathaniel Chantale Couture

DEWITT,
Baylee Jaden, b. 7/27/2002 in Colebrook; Michael DeWitt and Susan DeWitt

DOBSON,
Betty Jo, b. 10/31/1973; Brandon James Dobson and Janice Hope Clogston
Tina Marie, b. 8/12/1967; Brandon James Dobson and Janice Hope Clogston

DORE,
daughter, b. 5/12/1928; M/M Cleveland Dore
Christine May, b. 9/9/1952 in Nueces, TX; Cleveland H. Dore, Jr. and Rosalie J. Andrews

DORMAN,
daughter, b. 8/23/1910; M/M Walter Dorman
son, b. 2/7/1927; M/M Thomas Dorman
son, b. 4/4/1931; M/M Thomas Dorman
Angela Jean, b. 1/16/1980; Wayne Edward Dorman and Beverly Jean Gadwah
Benjamin French, b. 12/8/1943 in W. Stewartstown; Thomas Dorman and Evelyn E. Haynes
Betsey E., b. 2/22/1941 in Pittsburg; Thomas Dorman and Evelyn E. Haynes
Brian Thomas, b. 2/20/1981; Walter Douglas Dorman and Brenda Emily Barton

Courtney Lee, b. 4/19/1983; Wayne Edward Dorman and Beverly Jean Gadwah
Emily Marion, b. 9/17/1979; Walter Douglas Dorman and Brenda Emily Barton
Erica Lynn, b. 6/23/1976; Wayne Edward Dorman and Beverly Jean Gadwah
Gloria Evelyn, b. 8/26/1933; Thomas Edward Dorman and Evelyn E. Haynes
Lance Michael, b. 12/14/1984; Winston Arnold Dorman and Sherry Lynn Bryant
Melissa Ann, b. 9/1/1977; Sherman Alan Dorman and Janet Lee Young
Sherman A., b. 8/15/1936; Thomas Dorman and Evelyn Haynes
Walter Douglas, b. 8/23/1957; Thomas Edward Dorman, Jr. and Ervina Hicks Dorman
Wanda Jean, b. 3/23/1961; Thomas Edward Dorman, Jr. and Ervina Marilyn Hicks
Wayne Edward, b. 12/26/1952 in W. Stewartstown; Thomas Dorman, Jr. and Ervina M. Hicks
Wendell Lindon, b. 12/1/1954; Thomas Edward Dorman, Jr. and Ervena Hicks
Winston Arnold, b. 1/29/1956; Thomas Edward Dorman, Jr. and Ervena Marilyn Hicks

DORR,
son, b. 1/23/1919; M/M Cleveland Dorr

DUBE,
daughter, b. 5/30/1923; M/M Meryle Dube
Collin Richard Reeves, b. 4/11/1998 in Colebrook; Richard Norman Dube II and Stephanie Jo Dube
Jeremy Michael, b. 3/26/1984; Jean Marcel Dube and Linda Rose Smith
Madison Crystal Patricia, b. 4/27/2001 in Colebrook; Richard Dube and Stephanie Dube

Richard, b. 7/9/1953 in W. Stewartstown; Eugene A. Dube and Alice I. Brousseau

DUCETT,
daughter, b. 3/2/1925; M/M Nelson Ducett

DUNSTAN,
Jesse Bernard, b. 2/20/1997 in Colebrook; Thomas Frank Dunstan and Susan Jean Reich Dunstan

DUQUETTE,
daughter, b. 5/22/1925; M/M Narcisse Duquette
daughter, b. 2/2/1927; M/M Nelson Duquette

DURENLEAU,
son, b. 4/7/1922; M/M A. Durenleau

DWINALLE,
son, b. 4/29/1923; M/M Azero Dwinalle

EDWARDS,
Donald Roy, b. 7/9/1968; Roy Douglas Edwards and Myrna Lee Washburn

EGAN,
Brennan Joseph, b. 11/6/2003 in Lancaster; Christopher Egan and Kimberly Egan

ELLIOTT,
Lesett Lynn, b. 7/13/1972; Douglas James Elliott and Sandra Joann Harris

FAHERRIEN,
Joseph Roger, b. 10/25/1934; Oliver Faherrien and Evone Benoit

FARNSWORTH,
daughter, b. 2/26/1916; M/M Earl C. Farnsworth
daughter, b. 9/2/1918; M/M Earl Farnsworth

FARRAR,
Cedric Ivan, b. 7/31/1941 in W. Stewartstown; Herman Farrar
    and Leona P. Merrill
Curtis Wayne, b. 12/15/1938 in W. Stewartstown; Wayne Farrar
    and Leona P. Merrill
Faye Louise, b. 10/3/1936; Wayne Farrar and Leone Merrill
Linda Irene, b. 5/1/1940 in W. Stewartstown; Herman W. Farrar
    and Leona P. Merrill

FIRSETTE,
daughter, b. 7/10/1909; M/M George Firsette

FISH,
Blaine Delma, b. 2/15/1952 in W. Stewartstown; Delma H. Fish
    and Bernice R. Schoff
Jarvis Thurman, b. 2/20/1944 in W. Stewartstown; Delma H. Fish
    and Bernice R. Schoff
Marshall S., b. 11/16/1940 in W. Stewartstown; Delma H. Fish
    and Bernice R. Schoff
Rosalie, b. 6/3/1939 in W. Stewartstown; Delma Hall Fish and
    Bernice Ruth Schoff
Tia Charlene, b. 10/12/1962; Marshall Schoff Fish and Jane
    Harriet Masters

FLANDERS,
Nina Marie, b. 4/21/1943 in Pittsburg; Gordan Flanders and
    Jeanne Paquette
Randall Everett, b. 6/5/1954; Robert Brooks Flanders and Mary
    Lou Holden
Sandra, b. 12/27/1935; Gordon M. Flanders and Bernice R.
    Schoff

FOGG,
Meredith A., b. 9/30/1942 in Pittsburg; Leland M. Fogg and Katherine Shallow
Miriam Kay, b. 12/28/1944 in W. Stewartstown; Leland Fogg and Katherine Shallow
Muriel Louise, b. 5/30/1941 in Pittsburg; Leland Fogg and Katherine Shallow

FOOTE,
Brenda Kay, b. 2/13/1962; Frederick James Foote and Joanne Elaine Covell
Jarvis Nathan, b. 6/25/1960; Frederick James Foote and Joanne Elaine Covell
Nathan Frederick, b. 11/17/1987; Jarvis Nathan Foote and Jane Marie Waterhouse
Tyler Andrew, b. 6/16/1992; Jarvis Nathan Foote and Jane Marie Waterhouse

FORTIER,
Joseph R. K., b. 8/10/1940 in Berlin; Arthur Fortier and Juliette F. Belanger

FRENCH,
son, b. 9/2/1920; M/M Azel French
son, b. 6/5/1924; M/M Wilbur G. French
daughter, b. 5/28/1925; M/M Wilbur French
Ann Marie, b. 4/23/1979; Melvin Otis French and Linda Ann Crawford
Brian Azel, b. 2/29/1948 in W. Stewartstown; Lovell L. French and Daphyne Clogston
Bruce Neil, b. 10/6/1938 in Pittsburg; Azel H. French and Leone Lapoint
Cheryl Lynn, b. 1/16/1949 in W. Stewartstown; Lovell L. French and Daphne Clogston

Dale Brian, b. 3/28/1966; Brian Azel French and Jennifer Lee
    Brown
Gail Elaine, b. 7/22/1944 in W. Stewartstown; Lovell French and
    Daphyne Clogston
Janet Louise, b. 10/16/1950 in W. Stewartstown; Wayland
    French and Erma Covill
Maureen Burke, b. 8/31/1998 in Colebrook; Daniel McNeil
    French and Hilary Pagel French
Melvin Otis, b. 7/31/1949 in W. Stewartstown; Otis E. French and
    Julia Dobson
Peggy Wanda, b. 2/28/1977; Melvin Otis French and Linda Ann
    Crawford
Rachel Violet, b. 9/8/1949 in W. Stewartstown; Wayland W.
    French and Emma Covill
Sally Faye, b. 5/7/1934; Azel French and Leone LaPoint

FRESETTE,
son, b. 9/11/1907; M/M George H. Fresette

FRIZZELL,
Blaine Carl, b. 5/7/1988; Bradley Alan Frizzell and Heidi Lynne
    Curtis
Bronson Gray, b. 7/22/1985; Wayne Alpheus Frizzell and
    Pamela Jane Gray
Hannah Lynne, b. 12/16/1983; Bradley Alan Frizzell and Heidi
    Lynne Curtis

FULLER,
daughter, b. 6/11/1914; M/M Frank Fuller
son, b. 1/18/1915; M/M Andrew C. Fuller
daughter, b. 2/28/1916; M/M Frank Fuller
son, b. 8/1/1916; M/M Andrew Fuller
son, b. 2/6/1918; M/M Andrew Fuller
David James, Jr., b. 2/27/1977; David James Fuller, Sr. and
    Katharyn Margaret Bishop

GALIPEAU,
Olivia, b. 8/30/2008 in Berlin; Anthony Galipeau and Brittany Fernald

GARCELON,
Deborah Jean, b. 5/10/1963; David C. Garcelon and Helen K. Mousseau
Jan Helen, b. 4/25/1964; David Charles Garcelon and Helen K. Mousseau

GILBERT,
daughter, b. 5/28/1925; M/M Austin Gilbert

GLEASON,
Gavin Martin, b. 5/26/2004 in Lebanon; Michael Gleason and Monica Evans

GOODWIN,
Dana Allen, b. 1/29/1973; Douglas Stewart Goodwin and Constance Violet Haynes

GOULETTE,
David Ralph. Jr., b. 11/6/1964; David Ralph Goulette and Frances Alberta Sweeney
Loren Raymond, b. 9/25/1992; David Ralph Goulette, Jr. and Lisa Marie Harding

GRAY,
son, b. 4/23/1925; M/M Leroy Gray
son, b. 7/1/1928; M/M Merrill A. Gray
son, b. 4/27/1931; M/M Merrill Gray
Aidan Owen, b. 5/19/2008 in Berlin; Seth Gray and Jamie Gray
Arnold Edson, b. 10/18/1960; Robert Young Gray and Donna Adeline Bumford

Ashley Nicole, b. 1/28/1987; Arnold Edson Gray and Lucie Aline Madore
Christopher Robert, b. 12/16/1983; Arnold Edson Gray and Lucie Aline Madore
Harold Winston, b. 6/25/1954; Tabor Patrick Gray and Eunice Elaine Jeffers
Heather, b. 9/5/1962; Robert Young Gray and Donna Adeline Bumford
Holly Ruth, b. 12/30/1954; Robert Young Gray and Donna Adeline Bumford
Karen Lee, b. 7/28/1956; Robert Young Gray and Donna Adeline Bumford
Keith Elwin, b. 9/29/1961; Tabor Patrick Gray and Eunice Elaine Jeffers
Laurel Joyce, b. 6/30/1951 in W. Stewartstown; Robert Y. Gray and Donna Bumford
Leonard Roy, b. 8/26/1957; Tabor Patrick Gray and Eunice Elaine Jeffers
Lindsey Robert, b. 11/21/1952 in W. Stewartstown; Robert Y. Gray and Donna A. Bumford
Marilyn Rachel, b. 7/15/1985; Lindsey Robert Gray and Ann Marden Getchell
Melanie Beth, b. 11/7/1987; Lindsey Robert Gray and Ann Marden Getchell
Pamela Jane, b. 5/5/1958; Robert Young Gray and Donna Adeline Bumford
Sarah Louisa, b. 9/9/1980; Lindsey Robert Gray and Ann Marden Getchell
Seth Patrick, b. 12/23/1982; Lindsey Robert Gray and Ann Marden Getchell

GROVER,
son, b. 3/6/1930; M/M Glen Grover
Aneka Marie, b. 1/25/1988; William A. Grover and Judith Ann Coutts

Brendon Adna, b. 12/11/1932; M/M Glen Grover
Brendon Bradley, b. 5/12/1990; William A. Grover and Judith
 Ann Coutts
Brittany Ann, b. 6/18/1992; William A. Grover and Judith Ann
 Coutts
Cathy Ramona, b. 1/2/1958; Brendon Adna Grover and Joan
 Mae Day
Peter Brendon, b. 11/12/1967; Brendon Adna Grover and Joan
 Mae Day
Veronica Jean, b. 9/29/1953 in W. Stewartstown; Brendon A.
 Grover and Jean M. Day
William A., b. 6/17/1962; Brendon Adna Grover and Joan Mae
 Day

GUAY,
son, b. 7/26/1919; M/M Omar Guay
daughter, b. 7/20/1920; M/M Homer Guay
daughter, b. 5/22/1922; M/M Homer Guay

GUILMETTE,
Caleb James, b. 6/18/2004 in Lancaster; Jeremy Guilmette and
 Ann Guilmette
Summer Ann, b. 4/4/2006 in Lancaster; Jeremy Guilmette and
 Ann Guilmette

HALEY,
Kirk Philip, b. 3/19/1988; Philip Edward Haley and Sharon Lee
 Boucher

HALL,
son, b. 5/14/1925; M/M George Hall
son, b. 7/9/1929; M/M Vernon Hall
daughter, b. 1/9/1931; M/M Vernon Hall
Alberta Geneva, b. 11/30/1935; Vernon Hall and Christie Hawes

Burton Hawes, b. 7/13/1934; Vernon Haynes Hall and Christie Rebecca Hall

David George, b. 9/30/1938 in W. Stewartstown; Vernon Hall and Christie Hawes

Michael David, b. 3/8/1964; David George Hall and Elsie June Eames

Neal George, b. 9/16/1958; Burton Hawes Hall and Fay Anita Locke

Richard Burton, b. 7/18/1955; Burton Hawes Hall and Fay Anita Locke

Terri Lynne, b. 8/5/1961; David George Hall and Elsie June Eames

Verna Ruth, b. 3/7/1932; M/M Vernon Hall

HANN,

Ashley Marie, b. 3/29/1987; David Edward Hann and Mishawn Cassandra Grinnell

Beverly Lillian, b. 10/2/1938 in W. Stewartstown; Austin Hann and Lillian Wheeler

Bradley Austin, b. 9/9/1945 in W. Stewartstown; Austin Hann and Lillian Wheeler

Dakota Scott, b. 11/4/1989; Kelly Scott Hann and Lorraine Faith Ladd

David Edward, b. 10/6/1962; Gerald Edward Hann and Eva Elnora Huggins

Jade Elizabeth, b. 9/3/1988; Kelly Scott Hann and Lorraine Faith Ladd

Jamie Marie, b. 12/1/1963; Gerald Edward Hann and Eva Elnora Huggins

Kelly Scott, b. 12/24/1960; Gerald Edward Hann and Eva Elnora Huggins

Kenneth K., b. 5/30/1943 in W. Stewartstown; Kenneth W. Hann and Irene M. Harmon

HARDEN,
Daniel Arthur, b. 6/18/1966; James Patrick Harden and Margaret Ann Stuekey

HAWES,
son, b. 8/4/1904; M/M B. A. Hawes
son, b. 1/20/1905; M/M A. J. Hawes
daughter, b. --/--/1905; M/M L. A. Hawes
daughter, b. 12/1/1920; M/M George W. Hawes
son, b. 10/6/1928; M/M Vernon R. Hawes
Sophie Geneva, b. 2/4/1952 in W. Stewartstown; Russell Hawes and Mabel M. Haynes
Stephen Warren, b. 10/9/1948 in W. Stewartstown; Russell V. Hawes and Majel M. Haynes

HAWKINS,
Clyde Lee, b. 3/27/1963; Everett Owen Hawkins and Martha Ada DesChene
Desiree Marie, b. 8/28/1983; George Owen Hawkins and Any Ellen Farrar
George Owen, b. 8/1/1961; Everett Owen Hawkins and Martha Ada Deschene
Jamie Arlene, b. 11/27/1984; George Owen Hawkins and Amy Ellen Farrar
William David, b. 11/2/1964; Everett Owen Hawkins and Martha Ada Deschene

HAYNES,
son, b. --/--/1904; M/M Frank Haynes
daughter, b. 7/7/1918; M/M Stewart Haynes
daughter, b. 12/1/1919; M/M Stewart Haynes
daughter, b. 5/9/1922; M/M Wilbur Haynes
daughter, b. 9/11/1923; M/M Wilbur Haynes
daughter, b. 12/25/1923; M/M Stewart Haynes
daughter, b. 6/27/1928; M/M Stewart Haynes

son, b. 11/13/1930; M/M Stewart Haynes
Beverly Lee, b. 2/12/1941 in Pittsburg; Stewart Haynes and
    Hazel Danforth
Constance Violet, b. 4/13/1956; Bradley Haynes and Mona
    Eileen Hicks
Elwood Orson, b. 8/17/1937 in Pittsburg; Orson Haynes and
    Elizabeth Wheeler
Gerald Adna, b. 5/8/1938 in W. Stewartstown; Charlie Haynes
    and Evelyn Cummings
Jeffrey Scott, b. 7/27/1984; Scott Nathan Haynes and Roxanne
    Sheila Wheeler
Leslie Roy, b. 10/3/1944 in W. Stewartstown; Warren L. Haynes
    and Beatrice Knapp
Shirley Elaine, b. 8/23/1943 in W. Stewartstown; Warren Haynes
    and Beatrice Knapp
Terrance Owen, b. 10/8/1951 in W. Stewartstown; Bradley P.
    Haynes and Mona Hicks
Valorie Phil, b. 2/13/1950 in W. Stewartstown; Bradley P.
    Haynes and Mona Hicks
Wayne Owen, b. 2/13/1936; Stewart Haynes and Hazel Danforth

HEATH,
son, b. 2/13/1911; M/M Archie Heath
daughter, b. 9/26/1912; M/M Archie Heath
daughter, b. 10/22/1915; M/M Archie Heath
daughter, b. 5/13/1917; M/M Archie R. Heath
son, b. 3/26/1924; M/M Archie R. Heath
Elizabeth, b. 10/8/1919; Archie R. Heath and Laura Wood (1978)

HEBERT,
Beth Marie, b. 4/12/1988; Mark Roger Hebert and Joy Ellen
    Earle
Joseph Gerard G., b. 1/5/1955; Gerard Pierre Hebert and Claire
    Rose Lesieur

Marie Suzanne D., b. 5/29/1956; Gerald Pierre Hebert and Claire Rose Hebert
Samantha Lea, b. 6/9/1986; Mark Roger Hebert and Joy Ellen Earle

HEWSON,
Eric Christopher, b. 12/21/1970; Martin Gerard Hewson, Sr. and Anne Rosalie Miner

HIBBARD,
son, b. 4/8/1904; M/M Edward Hibbard
daughter, b. 7/4/1906; M/M Edd Hibbard
daughter, b. 8/14/1910; M/M Edward G. Hibbard
son, b. 5/6/1913; M/M Edward Hibbard
son, b. 1/18/1915; M/M Edwin G. Hibbard
Carol Muriel, b. 6/20/1954; George Ellis Hibbard and Irene Muriel Young
Edwin Claude, b. 9/26/1954; Maurice Edward Hibbard and Jennie Ada Howe
Elliot Justin, b. 2/23/1962; Maurice Edward Hibbard and Jennie Ada Howe
Elsie Etta, b. 5/24/1953 in W. Stewartstown; Maurice E. Hibbard and Jennie A. Howe
Erwin Maurice, b. 7/14/1957; Maurice Edward Hibbard and Jennie Ada Howe
Jean Anne, b. 11/7/1951 in W. Stewartstown; George E. Hibbard and Irene Young
Julie Christine, b. 3/3/1987; Wade Ellis Hibbard and Susan Lenore Carpenter
Karrie Rebecca, b. 6/13/1979; Wade Ellis Hibbard and Susan Lenore Carpenter
Laura Elizabeth, b. 11/4/1983; Wade Ellis Hibbard and Susan Lenore Carpenter
Peter George, b. 5/23/1982; Wade Ellis Hibbard and Susan Lenore Carpenter

Wade Ellis, b. 6/27/1953 in W. Stewartstown; George E. Hibbard
 and Irene M. Young
Winnie Laura, b. 9/22/1933; Maurice Hibbard and Mary Dorman

HICKS,
daughter, b. 12/1/1927; M/M Carmi Hicks
daughter, b. 3/12/1931; M/M Carmi Hicks
Donald Roy, b. 2/13/1972; Irving Alba Hicks and Rose Marie
 Gray
Irvena Mirilyn, b. 8/6/1933; Carmi Hicks and Marion Day
Irving Alba, b. 7/27/1944 in W. Stewartstown; Alba Hicks and
 Freda Howe
Mona Arlene, b. 8/13/1932; M/M Carmi Hicks
Verna Myrtie, b. 9/12/1937 in Pittsburg; Carmi Hicks and Marion
 Day

HILLIARD,
daughter, b. 3/12/1915; M/M Merton L. Hilliard
son, b. 3/5/1922; Mrs. Frank Hilliard

HINDS,
Rachelle Inez, b. 6/11/2008 in Littleton; Kevin Hinds and Rachel
 Hinds

HODGMAN,
Ervin Wyatt, b. 2/1/1953 in W. Stewartstown; Wyatt E. Hodgman
 and Hazel A. Berg

HOLDEN,
son, b. 3/13/1931; M/M Willie J. Holden
daughter, b. 12/27/1935; Willie J. Holden and Louise Lee
son, b. 12/13/1936; Willie J. Holden and Louise Lee
Frank Leslie, b. 12/27/1932; M/M Will Holden

HOLMES,
daughter, b. 1/29/1905; M/M A. J. Holmes
daughter, b. 9/20/1907; M/M A. J. Holmes
son, b. 6/15/1910; M/M A. J. Holmes

HOWE,
son, b. 12/26/1913; M/M Tilly Howe
daughter, b. 4/23/1916; M/M Tilly Howe
daughter, b. 3/20/1921; M/M Tilly Howe
son, b. 7/3/1924; M/M Tilly Howe
daughter, b. 7/28/1928; M/M Tilly Howe
Laurie Ann, b. 10/31/1961; Floyd Herbert Howe and Barbara Jean Straw
Letty Bessie, b. 2/13/1947 in W. Stewartstown; Kenneth Leroux and Jennie Howe
Lisa May, b. 1/26/1964; Floyd Herbert Guy Howe and Barbara Jean Straw
Wayne Anthony, b. 10/31/1967; Floyd Hebert Guy Howe and Barbara Jean Straw

HOWLAND,
son, b. 8/30/1917; M/M Roscoe Howland
son, b. 3/21/1928; M/M Roscoe Howland
Brenda Nancy, b. 7/27/1942 in W. Stewartstown; Bernard R. Howland and Margaret Ouellette
David Richard, b. 6/25/1963; Richard Ralph Howland and Barbara Ann Osiensky
Jason Michael, b. 10/3/1986; David Richard Howland and Corinne Marie Paquette
Kevin Brian, b. 6/14/1965; Richard Ralph Howland and Barbara Ann Osiensky
Richard R., b. 4/1/1941 in Pittsburg; Bernard Howland and Margaret Ouellette
Sheila Margaret, b. 8/24/1943 in Laconia; Bernard R. Howland and Margaret L. Ouillette

HOWLETT,
Torrie Lee, b. 7/7/2002 in Littleton; Timothy Howlett and Penny Howlett

HUGGINS,
son, b. 1/28/1911; M/M Frank Huggins
daughter, b. 12/8/1927; M/M Harry Huggins
daughter, b. 11/7/1928; M/M Harry Huggins
child, b. 6/3/1941 in Pittsburg; Ralph Huggins and Ruth Osgood
Eva Elnora, b. 11/18/1935; Ralph Huggins and Ruth E. Osgood
Hallie Ruth, b. 6/14/1943 in Pittsburg; Ralph Huggins and Ruth Osgood
Marjorie Grace, b. 1/24/1938 in Pittsburg; Ralph Huggins and Ruth Osgood

HURLBERT,
Amanda Sue, b. 3/10/1984; Lawrence Mainard Hurlbert and Helen Mavis Day

HURLBURT,
child, b. 5/16/1943 in Littleton; Burnham Hurlburt and Gertrude Nason

HURLEY,
Megan Marie, b. 11/15/1974; Kevin Thomas Hurley and Sharon Anne Young

INGERSOLL,
child, b. --/--/1905; M/M Bert Ingersoll

INKEL[L],
Brian Denis, b. 10/27/1970; Denis Gerald Inkel and Pauline Yvette Marquis

Sylvie Pauline, b. 5/31/1972; Denis Gerald Inkell and Pauline Yvette Marquis

JAMASON,
Donald Gerard, b. 7/8/1980; John Joseph Jamason and Debra Gail Hankel

JEWELL,
Roy Albin, b. 12/15/1937 in Pittsburg; John Jewell and Bertha M. Placy

JOCK,
Blake Elizabeth, b. 7/12/1999 in Littleton; Brett Jock and Mary Ann Jock
Brett Michael, b. 1/25/1974; Dale James Jock and Gloria Jeanne Chase
Casey Jean, b. 7/24/2000 in Littleton; Brett Jock and Mary Ann Jock
Garrett Michael, b. 7/19/2000 in Colebrook; Darrin Charles Jock and Robin Maureen Brooks

JOHNSON,
son, b. 10/24/1919; M/M Arthur Johnson
daughter, b. 7/27/1921; M/M Arthur E. Johnson
son, b. 12/1/1928; M/M William E. Johnson
Craig Rodney, b. 6/25/1955; Rodney Bradley Johnson and Betty Joyce Masters
Heidi Lynn, b. 3/20/1963; Embret Alton Johnson and Ida Beryl Locke
Inger Marie, b. 4/11/1965; Embert Alton Johnson and Ida Beryl Locke
Kim Rhonda, b. 5/10/1959; Rodney Bradley Johnson and Betty Joyce Masters
Leanna Jean, b. 4/21/1957; Rodney Bradley Johnson and Betty Joyce Masters

Lori Anne, b. 8/20/1975; Rodney Bradley Johnson and Betty Joyce Masters
Parker Edwin, b. 5/4/1979; Frank Dexter Johnson and Beverly Joan Cady

JUDD,
son, b. 3/4/1910; M/M W. N. Judd
Archie Nathan, b. 5/3/1935; Burnham Judd and Olive Heath
Archie Nathan, Jr., b. 1/12/1957; Archie Nathan Judd and Hazel Arlene Berg
Brooke Mae, b. 4/2/1993 in Lancaster; Richard A. Judd and Sheli Mae Judd
Burnham Alton, b. 8/27/1933; Burnham Judd and Olive A. Heath
Hunter Richard, b. 11/9/1991; Richard Alton Judd and Sheli Mae Machos
Jeffrey Thomas, b. 8/1/1979; Archie Nathan Judd, Jr. and Jhody Lynn Straw
Jensen Janice, b. 6/6/1992; Willie Dennison Judd, Jr. and Nancy Jean Kenney
Kevin Don, b. 6/24/1960; Willie Dennison Judd and Janice Irene Straw
Kim Rae, b. 1/5/1964; Willie Dennison Judd and Janice Irene Straw
Kirby Lyn, b. 7/3/1997 in Colebrook; Willie Dennison Judd, Jr. and Nancy Jean Kenney Judd
Lincoln Nathaniel, b. 9/15/1988; Kevin Don Judd and Ruth Susan Lincoln
Lindsey Lee, b. 9/15/1988; Kevin Don Judd and Ruth Susan Lincoln
Morgan Jean, b. 4/26/1987; Kevin Don Judd and Ruth Susan Lincoln
Nathan Robert, b. 1/17/1978; Archie Nathan Judd, Jr. and Jhody Lynn Straw
Richard Alton, b. 12/5/1957; Willie Dennison Judd and Janice Irene Straw

Vincent Vaughn, b. 7/23/1968; Willie Dennison Judd and Janice
    Irene Straw
Willie Dennison, b. 10/3/1936; Burnham Judd and Olive Heath
Willie Dennison, Jr., b. 7/15/1956; Willie Dennison Judd and
    Janice Irene Straw

KELLY,
James Thomas, b. 11/9/1996 in Colebrook; Sean Patrick Kelly
    and Donna Karen Kelly
Rebecca Lynn, b. 2/11/1998 in Colebrook; Sean Patrick Kelly
    and Donna Karen Kelly

KEYSER,
daughter, b. 1/8/1904; M/M George L. O. Keyser

KUNCIO,
Jacob Ronald Paul, b. 5/8/1989; Ronald Paul Kuncio, Jr. and
    Patricia Ann Powers
Samantha Audrey, b. 6/8/1994 in Colebrook; Ronald Paul
    Kuncio, Jr. and Patricia Ann Kuncio

LABRECQUE,
Alfred P., b. 8/8/1941 in Pittsburg; Joseph A. Labrecque and
    Cora B. Elliot
Joseph R. E., b. 6/27/1940 in Pittsburg; Armand Labrecque and
    Cora Beatrice Elliott

LACHANCE,
son, b. 6/12/1924; M/M Omar Lachance
Helen Sylvia, b. 6/29/1948 in W. Stewartstown; Henry J.
    Lachance and Sylvia M. Robie

LADD,
Jamie Barbara, b. 5/22/1979; Allen Earle Ladd and Ginette
    Leonie Marquis

LAGASSIE,
twin son and daughter, b. 1/--/1905; M/M Charles Lagassie

LALONDE,
John Paul, II, b. 10/2/1981; John Paul LaLonde and Milissa Mary Walker

LAMPRON,
Rachel Ann, b. 2/2/1981; Ronald Richard Lampron and Linda Anne Janules
Richard Ronald, b. 12/30/1981; Ronald Richard Lampron and Linda Anne Janules

LANCOTTE,
son, b. 9/26/1925; M/M Arthur Lancotte

LANSCOTT,
son, b. 4/4/1924; M/M Arthur Lanscott

LAPELLE,
daughter, b. 7/5/1914; M/M Jennette Lapelle

LAPERLE,
son, b. 5/28/1917; M/M Peter Laperle
son, b. 5/10/1919; M/M Flemion LaPerle
daughter, b. 9/17/1925; M/M Frank Laperle
Donald Robert, b. 5/20/1945 in W. Stewartstown; Roland Laperle and Leona Brown
Elaine Cecile, b. 4/10/1944 in W. Stewartstown; Roland LaPerle and Leona Brown
Joseph Guy L., b. 8/8/1951 in W. Stewartstown; Homer Laperle and Adrienne Belonger
Marie Louise V., b. 6/16/1943 in Pittsburg; Leon Laperle and Adriene Belanger

Murielle Ruth Colletti, b. 8/26/1945 in W. Stewartstown; Leon Laperle and Andrienne Belouge
Raymond Marcella, b. 5/1/1944 in W. Stewartstown; Leon LaPerle and Andrienne Belanger
Rosella Lillian, b. 12/13/1946 in W. Stewartstown; Leon Laperle and Adrienne Belonger

LAPOINT,
Faith Kelley, b. 2/5/1974; Richard Ernest Lapoint and Cathy Ann Delong
Shelley Lynn, b. 5/28/1976; Richard Ernest Lapoint, Jr. and Cathy Ann DeLong

LAPOINTE,
Caroline Claudette, b. 6/17/1970; Andre Claude Lapointe and Claudette Lucille Robinson

LARODU,
daughter, b. 6/17/1914; M/M Edd. Larodu

LASSONDE,
Garrett Joshua, b. 6/9/2004 in Lancaster; Kevin Lassonde and Stephanie Lassonde

LAVOSH,
son, b. 9/11/1913; M/M Ed. Lavosh

LAWRENCE,
daughter, b. --/--/1904; M/M Lewis Lawrence
son, b. 7/31/1906; M/M Louis Lawrence
daughter, b. 2/15/1912; M/M Louis Lawrence

LAWTON,
Herbert James, b. 12/28/1952 in W. Stewartstown; Donald J. Lawton and Nella M. Dorman

LECLERE,
son, b. 8/20/1920; M/M Augustus Leclere

LECLERCQ,
Joshua Michael, b. 10/6/1980; Michael Joseph Leclercq and Robin Anne Day

LEIGH,
Lester Covill, b. 6/12/1952 in W. Stewartstown; Lester R. Leigh and Virginia M. Covill
Richard Shirley, b. 11/21/1955; Lester Robert Leigh and Virginia May Covill
Suzanne Elaine, b. 6/7/1951 in W. Stewartstown; Lester R. Leigh and Virginia Covill

LEMIRE,
Nicholas Robert, b. 3/30/1983; Larry Robert Lemire and Teenia Marie Mandeville

LEVESQUE,
Nelson, b. 12/2/1940 in Pittsburg; Theophile Levesque and Sylvia M. Robie

LINCOLN,
Joseph Andrew, b. 11/8/1985; Daniel Allen Lincoln and Michelle Theresa Hebert

LITTLE,
Theresa Marie, b. 6/29/1975; William Bassett Little and JoAnne Marie White
Timothy William, b. 10/11/1978; William Bassett Little and JoAnne Marie White

LORD,
daughter, b. 6/6/1911; M/M Allen J. Lord
son, b. 4/17/1912; M/M William E. Lord
daughter, b. 6/22/1914; M/M Charles H. Lord
son, b. 1/21/1915; M/M William H. Lord
son, b. 8/3/1916; M/M Charles Lord, Jr.
daughter, b. 10/12/1917; M/M Henry Lord
son, b. 4/2/1919; M/M Charles H. Lord
daughter, b. 12/10/1919; M/M Henry C. Lord
daughter, b. 3/4/1925; M/M Charles Lord
son, b. 5/24/1927; M/M Charles Lord, Jr.
son, b. 9/20/1928; M/M Charles G. Lord
daughter, b. 12/6/1931; M/M Austin Lord
Andrea May, b. 4/20/1952 in W. Stewartstown; William E. Lord and Kate Fuller
Ariana Theresa, b. 2/16/2005 in Lancaster; Corey Lord and Theresa Lord
Corey Steven, b. 3/21/1976; Leslie George Lord and Beverly Jean Frizzell
Edith E., b. 9/20/1942 in Pittsburg; Austin P. Lord and Mabel Kane
Keaton Thomas, b. 1/9/2003 in Colebrook; Corey Lord and Theresa Lord
Leslie William, b. 12/21/2000 in Colebrook; Corey Lord and Theresa Lord
Myra June, b. 6/16/1932; M/M Henry Lord
Roger Allen, b. 10/18/1935; Austin Lord and Mabel Kane
Shaun Michael, b. 3/30/1978; Leslie George Lord and Beverly Jean Frizzell
Stephen W., b. 3/7/1941 in W. Stewartstown; William E. Lord and Kate Fuller

LUTHER,
son, b. 7/1/1909; M/M Sidney P. Luther
son, b. 1/29/1912; M/M Sydney P. Luther

son, b. 2/8/1912; M/M Sidney Luther
son, b. 6/25/1912; M/M John Luther

MADORE,
Helene Marie Camille, b. 7/5/1959; Eusebe Gilles Madore and Suzanne Adelina Paquette

MAILLOUX,
Brett Christian, b. 9/4/1994 in Lancaster; Christian Roger Mailloux and Ruth Ann Mailloux
Emily Anita, b. 6/20/1991; Christian Roger Mailloux and Ruth Ann Tucker

MAJOR,
David Roger, b. 6/11/1972; Raymond Joseph Major and Denise Odelie Goulet

MARCHASSAULT,
son, b. 6/23/1930; M/M Onile Marchassault

MARCHESSEAULT,
son, b. 4/22/1922; M/M O. Marchesseault

MARCHESSEONAULT,
son, b. 12/1/1919; M/M O. Marchesseaonault

MARQUIS,
Christine Lise, b. 5/16/1971; Ronald Leo Marquis and Lise Marthe Roy
Daniel Gilles, Jr., b. 4/26/1996 in Colebrook; Daniel Gilles Marquis, Sr. and Ann Marie Marquis
Julie Kathy, b. 2/28/1969; Gilles Paul Marquis and Claudette Anita Drouin
Linda M. A., b. 4/17/1965; Gilles Paul Marquis and Claudette Anite Drouin

Marie G. A., b. 6/22/1942 in Pittsburg; Adelard Marquis and Yvonne Chaloux
Marie Rose Deline Cecile, b. 11/2/1935; Adelard Marquis and Yvonne Chaloux
Mary Alberta Lucille, b. 2/3/1937 in Pittsburg; Adelard Marquis and Evon Chaloux
Nancy M. C., b. 12/1/1966; Gilles Paul Marquis and Claudette Anita Drouin
Normand Yvon, b. 9/23/1958; Leon Paul Marquis and Edith Delina Maurais
Yolande A. M., b. 5/31/1938 in Pittsburg; Adelard Marquis and Evonne Chaloux

MARSH,
son, b. 1/11/1916; M/M Robert Marsh
daughter, b. 5/11/1931; M/M Robert Marsh
Helen E., b. 5/25/1941 in W. Stewartstown; Walter E. Marsh and Pauline Deschene
Robert Edwin, b. 10/6/1933; Robert Marsh and Mildred Davis

MARTEL[L],
daughter, b. 3/10/1917; M/M Alfred Martell
Adam Thomas, b. 1/5/1979; Randall Louis Martell and Sandra Lea Grant
Amber Lea, b. 5/9/1980; Randall Louis Martel and Sandra Lea Grant

MARVIN,
Ronald Lee, b. 5/3/1937 in Pittsburg; Raymond Marvin and Veata Howland

MASTERS,
child, b. 7/20/1909; M/M William H. Masters
daughter, b. 5/22/1912; M/M William H. Masters
daughter, b. 3/17/1925; M/M Weldon Masters

son, b. 12/23/1927; M/M Weldon Masters
daughter, b. 1/25/1930; M/M Weldon Masters
son, b. 4/24/1931; Arlene Masters
son, b. 9/15/1931; M/M Weldon Masters
daughter, b. 4/23/1944 in W. Stewartstown; Weldon Masters and Florence Foster
Betty Joyce, b. 5/22/1934; Weldon Masters and Evelyn Foster
Bruce Elliot, b. 11/4/1962; Randall Ray Masters and Judith Gertrude Washburn
Chris Wesley, b. 3/11/1957; Russell Earl Masters and Verna Ruth Hall
Dana Russell, b. 5/10/1955; Russell Earl Masters and Verna Ruth Hall
Ethel Mae, b. 9/28/1938 in W. Stewartstown; Weldon Masters and Florence Foster
Jame Harriet, b. 10/10/1942 in Pittsburg; Leland Masters and Maud F. Foster
Janice L., b. 7/11/1941 in Pittsburg; Leland Masters and Maud Foster
Jeffrey Alan, b. 8/8/1952 in W. Stewartstown; Russell Masters and Verna R. Hall
Juanita Evelyn, b. 10/9/1938 in W. Stewartstown; Weldon Masters and Florence Fuller
Kyle Jeffrey, b. 6/7/1976; Jeffrey Alan Masters and Dottie-Jane Amey
Larry C., b. 7/30/1942 in W. Stewartstown; Weldon I. Masters and Florence E. Foster
Laurna Marie Rita, b. 4/6/1969; Ray Leland Masters and Linette Terry Crete
Pearl Florence, b. 6/3/1947 in W. Stewartstown; Weldon Masters and Florence Foster
Peter Cory, b. 3/26/1956; Russell Earl Masters and Verna Ruth Hall
Randall R., b. 3/22/1941 in Pittsburg; Weldon Masters and Florence Foster

Randall Ray, Jr., b. 1/29/1961; Randall Ray Masters and Judith Gertrude Washburn
Ray Leland, b. 8/16/1945 in Pittsburg; Leland R. Masters and Maude Frances Foster (1952)
Scott Frederick, b. 3/21/1968; Larry Charles Masters and Norma Lea Hodge
Veronica Sue, b. 12/4/1966; Larry Charles Masters and Norma Lea Hodge
Weldon Stanley, b. 10/4/1932; M/M Weldon Masters

MATHIEU,
Joseph Roland Denis, b. 9/20/1957; Roland Manuel Mathieu and Louise Elizabeth Giguerre
Ronald Joseph, b. 1/7/1959; Roland Emanuel Mathieu and Louise Elizabeth Giguere

MATTHEWS,
Donald, Jr., b. 10/3/1944 in W. Stewartstown; Donald Matthews and Edna Currier

MAUROIS,
son, b. 5/11/1922; M/M Audeau Maurois

McCOMISKEY,
Melanie Mae, b. 3/6/1971; Walter George McComiskey and Catherine Emily Frizzell

McKEAGE,
son, b. 3/27/1925; M/M Ivo McKeage
daughter, b. 8/23/1928; M/M Ivo McKeage
son, b. 8/18/1930; M/M Ivo McKeage
Brendon Dale, b. 4/1/1948 in W. Stewartstown; Willard McKeage and Irene Hicks
Brendon Keith, b. 4/19/1966; Brendon Dale McKeage and Crystal Ann Clogston

Ivona Ida, b. 5/21/1932; M/M Ivo McKeage
Penny Lea, b. 6/2/1965; Brendon Dale McKeage and Crystal Ann Clogston
Randall Ellis, b. 6/3/1946 in W. Stewartstown; Willard McKeage and Irene Hicks
Ricky Dale, b. 12/6/1967; Brendon Dale McKeage and Crystal Ann Clogston
Stephanie Jo, b. 5/11/1973; Brendon Dale McKeage and Crystal Ann Clogston
Tanner Roland, b. 7/27/1998 in Colebrook; Ricky Dale McKeage and Tanya-Marie McKeage

McKINNON,
Melissa Helen, b. 4/11/1998 in Littleton; Richard Carl McKinnon and Holli Lynn McKinnon

McLAUGHLIN,
son, b. 6/21/1917; M/M George McLaughlin
son, b. 5/27/1918; M/M George H. McLaughlin
son, b. 9/19/1919; M/M George McLaughlin
daughter, b. 11/17/1920; M/M George McLaughlin
daughter, b. 12/17/1921; M/M George McLaughlin

McLEAN,
Sophie Grayce, b. 7/2/2008 in Berlin; Shawn McLean and Doreen McLean

MERRILL,
daughter, b. 8/26/1910; M/M Chauncey Merrill
daughter, b. 10/13/1917; M/M Fay Merrill
son, b. 5/15/1919; M/M Ed Merrill
son, b. 11/21/1928; M/M Willie G. Merrill
daughter, b. 5/26/1931; M/M Willie G. Merrill
Aimee-Lynn Ann, b. 2/1/1984; Scott Patrick Merrill and Diane Ann Brooks

Amanda Jean, b. 7/7/1986; Glen Peter Merrill and Wanda Jean Wright
Bradley Scott, b. 5/24/1979; Scott Patrick Merrill and Diane Ann Brooks
Donovan Edward, b. 3/21/1911; Edward Merrill and Sadie Pike (1973)
Geoffrey Everett, b. 3/9/1957; John Merrill and Helen Sanborn
Glen Peter, b. 12/3/1957; Gerald Patrick Merrill and Vanessa Margaret Brown
Hugh Stewart, b. 3/24/1948 in W. Stewartstown; Gerald P. Merrill and Venessa Young
John, b. 6/9/1938 in W. Stewartstown; Willie Merrill and Margaret Berry
Luke Gerald, b. 5/14/1990; Glen Peter Merrill and Wander Jean Wright
Monica Marie, b. 4/22/1988; Glen Peter Merrill and Wanda Jean Wright
Myrtle Maude, b. 1/8/1915; Edward George Merrill and Sadie Ethel Pike (1973)
Richard Earl, b. 1/9/1955; Glenford Charles Merrill and Geraldine Mae Young
Scott Patrick, b. 11/7/1951 in W. Stewartstown; Gerald P. Merrill and Vanessa Young
Sharon, b. 1/9/1940 in W. Stewartstown; Willie Merrill and Margaret Berry
Tia Lori, b. 12/13/1967; Hugh Stewart Merrill and Judith Ervena Frizzell

MIELNICKI,
Tracy Ann, b. 2/27/1971; Robert David Mielnicki and Carol Ann Covey

MILLER,
daughter, b. --/--/1906; M/M G. H. Miller
son, b. 10/26/1907; M/M Charles R. Miller

MITCHELL,
Joyce Cecil, b. 12/10/1942 in Pittsburg; Herve P. Mitchell and Erma R. Howland

MOORE,
daughter, b. 10/10/1960; Dana Charles Moore and Mary Jane Styles

MORAN,
Jennifer Mary, b. 7/7/1979; Timothy Gerard Moran and Nadine Ellen Taylor

MORANN,
Allison Priscilla, b. 8/18/1990; William Henry Morann and Verna Jolene Allen
Sarah Elizabeth, b. 8/16/1994 in Colebrook; William Henry Morann and Verna Jolene Morann

MOREAU,
son, b. 5/31/1917; M/M J. Henry Moreau

MORRISSEY,
Sandy Leigh, b. 10/14/1971; Walter John Morrissey and Susan Bea Allen

MORSE,
Shawn Richard, b. 3/2/1989; Doug George Morse and Wendy Lynn Berkoski

MOUSSEAU,
daughter, b. 9/8/1923; M/M Atlee Mousseau
Atlee Lawrence, b. 8/14/1976; Francis Alexander Mousseau and Marlena Mae Heath

Francis Alexander, b. 7/4/1947 in W. Stewartstown; Keane Mousseau and Katherine Smith

Helen Kay, b. 8/21/1942 in Pittsburg; Keane Mousseau and Katherine Smith

Julia Anna, b. 12/30/1940 in Pittsburg; Keane Mousseau and Katherine Smith

Melissa A., b. 2/18/1950 in W. Stewartstown; Keane A. Mousseau and Katherine Smith

Oliver Keane, b. 8/26/1944 in W. Stewartstown; Keane Mousseau and Katherine Smith

MUNN,
daughter, b. 10/9/1917; M/M Harry C. Munn
daughter, b. 1/21/1927; M/M Harry Munn

NORTHCOTT,
Marc Anthony, b. 5/28/1975; Alan Edward Northcott and Jane Eileen Boffitte

NOYES,
Allen Michael, b. 2/14/2001 in Newport, VT; Gordon Noyes and Jesse Noyes

Aubrey Marie, b. 8/4/1981; Alan Ira Noyes and Sherry Lee Goodwin

Garrett Alan, b. 8/11/1984; Alan Ira Noyes and Sherry Lee Goodwin

Michael Richard, b. 10/7/1964; George Allen Noyes, Jr. and Alice Grace Pariseau

Murray Howard, b. 9/1/1945 in W. Stewartstown; Howard Noyes and Margaret Allen

Pamela Jeanne, b. 9/19/1957; George Allen Noyes, Jr. and Alice Grace Pariseau

O'NEIL,
Robert Ashley, b. 10/23/1950 in W. Stewartstown; Wayne W. O'Neil and Jan Ashley

O'ROURKE,
Bridget Morgan, b. 5/27/2002 in Littleton; Michael O'Rourke and Robin O'Rourke

OAKES,
Robert Gordon, b. 2/26/1949 in W. Stewartstown; Gordon Oakes and Pauline Clogston

ODEL,
son, b. 1/11/1911; M/M Peter Odel

ORMSBEE,
Matthew John, b. 7/5/1993 in Colebrook; Willard Duane Ormsbee and Regina Lynne Ormsbee
Taylor Meredith, b. 3/8/1995 in Colebrook; Willard Duane Ormsbee and Regina Burnham Ormsbee

OWEN,
son, b. 2/11/1915; M/M Burton S. Owens
Andrew Carson, b. 7/10/2005 in Lancaster; Ronnie Owen and Kimberly DeGray
Connie Ruth, b. 10/1/1965; Edward Grant Owen and Hallie Ruth Huggins
Debra Ann, b. 2/24/1959; Roger Burton Owen and Lorraine Germaine LaRoche
Donnie Ralph, b. 7/3/1964; Edward Grant Owen and Hallie Ruth Huggins
Edwin Ralph, b. 3/10/1962; Edward Grant Owen and Hallie Ruth Huggins
Jimmy Mark, b. 1/24/1960; Edward Grant Owen and Hallie Ruth Huggins

Johnny Mike, b. 1/24/1960; Edward Grant Owen and Hallie Ruth Huggins
Ronnie Frank, b. 1/6/1961; Edward Grant Owen and Hallie Ruth Huggins
Scottie Edward, b. 2/2/1967; Edward Grant Owen and Hallie Ruth Huggins
Timmy James, b. 5/2/1970; Edward Grant Owen and Hallie Ruth Huggins

PAQUETTE,
Corrine Marie, b. 8/18/1964; Real Norman Paquette and Jane Rita Peterson
Cynthia Lynn, b. 9/6/1963; Andra Jacque Paquette and Solange Delia Rouleau
Joanne Marie, b. 8/13/1960; Real Normand Paquette and Jane Rita Peterson
Rachel Marie, b. 8/29/1962; Real Norman Paquette and Jane Rita Peterson
Robert Antonio, b. 3/11/1961; Andre Jacques Paquette and Solange Delia Rouleau
Yolande, b. 4/26/1941 in W. Stewartstown; Aldege Paquette and Claire Dupois

PAQUIN,
daughter, b. 6/6/1928; M/M Joe Paquin

PARKER,
Bryan Bernard Young, b. 1/12/1994 in Colebrook; Reginald Earl Young Parker and Jacquelyn Ruth Parker
David Clyde, b. 3/8/1979; David Curtis Parker and Sylvia Diane Lamontagne
Jennifer Ruby, b. 11/15/1973; David Curtis Parker and Veronica Jean Grover
Ryan Roberta, b. 3/17/1980; Reuben Robert Parker and Christine Kay Pinckney

Sarah Elizabeth Young, b. 1/12/1998 in Colebrook; Reginald Earl Young Parker and Jacquelyn Ruth Parker

PATTEE,
daughter, b. 6/24/1918; M/M Leon J. Pattee

PAULIN,
son, b. 3/20/1925; M/M Treffle Paulin

PEARSONS,
daughter, b. 1/15/1911; M/M Fay Pearsons

PERRY,
Erin Ann, b. 11/7/1983; David Ballard Perry and Mary Ann Pausha
Kevin David, b. 6/8/1980; David Ballard Perry and Mary Ann Pausha
Thomas Robert, b. 2/9/1987; David Ballard Perry and Mary Ann Pausha

PHILLIPS,
Devin James, b. 11/29/2000 in Colebrook; Patrick Phillips and Amanda Phillips
Landen Ryan, b. 8/8/2003 in Colebrook; Patrick Phillips and Amanda Phillips

PIERCE,
Jessica Jean, b. 6/17/1978; Dale Alan Pierce and Tammy Jean Carlson
Ryan Joseph, b. 6/19/1997 in N. Conway; Timothy Scott Pierce and Lynda Lee McLellan Pierce

PIKE,
son, b. 9/25/1917; Mrs. Dores Pike

PINCI,
Chelsea Woodbury, b. 12/29/1984; Donald David Pinci and Dana Faye Woodbury
Isaac Woodbury, b. 7/31/1990; Donald David Pinci and Dana Faye Woodbury

PIPER,
Jean Abbie, b. 11/8/1939 in Pittsburg; Roger H. Piper and Evelyn Lillian Piper
June, b. 6/5/1937 in Pittsburg; Roger H. Piper and Evelyn Bacon

POISSON,
Marie Rose J., b. 11/17/1942 in Pittsburg; Theodore Poisson and Marie R. Brulotte

POTTER,
Leona, b. 10/6/1942 in W. Stewartstown; Linwood Potter and Romona Marsh

POULIN,
son, b. 9/5/1928; M/M Trifle Poulin

PREHEMO,
Brielle Lea, b. 3/7/2002 in Colebrook; Dana Prehemo and Amy Prehemo
Carter Jeffrey, b. 6/9/2004 in Lancaster; Jeffrey Prehemo and Megan Prehemo
Cole Jeffrey, b. 7/27/1999 in Colebrook; Jeffrey Prehemo and Megan Prehemo
Dana Robert, b. 11/24/1976; Robert Wilfred Prehemo and Carlene Carol Straw
Gina Marie, b. 8/8/1971; Robert Wilfred Prehemo and Carlene Carol Straw
Jeffrey William, b. 7/10/1973; Raymond Arthur Prehemo and Gale Elena French

Neil Ray, b. 8/10/1971; Raymond Arthur Prehemo and Gale
    Elene French
Spencer Raymond, b. 10/13/2003 in Colebrook; Neil Prehemo
    and Karen Kidder-Prehemo

PROVO,
David William, III, b. 12/17/1988; David William Provo, Jr. and
    Barbara Anne Provo

PUGLISI,
Anthony Joseph, b. 8/30/1997 in Colebrook; Louis Joseph
    Puglisi III and Brenda Kay Foote Puglisi

PURRINGTON,
Benjamin Fales, b. 4/17/1970; Melvin Curtis Purrington and
    Jacqueline Birch

QUIMBY,
son, b. 9/13/1922; M/M Walter E. Quimby

RAINVILLE,
David Stewart, b. 1/31/1954; Stewart Albert Rainville and Winnie
    Laura Hibbard
Linda Sue, b. 4/16/1955; Stewart Albert Rainville and Winnie
    Laura Hibbard

RANCLOES,
Wanda Lou, b. 6/18/1948 in W. Stewartstown; Frank O.
    Rancloes and Glenna Knapp

RAY,
Samantha Sadie, b. 4/29/1989; Kirk Dietrich Ray and Helyn Lois
    Deamon
Sarah Jean, b. 2/7/1991; Jeffrey Michael Ray and Brenda Doris
    Wheeler

RAYMOND,
Andrew Jason, b. 12/19/1989; Glenn Daniel Raymond, Sr. and Norma Jean Lampron
Leah Nicole, b. 9/7/1994 in Lancaster; Glenn Daniel Raymond, Sr. and Norma Jean Raymond

REICH,
Jacob James, b. 1/3/1997 in Colebrook; Steven James Reich and Rebekah Lynn Dunstan Reich
Nathaniel Scott, b. 10/19/1998 in Littleton; Steven Reich and Rebekah Reich

REID,
Eric Michael, b. 9/3/1983; Howard Edwin Reid and Judith Joyce Miles

REMICK,
Matthew Leavitt, b. 11/26/1993 in Lancaster; Michael Howard Remick and Kimberly Marie Remick
Nicholas Howard, b. 5/13/1997 in Colebrook; Michael Howard Remick and Kimberly Marie Young Remick

REYNOLDS,
daughter, b. 6/6/1914; M/M Maynard Reynolds
son, b. 11/23/1930; M/M Carl Reynolds
Roy Bruce, b. 8/24/1932; M/M Carl Reynolds

RICH,
Patricia Susan, b. 8/15/1946 in Farmington, ME; Harold Rich and Kyra Gladden

RICHARDS,
Ann, b. 4/19/1947 in W. Stewartstown; Arthur Richards and Arlene Young

RIENDEAU,
Anthony Robert, b. 5/24/1959; Robert Joseph Riendeau and Shirley Fay McKearney
Jeffrey Alan, b. 9/7/1960; Robert Joseph Riendeau and Shirley Faye McKearney
Suzella, b. 3/24/1943 in Pittsburg; Archille Riendeau and Mary L. Marquis

ROBBINS,
son, b. 3/1/1931; Harold Tuttle and Mabel Foss Robbins
Margaret Ann, b. 7/17/1935; Burton G. Robbins and Ada E. Longlond
Ray Edward, b. 3/7/1937 in W. Stewartstown; Burton G. Robbins and Ada Longland

ROBIE,
son, b. --/--/1906; M/M Norman Robie
daughter, b. 7/30/1919; M/M Norman Robie
son, b. 1/25/1924; M/M Ezra Robie
son, b. 3/11/1925; M/M Gerald Robie
daughter, b. 6/12/1925; M/M Ezra Robie
son, b. 8/26/1928; M/M Ezra Robie
daughter, b. 10/8/1928; M/M Gerald M. Robie
Allyson Margaret, b. 8/12/1952 in W. Stewartstown; Edwin M. Robie and Wilma J. Hawes
Carolyn Ann, b. 12/21/1954; Edwin Myron Robie and Wilma Julia Hawes
Janice Lea, b. 5/2/1944 in W. Stewartstown; Chester L. Robie and Ruth Flanders
Lana Marie, b. 10/22/1938 in Pittsburg; Chester L. Robie and Ruth Ellen Flanders

ROBINSON,
stillborn child, b. 5/28/1915; M/M Harry Robinson

Armon, b. 7/6/1947 in W. Stewartstown; Eric Robinson and Evelyn Beloin
Claudette, b. 6/28/1946 in W. Stewartstown; Alex Robinson and Evelyn Beloin
Francine, b. 8/7/1953 in W. Stewartstown; Eric J. Robinson and Evelyn M. Beloin
Gerard, b. 8/7/1953 in W. Stewartstown; Eric J. Robinson and Evelyn M. Beloin
Henri Joseph, b. 9/22/1954; Eric Joseph Robinson and Evelyn Mary Beloin
Keith James, b. 10/24/1986; Jules Ernest Robinson and Madeleine Lise Brouillard
Michel Gerard, b. 1/1/1959; Eric Joseph Robinson and Evelyn Mary Beloin
Norman Claude, b. 8/5/1948 in W. Stewartstown; Eric Robinson and Evelyn Beloin
Pauline Mary, b. 2/2/1950 in W. Stewartstown; Eric J. Robinson and Evelyn Beloin

ROBY,
son, b. 2/6/1910; M/M Norman Roby
son, b. 3/18/1922; M/M Ezra Roby
Almeda Nellie, b. 6/16/1894; Hiram Grant Roby and Ada B. Danforth (1955)

RODRIQUE,
Arlene M., b. 8/1/1955; Henry Joseph Roderique and Regina Madeline Hicks
Carleen Ann, b. 10/20/1950 in W. Stewartstown; Henry Rodrique and Regina Hicks
Marlene Linda, b. 11/27/1949 in W. Stewartstown; Henry Rodrique and Regina Hicks
Michelle Cheri, b. 3/21/1971; Sheridan Joseph Rodrique and Sharon Hilda Chase

Sheridan Joseph, b. 4/20/1948 in W. Stewartstown; Henry J.
    Roderick and Regina M. Hicks
Shirley May, b. 4/21/1956; Roland Joseph Roderique and
    Patricia Ann Young

RONDEAU,
Philip Richard, b. 1/26/1994 in Colebrook; Leo Roland Rondeau
    and Faith Kelley Rondeau

ROPPEL,
Marie Leona, b. 7/31/1943 in Pittsburg; Norman Roppel and
    Arlene H. French

ROUGEAU,
Marcel Pierre, b. 11/15/1956; Rosaire Germain Rougeau and
    Therese Marie Hebert
Richard Marc, b. 2/19/1965; Rosaire Germain Rougeau and
    Therese Marie Hebert

ROUSEAN,
son, b. 9/21/1915; M/M Louis Rousean
daughter, b. 9/21/1915; M/M Louis Rousean

ROY,
Carl Henry, b. 8/9/1964; Percy Henry Roy and Jill Bumford

RUTHIER,
Hughette Theresa, b. 12/22/1945 in W. Stewartstown; Bernard
    Ruthier and Simone Couture

SAGE,
Spencer Ian, b. 7/3/1989; Stewart Purley Sage, Jr. and Melody
    Ann Jock

SCHOFF,
daughter, b. 1/16/1904; M/M Perley R. Schoff
son, b. 12/17/1904; M/M Perley R. Schoff
daughter, b. 6/1/1905; M/M E. A. Schoff
son, b. 11/29/1905; M/M Perley R. Schoff
son, b. --/--/1906; M/M P. R. Schoff
daughter, b. 5/12/1911; M/M Perley R. Schoff
daughter, b. 11/23/1915; M/M Perley Schoff
son, b. 3/20/1919; M/M Perley Schoff
son, b. 8/10/1919; M/M Ray Schoff
Juana Leah, b. 11/7/1939 in W. Stewartstown; Willis Washburn
    and Josephine J. Schoff

SCOTT,
twin sons, b. 8/13/1907; M/M Gilbert Scott
son, b. 8/27/1915; M/M Roderick Scott
daughter, b. 2/4/1922; M/M Fred T. Scott
son, b. 10/3/1924; M/M Arthur Scott
son, b. 12/12/1929; M/M Jesse Scott
Sherry Linda, b. 9/8/1950 in W. Stewartstown; Richard J. Scott
    and Romona Harris
Willard Charles, b. 1/1/1908; Roderick Scott and Mary Cairns
    (1969)
Zelma Elzina, b. 4/22/1902; Charles Andrew Scott and Lillian
    Willis (1961)

SEYMORE,
son, b. 11/9/1917; M/M Herbert Seymore

SEYMOUR,
son, b. 4/2/1923; M/M Wilfred Seymour

SHACKLETON,
Ruth Nora, b. 8/13/1933; John Shackleton and Alice Hawes

SHALLOW,
son, b. 4/24/1910; M/M James M. Shallow
Lurlyne Elizabeth, b. 12/19/1917; James Michael Shallow and
 Lizzie Belle Gay (1972)

SHIELDS,
Christopher Ian, b. 4/9/1991; Larry Edward Shields and Norma
 Jean Dupuis
Patrick James, b. 6/11/1995 in Colebrook; Larry Edward Shields
 and Norma Jean Shields

SMITH,
Barbara M., b. 2/16/1993 in Colebrook; Kevin Dale Smith and
 Debra Joan Smith
Jay R., b. 9/26/1991; Kevin Dale Smith and Debra Joan Davis
Keara Ellen, b. 8/9/1994 in Peterborough; Gregory Scott Smith
 and Deborah Jean Smith
Marion Alice, b. 7/26/1959; Oliver Orleans Smith and Patricia
 June Mousseau
Maxine Phillis, b. 5/30/1943 in Pittsburg; Oliver O. Smith and
 Patricia J. Mousseau
Ramon Ellis, b. 6/12/1952 in W. Stewartstown; Oliver O. Smith
 and Patricia J. Mousseau
Vance Lee, b. 6/11/1949 in W. Stewartstown; Oliver O. Smith
 and Patricia Mousseau

SPENCER,
Jennifer Lynne, b. 7/5/1988; Duane Edward Spencer and Joanne
 Lorraine Horner
Kelly Rae, b. 9/28/1984; Duane Edward Spencer and Joanne
 Lorraine Horner

STOHL,
Judd Anderson, b. 5/29/1973; Bruce Wayne Stohl and Kristina
 Gale Anderson

Vicki Lynn, b. 3/19/1971; Bruce Wayne Stohl and Kristina Gale Anderson

STOVER,
son, b. 3/27/1929; Mrs. Emma G. Stover

STRAW,
Jacquelyn Ruth, b. 12/10/1963; Bernard Austin Straw and Marjorie Grace Huggins
Jhody Lynn, b. 10/15/1959; Bernard Austin Straw and Marjorie Grace Huggins
Judy Lee, b. 12/5/1960; Bernard Austin Straw and Marjorie Huggins

SUITOR,
daughter, b. 12/29/1910; M/M Sidney G. Suitor

SWEATT,
Aaron Dale, b. 4/18/1982; John Wendell Sweatt and Kathy Ann Hunt
Jennifer Lynne, b. 2/26/1984; John Wendell Sweatt and Kathy Ann Hunt

SWEDBERG,
Marcus Lloyd Coffey, b. 4/1/1994 in Lancaster; Matthew Charles Swedberg and Christine Anne Swedberg

TABOR,
Sarah Jane, b. 7/14/1934; Parker W. Tabor and Nina M. Williams

TANNER,
Joshua Matthew, b. 7/2/1977; Thomas David Tanner and Lynn Marie Sullivan

TERRILL,
son, b. 6/--/1905; M/M Urban Terrill
daughter, b. 10/24/1909; M/M Harry E. Terrill

THEBARGE,
Carol Jean, b. 10/3/1954; Albert Francis Thebarge and Mary
    Elizabeth Hopps

THERRIEN,
Michael Allen, b. 5/11/1989; James Albert Therrien and Carolyn
    Leslie Bolton

THIBAULT,
son, b. 3/17/1917; M/M Fred Thibault
son, b. 4/4/1919; M/M Alfred Thibault
daughter, b. 8/10/1921; M/M Alfred Thibault
son, b. 3/23/1925; M/M Fred Thibault
son, b. 7/22/1931; M/M Joseph Thibault
Joseph Morris, b. 12/2/1943 in Pittsburg; Joseph Thibault and
    Rose Dola Marquis
Lucile Bernette, b. 2/13/1937 in Pittsburg; Wilfred Thibault and
    Evon Bissonette
Mary Lucille, b. 3/17/1935; Joseph Thibault and Rose Ida
    Marquis

THIBEAULT,
son, b. 2/17/1929; M/M Wilfred Thibeault
Claude Joseph, b. 8/3/1963; Raymond Gillis Thibeault and
    Louisette Gaetane Marchand
Denise M. R., b. 3/19/1962; Raymond Gilles Thibeault and
    Louisetta Gaetane Marchand
George R., b. 2/13/1939 in Pittsburg; Joseph Thibeault and Rose
    Ida Marquis
Raymond, b. 11/27/1939 in W. Stewartstown; Henry Thibeault
    and Annette Colombe

Richard Patrick, b. 9/12/1960; Raymond Gilles Thibeault and Louisette Gaetane Marchand

TILTON,
Curtis Edward, b. 2/4/1948 in W. Stewartstown; Edward E. Tilton and Addie Young
Earl Robert, b. 7/13/1948 in W. Stewartstown; Earl Tilton and Harriet Doolan
Katherine Mae, b. 3/11/1947 in W. Stewartstown; Edward Tilton and Addie Young
Larry Earl, b. 8/14/1945 in W. Stewartstown; Earl Tilton and Harriet Doolan
Richard Earl, b. 12/11/1949 in W. Stewartstown; Edward E. Tilton and Addie Young
Robert Gene, b. 4/6/1947 in W. Stewartstown; Earl Tilton and Harritt Doolan
Sylvia May, b. 5/16/1943 in W. Stewartstown; Earl R. Tilton and Harriet A. Doolan

TOWLE,
daughter, b. 5/12/1914; M/M Edward Towle
daughter, b. 8/19/1916; M/M Edwin Towle
daughter, b. 6/11/1917; M/M Edgar Towle
son, b. 4/3/1928; M/M Fred T. Towle
daughter, b. 8/4/1929; M/M Edgar Towle
son, b. 9/15/1930; M/M Tom Towle
daughter, b. 1/18/1931; M/M Edgar Towle
Brenda K., b. 9/8/1940 in W. Stewartstown; King E. Towle and Mildred Manseau
Charles William, b. 1/19/1934; Fred T. Towle and Barbara Woods
Earl William, b. 11/28/1958; Charles William Towle and Joy Celia Bresette
Gene Eric, b. 12/7/1943 in Pittsburg; King Eric Towle and Mildred Manseau

Lee Robert, b. 8/15/1934; King E. Towle and Mildred Manseau
Sheila Elvenia, b. 12/28/1938 in Pittsburg; Fred T. Towle and
    Barbara Wood

TRUDEL,
Richard Michael, b. 1/18/1950 in W. Stewartstown; William J.
    Trudel and Betty Worhal
William Russell, b. 1/10/1949 in W. Stewartstown; William J.
    Trudell and Betty Worhal

TURNER,
Jerusha Ruth, b. 12/12/1992; John David Turner, Jr. and
    Frances Ruth Fletcher

URAN,
Brenda Lee, b. 9/14/1956; Frank Ernest Uran and Zelma Evelyn
    Foster
Frank Ernest, Jr., b. 5/13/1952 in W. Stewartstown; Frank E.
    Uran, Sr. and Zelma E. Foster
Gloria Jean, b. 6/8/1951 in W. Stewartstown; Frank E. Uran and
    Zelma Foster
Robin Ann, b. 11/4/1976; Steven Charles Uran and Barbara
    Jean Ricker
Roger Dale, b. 12/27/1954; Frank Ernest Uran and Zelma Evelyn
    Foster
Stephen Charles, b. 12/7/1949 in W. Stewartstown; Frank E.
    Uran and Thelma Foster

VARNEY,
Carl Leslie, b. 4/25/1956; Edward Deleven Varney and Alberta
    Geneva Hall
Curtis Edward, b. 8/2/1954; Edward Delven Varney and Alberta
    Geneva Hall
Edward Delbert, b. 11/7/1933; Arthur L. Varney and Freda S.
    Bacon

Harold Curtis, b. 6/27/1937 in Pittsburg; Arthur L. Varney and Freda Bacon

WASHBURN,
daughter, b. 6/20/1905; M/M George H. Washburn
son, b. 3/24/1910; M/M Samuel J. Washburn
Barry Austin, b. 5/13/1950 in W. Stewartstown; William Washburn and Arlene Hann
Brent William, b. 2/11/1946 in W. Stewartstown; William Washburn and Arlene Hann
Bruce Samuel, b. 12/18/1937 in W. Stewartstown; Rueben Washburn and Eunice Fiske
Dallas A., b. 3/24/1941 in W. Stewartstown; Reuben Washburn and Eunice Fiske
Kent George, b. 3/12/1943 in Pittsburg; William H. Washburn and Arlene Hann
Linda Jean, b. 7/17/1943 in Pittsburg; Willis Washburn and Ruene Hilliard
Michael T., b. 8/27/1965; Malcolm Roger Washburn and Mary Theresa Gardocki
Michelle Eunice, b. 4/12/1975; Malcolm Roger Washburn and Mary Theresa Gardocki
Myrna Lee, b. 10/26/1945 in W. Stewartstown; Willis Washburn and Ruene Hilliard
Roger Malcolm, b. 3/20/1943 in Pittsburg; Rueben G. Washburn and Eunice Fiske
Roger W., b. 8/31/1951 in W. Stewartstown; Willis E. Washburn and Alice Hilliard
Samuel A., b. 6/8/1943 in W. Stewartstown; Kenneth Washburn and Elizabeth Heath
Sandra E., b. 2/8/1951 in W. Stewartstown; Kenneth R. Washburn and Elizabeth Heath

WESTBERG,
daughter, b. 2/12/1929; M/M Carl Westberg

WHEELER,
daughter, b. --/--/1905; M/M Clarence Wheeler
son, b. 7/12/1909; M/M Jubel Wheeler
daughter, b. 5/29/1912; M/M Jubel Wheeler
daughter, b. 8/4/1913; M/M Jubel Wheeler
twin daughters, b. 7/26/1919; M/M Jubal Wheeler
daughter, b. 12/6/1925; M/M Leonard Wheeler
Brenda Doris, b. 1/16/1968; Donald Raymond Wheeler and
    Sheila Margaret Howland
Cassandra Lee, b. 2/4/1988; Dennis Donald Wheeler and
    Pamela Ann Clark
Claude Arthur, b. 6/30/1935; Raymond A. Wheeler and Doris
    Chandler
Claudia Ann, b. 1/21/1970; Claude Arthur Wheeler and Alberta
    Annette Gagne
Derek Donald Wayne, b. 12/29/1989; Dennis Donald Wheeler
    and Pamela Ann Clark
Donald R., b. 1/20/1940 in W. Stewartstown; Raymond Wheeler
    and Doris F. Chandler
James Deland, b. 9/23/1959; Claude Arthur Wheeler and Alberta
    Annette Gagne
Jean Abbie, b. 7/28/1933; Sidney Wheeler and Cora Bunnell
Julie Melina, b. 5/18/1962; Claude Arthur Wheeler and Alberta
    Annette Gagne
Roxanne Sheila, b. 3/6/1964; Donald Raymond Wheeler and
    Sheila Margaret Howland
Sidney Leighton, b. 3/31/1936; Sidney L. Wheeler and Cora
    Bunnell
Tina Marie, b. 1/11/1972; Donald Raymond Wheeler and Sheila
    Margaret Howland

WHITE,
son, b. 1/24/1916; M/M Joseph White
son, b. 7/13/1917; M/M Joe White

daughter, b. 2/23/1919; M/M Joseph White

WIDLUND,
Stacey Ursula, b. 8/8/1977; Carl Johan-Arthur Widlund and Doris Marie Major

WIGGINS,
daughter, b. 10/17/1930; M/M Arthur D. Wiggins

WILLIS,
Esther Alena, b. 6/25/1949 in W. Stewartstown; Leslie J. Willis and Leora Heath

WILSON,
John, b. 11/13/1951 in W. Stewartstown; Francis Charles Wilson and Sophie Byk

WOODROW,
Renay, b. 5/31/1936; Carroll Woodrow and Frances Bacon

WRIGHT,
daughter, b. 9/22/1921; M/M Samuel Wright
daughter, b. 5/17/1931; M/M Sam Wright
Dennis Paul, b. 2/12/1959; Paul Dennis Wright and Loretta Jane Young
Karen Lee, b. 6/2/1980; Steven Robert Wright and Roxanne Lee Bryant
Kristen Marie, b. 11/19/1982; Steven Robert Wright and Roxanne Lee Bryant

YOUNG,
son, b. 11/24/1915; M/M Ivan Young
son, b. 1/9/1921; M/M Hollis Young
daughter, b. 7/3/1924; M/M Jesse Young
daughter, b. 12/22/1924; M/M Stewart Young

son, b. 8/6/1925; M/M Jesse Young
daughter, b. 4/3/1927; M/M Stewart Young
daughter, b. 3/20/1928; M/M Jesse W. Young
daughter, b. 1/7/1930; M/M Clayton Young
son, b. 2/5/1930; M/M Stewart Young
son, b. 5/26/1930; M/M Jesse Young
Adam Hall, b. 7/15/1999 in Colebrook; Sanford Young and Jill
  Young
Allyson Lynn, b. 3/12/1995 in Colebrook; Duane Richard Young
  and Luanne Marie Young
Andrew Phillip, b. 6/11/1977; Leonard William Young and Marilyn
  Anne White
Carleen Alida, b. 1/23/1946 in Pittsburg; Phillip Young and
  Mildred Andrews
Duane Richard, b. 5/31/1963; Phillip Leavitt Young and Mildred
  Alida Andrews
Howard Clayton, b. 2/25/1932; M/M Clayton Young
Jason Walter, b. 9/26/1976; Richard Wayne Young and Linda
  Jane Pierce
Jeremy Wayne, b. 10/4/1974; Richard Wayne Young and Linda
  Jane Pierce
Joel Sidney, b. 10/9/1981; Sidney Arnold Young and Denise
  Claire Desrosiers
Judith E., b. 7/18/1941 in Pittsburg; Phillip L. Young and Mildred
  Andrews
Leavitt Leroy, b. 4/16/1944 in Pittsburg; Phillip L. Young and
  Mildred A. Andrews
Leonard, b. 12/27/1947 in W. Stewartstown; Phillip Young and
  Mildred Andrews
Lorraine Eleanor, b. 5/22/1932; M/M Hollis Young
Lorretta Jane, b. 9/26/1940 in Pittsburg; Hollis H. Young and
  Melvina L. Young
Lynn Rae, b. 2/27/1956; Ivan George Young and Helen May
  Young

Marlene Florence, b. 6/21/1950 in W. Stewartstown; Ivan G. Young and Helen Young
Melinda Anne, b. 7/26/1993 in Colebrook; Duane Richard Young and Luanne Marie Young
Michaela Ann, b. 9/3/1995 in Colebrook; Sanford Wade Young and Jill Emily Young
Nancy Arleater, b. 1/23/1935; Stewart Young and Hilda Brown
Nathan Klaus, b. 2/28/1974; Leonard William Young and Marilyn Anne White
Roland Roy, b. 5/9/1938 in Pittsburg; William Young and Lottie Howe
Sanford Wade, b. 4/28/1961; Arnold Stewart Young and Lou Alberta Young
Sharon Ann, b. 10/23/1954; Arnold Stewart Young and Lou Alberta Young
Sheridan Roy, b. 2/8/1959; Arnold Stewart Young and Lou Alberta Young
Sidney Arnold, b. 9/1/1952 in W. Stewartstown; Arnold S. Young and Lou Alberta Young
Sonya Dee, b. 2/19/1980; Sidney Arnold Young and Denise Claire Desrosiers
Steven Howard, b. 2/1/1957; Arnold Stewart Young and Lou Alberta Young
Susan Jane, b. 10/17/1951 in W. Stewartstown; Ivan G. Young and Helen Young
Tami Adell, b. 3/12/1963; Ivan George Young and Helen May Young
Winston J., b. 10/8/1942 in Pittsburg; Phillip Young and Mildred Andrews

Marriages

ALDRICH,
Cecil Orin of Pittsburg m. Florence Carleen **Kane** of Pittsburg 11/13/1929
Darwin L. of Pittsburg m. Violet M. **Lang** of Littleton 11/1/1917
Henry W. of Pittsburg m. Mary A. **Rockelin** of PA 5/18/1904
Henry W. of Pittsburg m. Mary **Blank** of Allentown, PA 6/16/1917

ALLEN,
George of Pittsburg m. Constance **Hawes** of Beecher Falls, VT 9/18/1920
Harry S. of Pittsburg m. Angie **Roby** of Pittsburg 8/27/1913
Wilber m. Leona **Lantagne** 9/15/1964; H – 52, s/o Wilber D. Allen and Flora Akley; W – 36, d/o Leland Waters and Ila Rowe

ALLISON,
Rupert Nash m. Ann **Wright** 6/12/1953; H – 25, s/o Rupert E. Allison and Florence E. Nash; W – 22, d/o Samuel H. Wright and Flora M. Bacon

AMEY,
Holman J. of Pittsburg m. Mary H. **Sommers** of Burlington, VT 7/17/1923
Holman J. m. Dorothy **Sprague** 3/5/1949; H – 47, s/o Alfred E. Amey and Etta A. Young; W – 24, d/o Leroy W. Sprague and Ruth M. Richardson
John Holman m. Deborah Arline **Locke** 8/17/1974; H – 24, s/o Holman J. Amey and Dorothy Sprague; W – 20, d/o Leo Locke and Louise Smith
Mark Everett m. Heather Lyn **Mitchell** 7/5/1974; H – 22, s/o Holman J. Amey and Dorothy Sprague; W – 17, d/o Edmund Mitchell and Louise Gauthier
Paul R. of Pittsburg m. Arcia A. **French** of Gladwin, MI 9/15/1984

Roy Edward m. Laurel Joyce **Gray** 8/15/1970; H – 19, s/o Holman Amey and Dorothy Sprague; W – 19, d/o Robert Gray and Donna Bumford

ANDERSON,
Clint Edward of Pittsburg m. Darcy Lynn **Purrington** of Stewartstown 8/3/1991
Jon R. G. of Pittsburg m. Christine McCaffrey **Goulet** of Pittsburg 11/8/1997
Mallet A. m. Dorothy F. **Hawes** 6/13/1942; H – 26, s/o Carlton Anderson and Christine Swenson; W – 21, d/o George W. Hawes and Geneva Farnsworth
Michael B. m. Rhoda Lyn **Whitman** 7/2/1978; H – 34, s/o Mallett Anderson and Dorothy Hawes; W – 31, d/o Arthur Blaney and Hilda Blodgett
Raymond J. M. of Pittsburg m. Mellissa Lynn **Bennett** of Concord 8/13/1994

ARMSTRONG,
David D. of Pittsburg m. Marcia D. **Smith** of Otter River, MA 3/20/2005 in Pittsburg

ARSENAULT,
Kenneth Paul of Pittsburg m. Patty Joe **Robidoux** of Pittsburg 12/9/1998

BACON,
Claude S. m. Irma **Philbrook** 9/15/1934 in Colebrook; H – 25, s/o Willie H. Bacon and Nellie Sanborn; W – 21, d/o Earle Philbrook and Harriet Crocker
George A. of Pittsburg m. Myrtle **Goerson** of Canaan, VT 2/28/1918
James H. m. Thelma Beatrice **Fogg** 8/1/1938; H – 28, s/o Will H. Bacon and Nellie Sanborn; W – 20, d/o Austin Fogg and Carrie Dyette

John E. m. Norma **Masters** 5/1/1974; H – 26, s/o James H. Bacon and Thelma Fogg; W – 28, d/o Celon Hodge and Wilma Crawford

William Austin m. Laurie Ann **Little** 11/30/1968; H – 29, s/o James Bacon and Thelma Fogg; W – 18, d/o William Little and Beatrice Currier

BAGLEY,
Guy Andrew m. Ruth Martha **Currier** 7/17/1948; H – 28, s/o Guy E. Bagley and Ella G. Roberts; W – 26, d/o Andrew H. Currier and Nellie Witherell

BALDWIN,
George W. of Pittsburg m. Nettie N. **Blodgett** 2/4/1909

BALL,
Ernest James m. Alice Iona **Towle** 8/19/1937 in Pittsburg; H – 21, s/o Elwin Ball and Minnie Jackson; W – 20, d/o Edwin A. Towle and Alice Gordon

BARR,
Ronald Eugene of W. Stewartstown m. Patti Anne **Hutchinson** of W. Stewartstown 5/20/1989

BARRY,
Alton Charles m. Bertha M. **Cook** 8/6/1937 in Pittsburg; H – 21, s/o Thomas Barry and Elizabeth Clackey; W – 23, d/o Wheatly Cook and Grace Tillotson

BARTLETT,
Michael J. of Pittsburg m. Karin L. **Harper** of Pittsburg 5/23/2007 in Pittsburg

BARTON,
John Allen, Sr. m. Mary Ange **Fraser** 7/27/1974; H – 56, s/o Harry Barton and Ida M. LaFreniere; W – 63, d/o Arsene Venne and Melina Piche

BASWELL,
Harry W. of Beecher Falls, VT m. Mercy T. **Day** of Pittsburg 5/13/1906

BAUER,
August L. m. Rosalie E. **Beauchemin** 12/29/1961; H – 22, s/o August Bauer and Mary Miller; W – 19, d/o Lewis Beauchemin and Una Furgerson

BEAUCHEMIN,
Gene L. m. Virginia **Lagoulis** 9/3/1961; H – 24, s/o Lewis Beauchemin and Una Furgerson; W – 17, d/o Speros Lagoulis and Gertrude Smith
Lawrence George m. Marcia Louise **Langley** 12/24/1954; H – 20, s/o Lewis Beauchemin and Una Fergerson; W – 18, d/o William Langley and Norma Dal-Lero

BEECHER,
Leo of Pittsburg m. G. Beryl **Lawton** of Hereford, PQ 10/14/1920

BEGIN,
Richard Louis of Pittsburg m. July Ann **Jameson** of Columbia 8/16/1980

BELLOWS,
Carl W. of Essex Jct., VT m. Colette M. **Beloin** of Pittsburg 8/4/1979

BENNETT,
Anthony F. of Pittsburg m. Holly A. **Firda** of Pittsburg 5/23/1981

BENTLEY,
Christopher Robert of Salisbury m. Alicia Anne **Harris** of Salisbury 6/28/1999

BERGERON,
Leopold Rosaire m. Beverly Irene **MacLeod** 2/24/1973; H – 27, s/o Henry Bergeron and Margaret Gagnon; W – 21, d/o Fred MacLeod and Margaret Morrison
Paul A. of Pittsburg m. Jo-Anne M. **Fluet** of Derry 7/24/1982

BERNARD,
Peter L. m. Rose M. **Uran** 10/31/1964; H – 22, s/o Joseph C. Bernard and Louise Thiverge; W – 17, d/o Frank Uran and Thelma Foster

BERNHARDT,
William F. of Pittsburg m. Emily M. **Dorman** of Pittsburg 7/30/2005 in Pittsburg

BERRY,
Arthur Merton of Columbia m. Lena May **Wheeler** of Pittsburg 5/28/1931
Kenneth W. m. Mary E. **Mandigo** 9/15/1943; H – 41, s/o Frederick W. Berry and Minnie M. Hale; W – 32, d/o Arthur A. Mandigo and Lucia L. Harvey

BETTS,
Norman K. of Pittsburg m. Lizzie A. **Wheeler** of Pittsburg 11/5/1907

BIBBO,
James Vincent, III m. Nancy Lee **Newman** 3/1/1975; H – 27, s/o James V. Bibbo, Jr. and Ruth E. Cain; W – 28, d/o Clifford C. Cooper and Ethel M. Schofield

BILLINGS,
Christopher Cooper of New Egypt, NJ m. Amy Marie **Malsbury** of New Egypt, NJ 10/8/1999

BILODEAU,
Raymond Joseph of Pittsburg m. Paula Marie **Kench** of Pittsburg 5/20/1995

BIRON,
Michael A. of Clarksville m. Raelene M. **Bryant** of Pittsburg 7/26/1980

BLAIS,
Dennis G. m. Louise M. **Labbe** 12/22/1970; H – 19, s/o Howard Blais and Madeline Tenney; W – 19, d/o John Labbe and Marcelle Roy

Rowland Roy m. Leona Effie **Edes** 8/5/1944; H – 22, s/o Roy Blais and Violet McKeage; W – 18, d/o Guy Edes and Bessie Rogers

Roy of Pittsburg m. Violet **McKeage** of Pittsburg 1/29/1921

BLAKELY,
Lawrence F., Jr. of Pittsburg m. Jacqueline M. **Brungot** of Pittsburg 9/15/1990

BLANCHARD,
Jesse A. of Pittsburg m. Pearl M. **Martin** of Glendale, CA 9/30/1922

Jesse A. of Pittsburg m. Pearl M. **Blanchard** of Glendale, CA 7/28/1931

Roy George m. Bernadine Adelaide **Hicks** 7/25/1946; H – 27, s/o Guy Blanchard and Helen Maranville; W – 18, d/o Carmi Hicks and Marion Day

BLODGETT,
Arthur of Pittsburg m. Blanch **Merrill** of Pittsburg 9/17/1906

BOLDUC,
Michael Leslie of Pittsburg m. Kathy Ann **Bourassa** of Pittsburg 10/8/1988

BOLENS,
William F. of Pittsburg m. Brandy L. **Estes** of Pittsburg 7/10/2004
William Fredrick of Pittsburg m. Michelle Cheri **Rodrique** of Pittsburg 4/24/1993

BOLTON,
William E. of Pittsburg m. Dianna M. **Correll** of Littleton 9/30/1995

BOUCHARD,
Aurele William m. Marion Angeline **Dion** 12/9/1940; H – 22, s/o Joseph Bouchard and Lea Cote; W – 18, d/o Pete Dion and Anna Marie Labbee

BOURGOINE,
Anthony E. of Farmington m. Laurie A. **Wake** of Pittsburg 10/12/2002

BOUTIN,
Gerald of Pittsburg m. Kelly **Gould** of Colebrook 7/19/1980
Gerald G. of Pittsburg m. Catherine Ann **Belanger** of Pittsburg 11/20/1992
Ivon J. of Pittsburg m. Lisa R. **Clark** of Pittsburg 4/17/2000

BRISTOL,
Melvin L. of Sherman, CT m. Diana H. **Knapp** of Sherman, CT 7/5/1982

BROOKS,
Clinton W. m. Dorothy K. **Meiggs** 10/10/1943; H – 34, s/o Francis Brooks and Lena Potter; W – 34, d/o Johnny Meiggs and Jessie M. Page
Glen C. m. Nettie W. **Crawford** 1/8/1949; H – 28, s/o Harold L. Brooks and Marion E. McConnell; W – 17, d/o Carroll E. Crawford and Caroline M. Dorman
Lawrence H. m. Myra J. **Lord** 4/25/1953; H – 31, s/o Harold L. Brooks and Marion E. McConnell; W – 20, d/o Henry C. Lord and Ella Currier
Leo M. m. Margaret N. **Allen** 7/8/1933 in Pittsburg; H – 27, b. Pittsburg, s/o Fred E. Brooks and Rose B. Coates; W – 18, b. Pittsburg, d/o Harry S. Allen and Angie E. Roby
Leo Manfred m. Winifred Lucille **Harding** 12/4/1948; H – 43, s/o Fred E. Brooks and Rose Coates; W – 25, d/o Gerald Harding and Ethel Brown
Roy Everett m. Carleen Ann **Rodrique** 7/13/1972; H – b. 8/28/1931, s/o Harold Brooks and Marian McConnell; W – b. 10/20/1950, d/o Henry Rodrique and Regena Hicks
Russell E. m. Elaine C. **Holt** 1/29/1958; H – 20, s/o Leo M. Brooks and Margaret Allen; W – 19, d/o Charles W. Holt and Ellen O. Leary

BROUSSEAU,
Waldo Charles m. Esther Alena **Willis** 9/27/1969; H – 38, s/o Dona Brousseau and Cora Dyette; W – 20, d/o Leslie Willis and Leora Heath

BROWN,
Alfred m. Virginia **Brown** 7/19/1952; H – 29, s/o Herbert Brown and Doris Hibbard; W – 22, d/o Clifton Clogston and Evelyn Day
Alfred P. m. Virginia L. **Clogston** 12/14/1946; H – 23, s/o Herbert Brown and Doris Hibbard; W – 17, d/o Clifton Clogston and Evelyn Day

Allen m. Harriet **Fuller** 7/5/1938 in Pittsburg; H – 30, s/o Elwin Brown and Margaret Brown; W – 20, d/o Reuben Fuller and Florence Bunnell

George Franklin, Jr. m. Beverly Jane **Bumford** 10/8/1955; H – 29, s/o George Brown and Hattie Ellingwood; W – 21, d/o Edson Bumford and Viola Schoff

George L. of Pittsburg m. Maple **Mills** of W. Stewartstown 8/5/1904

Herbert of Pittsburg m. Dorris **Hibbard** of Pittsburg 1/7/1918

Herbert m. Freda S. **Varney** 9/18/1949; H – 51, s/o Isaac Brown and Delila Carey; W – 51, d/o William H. Bacon and Nellie Sanborn

Herbert L. m. Nettie A. **Currier** 1/11/1933 in Bloomfield, VT; H – 35, b. Brookfield, MA, s/o Isaac Brown and Delila Curie; W – 39, b. W. Hamp., MA, d/o George Witherell and Minerva Holdridge

Isaac of Pittsburg m. Mebal R. **Merrill** of Pittsburg 9/27/1926

Otis J. m. Barbara R. **LaPoint** 7/7/1937 in Colebrook; H – 20, s/o Elwin Brown and Margaret Lord; W – 20, d/o Ernest LaPoint and Edith Terrill

William Dean m. Maureen Evelyn **Brown** 2/17/1962; H – 23, s/o Allen W. Brown and Harriet Fuller; W – 19, d/o Fred Walter Brown and Josephine Downs

BRUNELLE,

Billy m. Shirley A. **Richards** 7/2/1960; H – 19, s/o Alfred Clark Brunelle and Hazel Anderson; W – 21, d/o Clovis Richards and Armoza Paradis

David A. m. Colleen A. **Washburn** 4/8/1961; H – 19, s/o Alfred Clark Brunelle and Hazel Anderson; W – 19, d/o George Washburn and Gertrude Collins

Lawrence Albert of Pittsburg m. Bibiane Emily **D'Anjou** of Pittsburg 9/7/1996

BRUNGOT,
Norman S., Jr. m. Jacqueline M. **Covey** 10/9/1965; H – 20, s/o
 Norman S. Brungot, Sr. and Lois Ann Clawson; W – 19,
 d/o Charles Arthur Covey, Sr. and Sophia Makarawicz
Norman S., III of Pittsburg m. Jennifer Lee **Davis** of Salem
 8/11/1995

BRYANT,
Ray Allen m. Grathia Janet **Ladd** 4/10/1965; H – 29, s/o Victor
 Bryant and Gladys Hutchins; W – 35, d/o Wesley Ladd and
 Ella McPheters

BUFFINGTON,
Elmer E. m. Leora **Marsh** 12/6/1939; H – 21, s/o Leon Buffington
 and Alice Bunnell; W – 18, d/o Robert Marsh and Mildred
 G. Davis

BUMFORD,
Fredric S. m. Sharon **Merrill** 1/31/1958; H – 20, s/o Edson M.
 Bumford and Viola Doris Schoff; W – 18, d/o Willie Merrill
 and Margaret Berry

BUNNELL,
Clifford A. of Pittsburg m. Shirley A. **Ray** of Pittsburg 4/21/1979
Everett M. m. Rilma **Marsh** 10/22/1942; H – 22, s/o Nelson
 Bunnell and Flora Martin; W – 18, d/o Robert Marsh and
 Mary Davis
Holman G. m. Glendwen J. **Haynes** 8/22/1936 in Colebrook; H –
 29, s/o Dan B. Bunnell and Martha Forrest; W – 18, d/o
 Stewart Haynes and Hazel Covill

BURGES,
Albert N. of Pittsburg m. Nora M. **Stevens** of Pittsburg 1/29/1919

BURNS,
Robert John m. Norma Elnora **Huggins** 6/4/1949; H – 21, s/o Benjamin S. Burns and Lena L. Caron; W – 21, d/o Harry F. Huggins and Althea Hurlbert

BURRILL,
Paul Kingman of Pittsburg m. Wanda June **White** of Pittsburg 4/16/1988

BURTCHNELL,
William Edward m. Aline Beulah **Bourassa** 12/18/1976; H – 41, s/o William E. Burtchnell and Nettie Smith; W – 34, d/o David C. Pond and Beulah Shatney

BUTEAU,
Andre m. Edith E. **Lord** 6/15/1961; H – 38, s/o Emile Buteau and Emma Paquin; W – 18, d/o Austin P. Lord and Mable Kane

BUTLER,
Rick E. of Pittsburg m. Constance V. **Carter** of Pittsburg 6/18/2005 in Pittsburg

CAMARDA,
Phillip m. Elinor Ruth **French** 3/28/1947; H – 29, s/o Salvatore Camarda and Francis Mione; W – 21, d/o Wilbur French and Viola Brown

CAMERON,
Donald A. m. Lorraine E. **Young** 9/30/1951; H – 21, s/o Ewen U. Cameron and Helen E. Menchim; W – 19, d/o Hollis H. Young and Melvina I. Young
George A. m. Corinne **Brown** 12/11/1973; H – 19, s/o Fred Cameron and Rose Mickelboro; W – 15, d/o George Brown and Beverly Bumford

Warren J. of Pittsburg m. Ramona J. **Chamberlain** of Pittsburg 8/4/1984

CARLETON,
David John of Pittsburg m. Theresa Marie **Hufault** of Pittsburg 5/26/1990

CARLSON,
Carl T. m. Joanne I. **Jackson** 12/11/1963; H – 32, s/o Carl E. Carlson and Mary O. Chivers; W – 24, d/o Carroll Jackson and Pauline Mason

CARON,
Charles Robert of Pittsburg m. Heather **Gray** of Pittsburg 1/9/1999
Leo Paul of Pittsburg m. Christine Alice **Fortier** of Pittsburg 1/7/1995

CARRIER,
Bernard P. m. Suzanne M. **Beloin** 7/27/1974; H – 21, s/o Armand Carrier and Doris Lavertue; W – 22, d/o Alcide Beloin and Yvette Maurais

CASS,
Earnest E. of Columbia m. Lois M. **Gray** of Pittsburg 5/21/1921

CASTINE,
Peter H. of Pittsburg m. Elaine P. **Holland** of Pittsburg 11/5/2002

CASTONGUAY,
Donald O. m. Phyllis Louise **Brown** 5/3/1952; H – 23, s/o Orlando Castonguay and Beatrice Haynes; W – 21, d/o Isaac Brown and Mabel R. Merrill

CHALOUX,
Leo N. m. Therese Noella **Dube** 6/9/1962; H – 18, s/o Leon Chaloux and Jeanette Maller; W – 19, d/o Vezina Dube and Alma Benoit
Lionel G. m. Billie E. **Statkum** 7/18/1953; H – 19, s/o Joseph Chaloux and Celanise Benoit; W – 17, d/o Walter Statkum and Vivian Sarsfield
Lionel G. m. Jean **Bryant** 11/21/1962; H – 28, s/o Joseph Chaloux and Celanaire Benoit; W – 25, d/o George Crawford and Emma Johnson

CHAMBERLAIN,
William A. m. Audrey E. **Hilliard** 5/24/1941; H – 26, s/o Charles Chamberlain and Lula Lovering; W – 18, d/o George Hilliard and Ada Crawford

CHANDONNET,
Eugene W. of Manchester m. Karen L. **Lacoy** of Pittsburg 6/3/1985

CHASE,
Christopher James of Pittsburg m. Linda Susan **Baird** of Lancaster 5/20/1994
Ronald Warren m. Dallas Ann **Washburn** 6/23/1962; H – 26, s/o Frank Chase and Lena Ripley; W – 21, d/o Rueben Washburn and Eunice Fiske
Warren E. of Pittsburg m. Kim R. **Judd** of Pittsburg 6/14/1987

CILLEY,
Clifton Cleve, Jr. of Pittsburg m. Joanne Marie **Burrill** of Pittsburg 8/9/1997

CLARK,
Kenneth R. m. Ruth M. **Covell** 7/1/1933 in Pittsburg; H – 25, b.
  Pittsburg, s/o Willie P. Clark and Annie E. Brown; W – 22,
  b. Pittsburg, d/o Everett Covell and Birdie M. Cody
Willie P. of Pittsburg m. Annie E. **Brown** of Pittsburg 10/21/1906

CLARKE,
Andrew Edward of Melrose, MA m. Deborah Anne **Zub** of
  Melrose, MA 10/14/2000

CLOGSTON,
Bruce Wayne m. Cheryl Elaine **Owen** 6/29/1974; H – 20, s/o
  Clifton Clogston, Jr. and Irma Lord; W – 23, d/o Shirley
  Owen and Gertrude Wheeler
Clifton W. of Pittsburg m. Evelyn B. **Day** of Pittsburg 12/2/1925
Clifton W., Jr. m. Irma F. **Lord** 7/16/1949; H – 17, s/o Clifton
  Clogston, Sr. and Evelyn Day; W – 17, d/o Austin Lord and
  Mabel Kane
Edmund L. m. Barbara A. **Nichols** 9/19/1959; H – 25, s/o Clifton
  Clogston and Evelyn Day; W – 24, d/o Willis Bennett and
  Clara Johnson
Edmund L. m. Linda J. **Washburn** 11/9/1963; H – 29, s/o Clifton
  W. Clogston, Jr. and Evelyn Day; W – 20, d/o Willis E.
  Washburn and A. Ruene Hibbard
Edmund Linden m. Geneva Maude **Covill** 8/27/1952; H – 18, s/o
  Clifton W. Clogston and Evelyn B. Day; W – 18, d/o Forest
  Covill and Hilda Dearth
Keith W. m. Dorothy E. **Dalton** 8/8/1946; H – 17, s/o Clifton
  Clogston and Evelyn Day; W – 19, d/o Albert Dalton and
  Lois Gray
Paul W. of Pittsburg m. Alta **Wheeler** of Pittsburg 6/19/1926
Ricky C. of Pittsburg m. Helene C. **Madore** of Pittsburg 7/7/1979
William Chester m. Ivona Ada **McKeage** 8/21/1954; H – 25, s/o
  Paul W. Clogston and Alta M. Wheeler; W – 22, d/o Ivo R.
  McKeage and Vena E. Washburn

COLCORD,
Charles Foster m. Ernestine Helen **Chase** 4/4/1969; H – 36, s/o Clyde Colcord and Elizabeth Dudley; W – 45, d/o Ernest Lapoint and Edith Terrill

COLE,
Herman C. of Pittsburg m. Ada L. **Washburn** of Pittsburg 12/10/1919

CONGDON,
Robert N. m. Brenda N. **Howland** 6/30/1962; H – 21, s/o Clarence Congdon and Esther Rines; W – 19, d/o Bernard R. Howland and Margaret Ouellette

CONNOR,
William Allan of Turners Falls, MA m. Melisa A. **Harrison** of Westminster, VT 9/16/1996

CONROY,
Robert Edward m. Marie Leona **Ropple** 7/21/1963; H – 27, s/o Walter J. Conroy and Lillian Becktold; W – 19, d/o Norman Ropple and Arlene French

COOK,
Roland Simpson m. Doris Gray **Fissette** 10/8/1966; H – 60, s/o George Cook and Mable Gray; W – 55, d/o Walter Gray and Elvira Gray

COONEY,
Joseph J. m. Mary A. **Robideau** 5/28/1951; H – 45, s/o Joseph A. Cooney and Phoebe Morey; W – 35, d/o Jacob Gadomski and Magdeline Karpowitz

CORON,
John of Pittsburg m. Rosie **Lagasce** of Pittsburg 2/11/1910

COTE,
Gerard m. Roena **Hayes** 6/20/1942; H – 23, s/o Isidore Colte and Eva L. Favreau; W – 23, d/o Stewart Haynes and Hazel Danforth
Paul A. m. Cheryl Ann **Noyes** 10/25/1969; H – 26, s/o Eugene J. Cote and Desnieges Thibeault; W – 22, d/o George A. Noyes and Alice Pariseau

COUTURE,
Neil Paul m. Beverly Lee **Haynes** 6/17/1961; H – 19, s/o Joseph P. Couture and Theresa Gendron; W – 20, d/o Stewart H. Haynes and Hazel E. Danforth
Rick Paul of Pittsburg m. Riana Frost **Carroll** of Pittsburg 7/17/1988

COVELL,
Dwayne Otis of Pittsburg m. Michelle Ann **Cameron** of Pittsburg 7/28/1990
Dwayne Otis of Pittsburg m. Kathleen Marie **Scott** of Stratford 11/27/1993
Everett H. of Pittsburg m. Birdie M. **Codey** of Pittsburg 12/23/1904
Forest A. of Pittsburg m. Hilda **Dearth** of Pittsburg 1/4/1926
Garland T. m. Leone D. **Day** 1/18/1936 in Colebrook; H – 23, s/o Francis Covill and Nora Mayberry; W – 19, d/o Rufus E. Day and Nora M. Haynes
Gary Winston m. Hilda Francese **Brown** 8/19/1959; H – 18, s/o Forest Covell and Hilda Dearth; W – 18, d/o Otis J. Brown and Barbara LaPointe
Leslie Lafe m. Ruth Helen **Foote** 3/7/1959; H – 19, s/o Forest Covell and Hilda Dearth; W – 15, d/o Onie Foote and Helen Rathbun

Roy E. of Pittsburg m. Margaret **Penn** of Clarksville 8/30/1924
Shirley J. of Pittsburg m. Elaine **Dearth** of Pittsburg 6/20/1927

COVEY,
Charles Arthur, Jr. m. Dorothy Anne **Phillips** 9/21/1968; H – 26, s/o Charles A. Covey, Sr. and Sophia Makarowicz; W – 20, d/o Bert Phillips and Evelyn Holden

COVILL,
Bernard A. m. Catherine M. **Banks** 12/31/1947; H – 20, s/o Forest Covill and Hilda A. Dearth; W – 17, d/o Chester Banks and Mable Johnson

Clesson m. Alice J. **Chappell** 12/14/1937 in Brookline; H – 29, s/o Grant Covill and Maude Merrill; W – 19, d/o Irving G. Chappell and Rose Currier

David G. of Pittsburg m. Cheryl A. **Mackey** of Pittsburg 10/9/1982

Dennis Lindsey m. Jean Anne **Hibbard** 5/20/1972; H – b. 3/3/1950, s/o Lindsey Covill and Roberta Merrill; W- b. 12/7/1951, d/o George E. Hibbard and Irene Young

Earle Wilbur m. Nancy Arleta **Young** 7/14/1952; H – 19, s/o Wilbur D. Covill and Ladora Philbrook; W – 17, d/o Stewart Young and Hilda Brown

Forrest A. of Pittsburg m. Sheila M. **Thurber** of Pittsburg 7/3/1999

Forrest Alfred m. Linda Ellen **Keezer** 1/20/1968; H – 19, s/o Bernard Covill and Marjorie Keezer; W – 18, d/o Sidney Adams and Katherine Banks

Gordon L. m. Norma E. **Lynch** 5/25/1957; H – 30, s/o Forest Covill and Hilda Dearth; W – 22, d/o Kenneth Lynch and Dorothy Barker

Lindsey Leroy m. Roberta June **Merrill** 8/27/1949; H – 20, s/o Forest A. Covill and Hilda A. Dearth; W – 18, d/o Willie G. Merrill and Margaret S. Berry

Robert D. m. Margaret **Crawford** 6/29/1957; H – 26, s/o Forest Covill and Hilda Dearth; W – 16, d/o George Crawford and Emma Johnson

Roger G. of Pittsburg m. Deborah M. **Slack** of Pittsburg 7/5/1980

CRAWFORD,

Alfred J. of Pittsburg m. Matilda **Jackson** of Pittsburg 5/27/1906

Carrol of Pittsburg m. Caroline **Dorman** of Pittsburg 9/1/1928

Jay J. m. Dorothy **Holbrook** 6/14/1941; H – 42, s/o Myron Crawford and Bertha Shallow; W – 34, d/o Melvin T. Holbrook and Catherine E. Erowe

Orrie of Clarksville m. Mertie **Covill** of Pittsburg 9/23/1905

CROSS,

Dennis E. of Pittsburg m. Deborah C. **Pariseau** of Pittsburg 5/19/2001

Harlan of Pittsburg m. Mhilia **Hodge** of Sutton, PQ 1/29/1915

Harold W. m. Laura M. **Duquette** 1/11/1937 in Colebrook; H – 25, s/o Walter T. Cross and Bessie Hibbard; W – 22, d/o Nelson Duquette and Rose Ann DeBlois

Ricky D. of Stewartstown m. Penny L. **McKeage** of Pittsburg 2/18/1984

CUMMINGS,

William Elwin m. Sarah Jane **Tabor** 10/23/1955; H – 19, s/o Maurice Pike and Francis L. Cummings; W – 21, d/o Parker W. Tabor and Nina M. Williams

CURRIER,

Andrew H. m. Muriel V. **Keach** 8/12/1933 in Keene; H – 42, b. Pittsburg, s/o Andrew J. Currier and Martha N. Shoppee; W – 28, b. Pittsburg, d/o Herman W. Keach and Grace May Hilliard

DAGESSE,
Richard A. m. Mariette A. **Robinson** 10/20/1962; H – 17, s/o Levis Dagesse and Eva Lessard; W – 18, d/o Eric Robinson and Evelyn Beloin
Yvon Doris m. Monica Rita **Robinson** 7/2/1960; H – 24, s/o Levis Degasse and Eva Lessard; W – 17, d/o Eric Robinson and Evelyn Beloin

DALTON,
Merrill Albert m. Judith Eileen **Young** 7/27/1963; H – 23, s/o Albert H. Dalton and Lois Gray; W – 21, d/o Phillip J. Young and Mildred Andrews

DANFORTH,
Robert Henry m. Vivian Carleton **Emmons** 12/25/1949; H – 60, s/o Henry Danforth and Annie Young; W – 51, d/o George R. Bemis and Belle A. Merrill

DANIELS,
Stephen Allen of Pittsburg m. Michele Marie **Plante** of Pittsburg 6/19/1999

DAVIS,
Frank H. of Pittsburg m. Mildred **Bennett** of St. Johnsbury, VT 6/3/1919
James A. m. Ethel May **Creon** 6/30/1934 in Pittsburg; H – 45, s/o Joe Davis and Gertie E. Davis; W – 36, d/o John Gable and Florence Records
Ora M. of Pittsburg m. Florence **Bennett** of Pittsburg 2/27/1917

DAY,
Alfred Edwin m. Geraldine Marvis **Forbes** 2/10/1945; H – 22, s/o Lyle S. Day and Winifred M. Day; W – 18, d/o George W. Forbes and Eda J. Harriman
Edwin C. of Pittsburg m. Blanche **Alls** of Colebrook 8/24/1907

Gerald Alfred m. Anna Marie **Bruno** 3/27/1976; H – 29, s/o
Alfred Day and Geraldine Forbes; W – 19, d/o Peter Bruno
and June DeGray

Harry Lee of Pittsburg m. Glee Adell **Nason** of Colebrook
1/27/1931

Howard Edwin m. Terry Mae **Scott** 11/25/1971; H – 23, s/o
Alfred Day and Geraldine Forbes; W – 18, d/o Richard J.
Scott and Ramona Harris

Irving of Pittsburg m. Catherine **Wade** of W. Burke, VT 6/14/1910

Lloyd D. of Pittsburg m. Jessie R. **Huggins** of Pittsburg
6/24/1921

Wendall Waide m. Hallie Eliza **Clark** 8/23/1933 in Pittsburg; H –
22, b. Pittsburg, s/o Orie Irving Day and Katherine Waide;
W – 22, b. Pittsburg, d/o Willie P. Clark and Annie E.
Brown

DEARTH,

Warren William m. Rebecca Helen **Hall** 1/17/1949; H – 20, s/o
Isreal Dearth and Minnie McKeage; W – 18, d/o Vernon H.
Hall and Christine R. Hawes

DENEHER,

Michael of Ossining, NY m. Joan Marie Daly **Horkovich** of
Ossining, NY 9/27/1997

DESCHENE,

George O. of Pittsburg m. Geraldine M. **Day** of Pittsburg
4/2/1983

George Oliver m. Florence Eldora **Shatney** 10/26/1940; H – 21,
s/o John Deschene and Ada Bean; W – 15, d/o David
Shatney and Avis Tirrell

George Oliver m. Dorothy Shatford **Deschene** 10/11/1969; H –
50, s/o John Deschene and Ada Bean; W – 53, d/o Lester
Greenwood and Nora Shatford

DESROCHERS,
Michael Alan of Pittsburg m. Nathalie Chantale **Couture** of Pittsburg 7/28/1990

DION,
Charles J. m. Madeline M. **Covill** 12/23/1950; H – 18, s/o Pete Dion and Anna Labbe; W – 19, d/o Reginald Covill and Josephine Gilbert

Peter Edward m. Helen Sylvia **Lachance** 8/17/1968; H – 25, s/o Albert Dion and Rose Markovich; W – 20, d/o Henry Lachance and Sylvia Robie

DIONNE,
Serge Armand m. Deborah Ann **Dehl** 7/20/1974; H – 20, s/o Antonio Dionne and Alice Peloquin; W – 20, d/o Stephen Dehl and Beatrice Beaudette

DOBSON,
Brandon James m. Janice Hope **Clogston** 5/27/1966; H – 22, s/o James Dobson and Marguerite Keazer; W – 16, d/o Keith Clogston and Dorothy Dalton

Charles Thomas m. Gladys Flagg **Daggett** 12/25/1949; H – 60, s/o Isaiah Dobson and Annie Allwood; W – 56, d/o Frank Carbee and Annie Tewksbury

Jerry Earl m. Muriel Lee **Fogg** 10/14/1961; H – 19, s/o James M. Dobson and Marguerite L. Kayser; W – 20, d/o Leland M. Fogg and Katherine Shallow

DORE,
Cleveland H. of Pittsburg m. Myrtle F. **Wright** of Pittsburg 12/16/1917

DORMAN,
Sherman Alson m. Evelyn Grace **Owen** 5/10/1954; H – 17, s/o Thomas E. Dorman and Evelyn E. Haynes; W – 16, d/o Munn Owen and Gladys H. Bolton
Thomas E. of Canaan, VT m. Rosie **Gosselin** of Pittsburg 3/10/1909
Thomas E. of Pittsburg m. Bertha S. **Haynes** of Pittsburg 5/29/1926
Thomas, Jr. m. Ervena M. **Hicks** 6/15/1951; H – 20, s/o Thomas Dorman, Sr. and Evelyn Haynes; W – 17, d/o Carmi Hicks and Marion Day
Walter of Pittsburg m. Winnie **Haynes** of Pittsburg 3/9/1907
Walter Douglas m. Brenda Emily **Barton** 8/6/1977; H – 19, s/o Thomas E. Dorman, Jr. and Ervena Hicks; W – 24, d/o Kenneth K. Barton and Emily P. Marston
Wayne Edward m. Beverly Jean **Gadwah** 7/29/1972; H – b. 12/26/1952, s/o Thomas Dorman, Jr. and Ervena Hicks; W – b. 10/6/1953, d/o Lyman I. Gadwah and ----- Dwinnell
Wendell Lyndon m. Barbara Jean **Bedard** 6/28/1975; H – 20, s/o Thomas Dorman, Jr. and Ervina Hicks; W – 20, d/o Noel Bedard, Sr. and Sylvia Foster
Winston Arnold m. Sherry Lynn **Bryant** 6/26/1976; H – 20, s/o Thomas E. Dorman, Jr. and Ervena M. Hicks; W – 18, d/o Ray Bryant and Jean Crawford

DRAGON,
Alfred of Pittsburg m. Maria **Chaquet** of Hereford, PQ --/--/1904

DUBE,
Richard N., II of Pittsburg m. Stephanie Jo **McKeage** of Pittsburg 5/25/1996

DUMAIS,
John R. of Brunswick, ME m. Darlene K. **French** of Brunswick, ME 9/17/1983

DUNKLEE,
Alan Edward, Jr. of Wilder, VT m. Janelle Elizabeth Brown **Daubenschmidt** of Wilder, VT 3/29/1997

DUPUIS,
Romeo Gaston, Jr. of Manchester m. Catherine Marie **Gauvin** of Manchester 7/11/1998

DWYER,
Michael K. of Pittsburg m. Gloria D. **Duffy** of Pittsburg 3/1/2003

DYSART,
John E. of Brunswick, ME m. Lynn R. **Young** of Brunswick, ME 10/10/1987

EARLE,
Charles G. of Pittsburg m. Janice L. **Earle** of Pittsburg 11/28/1981

EDMOND,
Stuart Deane m. Arlene Helen **McMaster** 3/22/1941; H – 30, s/o Herman D. Edmond and Annie E. Hammond; W – 23, d/o Alexander McMasters and Hazel T. Howe

EKBERG,
Mark C. of Pittsburg m. Laurie A. **Lemanski** of Hillsborough 7/26/2008 in Laconia

ELDRIDGE,
Timothy W. of Ctr. Ossipee m. Karen B. **Eldridge** of Ctr. Ossipee 4/29/2000

ELEMONDE,
Jean-Paul m. Arlene Cecile **Chaloux** 7/18/1959; H – 27, s/o Antoine Elemond and Julienne St. Martin; W – 21, d/o Joseph Chaloux and Celanaire Benoit

ELLIS,
George Colin, Jr. of Pittsburg m. Bonnie Joyce **Howard** of Pittsburg 10/10/1998

EMMONS,
Merrill C. m. Dorothy F. **Lynch** 10/15/1954; H – 30, s/o Harold Emmons and Vivian Bemis; W – 30, d/o William Lynch and Ethel Riddle

FANDRICH,
Edgar Jacob m. Melissa Amelia **Mousseau** 9/10/1977; H – 20, s/o Christoph Fandrich and Gerda Landenberger; W – 27, d/o Keane Mousseau and Katherine Smith

FARNSWORTH,
Earl of Pittsburg m. Florence **Aldrich** of Clarksville 8/16/1911
Harry D. of Pittsburg m. Hattie **Hibbard** of Pittsburg 9/23/1905
Harry D. of Pittsburg m. Mrs. Lucy M. **Tilton** of Canaan, VT 11/1/1921

FILLION,
Donald m. Vivian **Laperle** 10/1/1977; H – 30, s/o Lucien Fillion and Anita Valliere; W – 34, d/o Leon Laperle and Adrienne Belanger

FISH,
Blaine Delma m. Sherry Ann **Ladd** 1/23/1971; H – 18, s/o Delma Fish and Bernice Schoff; W – 19, d/o Elwin Ladd and Lona Knapp

Jarvis Thurman m. Carlene Alida **Young** 6/22/1968; H – 24, s/o Delma Fish and Bernice Schoff; W – 22, d/o Philip Young and Mildred Andrews

Marshall Schoff m. Jane Harriet **Masters** 11/25/1961; H – 21, s/o Delma Fish and Bernice Schoff; W – 19, d/o Leland Masters and Maud Foster

FISSETTE,

George of Pittsburg m. Hazle **Fuller** of Pittsburg 9/5/1906

George H. of Pittsburg m. Alice **Smith** of Nashua 10/21/1922

Joseph H. of Pittsburg m. Delia **Nolan** of Berlin 5/4/1919

Robert Arthur m. Nerine Mae **Heath** 7/28/1961; H – 21, s/o Denail A. Fissette and Junie M. Haynes; W – 18, d/o Quinten C. Heath and Mae R. Chapple

Roger C. m. Doris E. **Gray** 8/28/1940; H – 29, s/o George H. Fissette and Hazel Fuller; W – 29, d/o Walter I. Gray and Elvira E. Gray

FLANDERS,

Gordan M. m. Bernice **Schoff** 11/14/1934 in Colebrook; H – 23, s/o Irving Flanders and Nellie Colby; W – 18, d/o Perley R. Schoff and Lizzie Johnson

Gordan M. m. Marie Jeanne **Paquette** 2/25/1941; H – 29, s/o Irving H. Flanders and Nellie Colby; W – 27, d/o Joseph E. Paquette and Marie Chouinard

Gordon M. m. Helen M. R. **Dionne** 9/1/1951; H – 40, s/o Irving Flanders and Nellie E. Colby; W – 36, d/o Arthur J. Dionne and Nellie T. Scanlon

Walter Wilfred m. Jacquelyn Ethyl **Bumford** 12/19/1948; H – 22, s/o Walter C. Flanders and Alice Brooks; W – 20, d/o Edson Bomford and Viola Schoff

FOGG,

James David of Tremont, PA m. Lori Ann **Shuler** of Tremont, PA 9/27/1997

Leland m. Katherine A. **Shallow** 5/17/1941; H – 26, s/o Austin Fogg and Carrie Deyette; W – 20, d/o James M. Shallow and Elizabeth Day

FOOTE,
Frederick James m. Joanne Elaine **Covell** 12/12/1956; H – 21, s/o Onie Foote and Helen Rathbun; W – 20, d/o Forest Covell and Hilda Dearth
Jarvis N. of Pittsburg m. Jane M. **Waterhouse** of Pittsburg 9/27/1987

FOSHER,
Thomas J. of Pittsburg m. Robin L. **Covill** of Pittsburg 7/14/1984

FOSTER,
Lawrence Bartlett m. Laura Bell **Davis** 12/19/1939; H – 26, s/o Walter Noah Foster and Leona C. Nichols; W – 23, d/o Harry I. Davis and Ruth Furgerson

FOX,
Kenneth Howard of W. Stewartstown m. Hannah Eile **Brown** of E. Hereford, PQ 6/5/1931

FRANCOEUR,
Clark Alan of Pittsburg m. Shelly J. **Wiswell** of Clarksville 6/19/1982

FRENCH,
Brian Azel m. Jennifer Lee **Brown** 8/20/1965; H – 17, s/o Lovell French and Daphyne Clogston; W – 18, d/o Isaac Brown and Leitha Young
Lovell L. m. Daphyne W. **Clogston** 1/20/1944; H – 17, s/o Azel H. French and Leone Lapoint; W – 17, d/o Clifton Clogston and Evelyn Day

Melvin Otis m. Linda Ann **Crawford** 5/31/1975; H – 25, s/o Otis French and Julia Dobson; W – 27, d/o Carroll Crawford and Caroline Dorman

Otis E. m. Julia M. **Dobson** 5/24/1947; H – 20, s/o Wilbur French and Viola Brown; W – 17, d/o Charles Dobson

Wayland W. m. Irma J. **Covill** 2/19/1949; H – 24, s/o Wilbur C. French and Viola Brown; W – 18, d/o Reginald Covill and Josephine Gilbert

FRIZZELL,
Bradley Alan of Pittsburg m. Heidi L. **Curtis** of Pittsburg 4/7/1979

Roy W. m. Janine C. **Klebe** 9/27/1969; H – 18, s/o Wilfred Frizzell and Natalie Whitehill; W – 18, d/o Curtis Klebe and Gloria Mullavey

Roy W. m. Nancy E. **Campbell** 7/1/1978; H – 27, s/o Wilfred Frizzell and Natalie E. Whitehill; W – 31, d/o Herman Cross and Gwendolyn Ellingwood

FULLER,
Andrew C. of Pittsburg m. Goldie **Smith** of Stewartstown 4/9/1912

Andrew C. of Pittsburg m. Freda **Bacon** of Pittsburg 6/6/1914

Andrew C. of Pittsburg m. Mildred Anna **Williams** of Pittsburg 6/18/1926

David James m. Katharyn Margaret **Bishop** 9/25/1976; H – 21, s/o William B. Fuller, Sr. and Muriel Lambert; W – 16, d/o Floyd Bishop and Mary McCarthy

Frank of Pittsburg m. Ella O. **Corkum** of Milan 4/5/1913

William E. m. Cecile A. **Cote** 6/13/1942; H – 21, s/o Andrew Fuller and Freda S. Bacon; W – 18, d/o Isidore Cote and Eva Favreau

FURBUSH,
George M. of Pittsburg m. Ellen **Terrill** of Pittsburg 9/21/1912

GADWAH,
Bruce Edwin m. Deborah Agnes **Rattigan** 3/8/1976; H – 27, s/o Lyman Gadwah and Katherine Dwinell; W – 24, d/o Edwin B. White and Olga Yaroma

Mervyn Oliver m. Eva S. **Scott** 12/24/1977; H – 59, s/o Victor A. Gadwah and Jessie A. Henson; W – 67, d/o Harley Smith and Maude Greenwood

GAGNE,
Rene m. Marie Claire **Chaloux** 8/19/1961; H – 20, s/o Laurent Gagne and Bernadette Dionne; W – 19, d/o Leon Chaloux and Jeanette Malleur

GALLAGHER,
Charles Thomas of Eldred, NY m. Christine Jon **Poillon** of Barryville, NY 2/13/1999

Frank L. of Groveton m. Eva H. **Scott** of Pittsburg 6/23/1923

GARCELON,
David C. m. Helen **Mousseau** 8/27/1960; H – 19, s/o C. Frederick Garcelon and Edyth M. Barker; W – 17, d/o Keane Mousseau and Katherine Smith

GATHERCOLE,
Roy C. of Pittsburg m. Grace **Fellows** of Clarksville 11/30/1905

GENDRON,
Phillip Ovila m. Patricia Ann **Masters** 4/23/1960; H – 21, s/o Ovila Gendron and Earline Greenwood; W – 21, d/o Leland Ray Masters and Maud Frances Foster

GEORGE,
Bertram E. of Colebrook m. M. J. **Frey** of Pittsburg 11/9/2004

GIBSON,
George Arthur of Pittsburg m. Suzanne Elaine **Blanchard** of Pittsburg 4/3/1994

GILBERT,
Dean Coolidge m. Pauline Matilda **McComiskey** 6/19/1954; H – 22, s/o Theodore A. Gilbert and Otlee M. Coolidge; W – 29, d/o Henry A. Gilbert and Alice E. Blodgette

GILSON,
Daniel of Pittsburg m. Lynn **Wolny** of Pittsburg 11/24/2006 in Pittsburg

GLEASON,
Michael F. of Pittsburg m. Monica C. **Evans** of Pittsburg 8/15/2004

GOERKE,
Arthur Wayne of Westford, MA m. Gail Ellen **Norgoal** of Westford, MA 4/17/1993

GOLDRUP,
Robert C. m. Anna C. **Spat** 10/21/1950; H – 21, s/o Ernest Goldrup and Blanche Savage; W – 18, d/o Esther Spat
William M. m. June S. E. **Tame** 4/21/1951; H – 20, s/o Ernest A. Goldrup and Blanche M. Savage; W – 17, d/o John L. Tame and Jeanette Anderson

GOODNOW,
Douglas Everett of Pittsburg m. Rebecca Lynn **Kubosiak** of Pittsburg 6/17/1995

GOODREAU,
Archie W. m. Nora Leone **Brooks** 3/6/1943; H – 32, s/o Joseph Goodreau and Rose McCarty; W – 18, d/o Francis Brooks and Lena Potter

GOODWIN,
Douglas Stewart m. Constance Violet **Haynes** 5/17/1971; H – 18, s/o Glen Goodwin and Laura Chase; W – 15, d/o Bradley Haynes and Mona Hicks

Harry Alton, Jr. m. Constance Violet **Goodwin** 10/27/1973; H – 27, s/o Harry A. Goodwin, Sr. and Elizabeth Gorman; W – 17, d/o Bradley Haynes and Mona Hicks

GOSSELIN,
Bernard M. of Pittsburg m. Susan O. **Gamsby** of Canaan, VT 11/25/1995

GOULETTE,
David Ralph m. Francese A. **Sweeney** 3/3/1962; H – 20, s/o Ralph Goulette and Celeste Phelps; W – 20, d/o Julius Sweeney and Dorothy Lunderville

GRAY,
Arnold E. of Pittsburg m. Lucie A. **Madore** of Pittsburg 10/4/1980

Harold m. Kimberly **Gadwah** 10/21/1978; H – 24, s/o Tabor Gray and Eunice Jeffers; W – 20, d/o Sylvia Gadwah

Leonard R. of Pittsburg m. Tammy L. **Havalotti** of Stewartstown 11/28/2003

Leroy E. of Pittsburg m. Linnie M. **Young** of N. Stratford 8/18/1924

Lindsey R. m. Ann M. **Getchell** 7/15/1978; H – 25, s/o Robert Gray and Donna Bumford; W – 25, d/o L. Forbes Getchell and Sylvia Fitts

Merrill A. of Pittsburg m. Velma **Hibbard** of Pittsburg 6/17/1922

Patrick Hibbard m. Thelma Iris **Robertshaw** 6/26/1952; H – 21, s/o Merrill Gray and Velma H. Hibbard; W – 18, d/o Harry Robertshaw and Eveline Hall

Robert Edward m. Marian Theresa **Kelley** 3/10/1945; H – 21, s/o Edward Gray and Bertha Hackett; W – 22, d/o Frank J. Kelly and Louise Reilly

Robert Y. m. Donna A. **Bumford** 9/16/1950; H – 24, s/o Leroy Gray and Linnie Young; W - 24, d/o Edson Bumford and Viola Schoff

Seth P. of Pittsburg m. Jamie N. **Owen** of Pittsburg 8/27/2005 in Whitefield

Tabor P. m. Eunice E. **Jeffers** 9/19/1953; H – 28, s/o Leroy E. Gray and Linnie M. Young; W – 18, d/o Miles C. Jeffers and Laura F. Blodgett

GREEN,

Frank Edward m. Brenda Hazel **Goulette** 9/5/1965; H – 29, s/o Kenneth Green and Blanche Brown; W – 29, d/o Ralph David Goulette and Celeste Eliza Phelps

GRIFFIN,

Wayne R. of Pittsburg m. Rita M. **Coleman** of Pittsburg 10/13/1983

GROVER,

Brendon m. Joan **Day** 6/14/1952; H – 19, s/o Glen Grover and Ruby Clark; W – 16, d/o Holman Day and Romona Haynes

Glen H. of Pittsburg m. Evelyn Ruby **Clark** of Colebrook 1/24/1929

William A. of Elizaville, NY m. Judith A. **Coutts** of Elizaville, NY 8/11/1984

GUAY,
Nelson m. Mary Rose **Duquette** 6/3/1935 in W. Stewartstown; H – 24, s/o Abraham Guay and Mary Louise Charette; W – 18, d/o Nelson Duquette and Roseando Deblonois

GUILMETTE,
Jeremy Ramon of Stewartstown m. Ann Marie **French** of Stewartstown 9/2/2000

HADLEY,
Chuck L. of Wilton m. Pamela J. **Sweet** of Wilton 6/27/1998

HALL,
Burton Hawes m. Fay Anita **Locke** 8/12/1954; H – 20, s/o Vernon H. Hall and Christie R. Hawes; W – 18, d/o Guy E. Locke and Rena A. Harrison
David George m. Elsie June **Eames** 7/16/1960; H – 21, s/o Vernon Haynes Hall and Christie Rebecca Hawes; W – 18, d/o Everett Rawson Eames and Mona Ernestine Bennett
Donald C. of Pittsburg m. Elaine A. **Champagne** of Pittsburg 7/5/1989
George D. of Clarksville m. Emma M. **Johnson** of Pittsburg 11/22/1924
Richard Burton m. Sandra Lee **Haynes** 9/1/1973; H – 18, s/o Burton Hall and Fay Locke; W – 18, d/o Donald E. Haynes and Joyce Hodson
Vernon R. of Clarksville m. Christie R. **Hawes** of Pittsburg 10/18/1928

HAMMERSLEY,
James E. of Franklin m. Kim C. **Reid** of Pittsburg 6/28/2003

HAND,
Jonathan M. of Pittsburg m. April L. **Connary** of Pittsburg 4/28/2007 in N. Stratford

HANN,
Austin Carl m. Lillian Ruth **Wheeler** 6/30/1934 in Lancaster; H – 26, s/o Frank Hann and Martha Ellingwood; W – 20, d/o Jubel Wheeler and Lillian Luther
Bradley m. Barbara Elaine **Brooks** 2/15/1964; H – 18, s/o Austin Hann and Lillian Wheeler; W – 18, d/o Holman Brooks and Eleanor Cater
David E. of Pittsburg m. Mishawn C. **Grinell** of Pittsburg 12/31/1987
Gerald Edward m. Eva Eleanor **Huggins** 10/18/1958; H – 20, s/o Herman Hann and Dorothy Owen; W – 22, d/o Ralph Huggins and Ruth Osgoods
Kelly S. of Pittsburg m. Lorraine F. **Ladd** of Pittsburg 3/29/1987
Kenneth U. m. Irene M. **Harmon** 6/22/1941; H – 21, s/o George Hann and Abbie Wheeler; W – 22, d/o Everett Harmon and Clara Shortt

HARDING,
Christopher Lewis of Pittsburg m. [illegible] of Pittsburg 10/16/1996
Michael Richard of Pittsburg m. Donna Susan **Elliott** of Pittsburg 7/18/1992

HARRIS,
Ernest John m. Sheila Margaret **Wheeler** 3/2/1977; H – 46, s/o John W. Harris and Florence Barnes; W – 33, d/o Bernard Howland and Margaret Ouellette

HARTSHORN,
Raymond V. m. Ivona Ada **McKeage** 8/5/1966; H – 42, s/o Raymond M. Hartshorn and Mae L. Wood; W – 34, d/o Ivo R. McKeage and Vena E. Washburn

HASTINGS,
James W. of Stewartstown m. Lila **Masters** of Pittsburg 2/28/1920

HATCH,
John J. of Pittsburg m. Wendy Sue **Sarazin** of Pittsburg 5/8/1982

HAWES,
Frank B. of Pittsburg m. Constance **Haynes** of Beecher Falls, VT 11/1/1914
George W. of Pittsburg m. Geneva **Farnsworth** 7/4/1904
Herbert m. Margaret **Noyes** 2/12/1949; H – 44, s/o Willie Hawes and Alzada K. Hawes; W – 33, d/o Harry F. Allen and Angie Roby
L. A. of Pittsburg m. Hattie **Fuller** of Pittsburg 8/2/1904
Russell V. m. Majel Mae **Haynes** 8/10/1947; H – 20, s/o Vernon Hawes and Pearl Bacon; W – 19, d/o Stewart Haynes and Hazel Danforth
Warren G. m. Carolyn M. **Stewart** 10/30/1953; H – 25, s/o Vernon Hawes and Pearl Bacon; W – 18, d/o Edgar Stewart and Rena Pierce

HAWKINS,
Everett m. Martha **Deschene** 10/29/1960; H – 23, s/o Owen Hawkins and Lois Young; W – 19, d/o George O. Deschene and Florence Shatney

HAYNES,
Bradley Phil m. Mona Eileen **Hicks** 6/30/1949; H – 22, s/o Stewart Haynes and Hazel Danforth; W – 16, d/o Carmi Hicks and Marion Day
Eldon Stewart m. Diane Ruth **Covell** 9/10/1977; H – 19, s/o Keith H. Haynes and Emily D. Harriman; W – 18, d/o Lesley L. Covell and Ruth H. Foote

Gary Charles m. Cheryl Lynn **French** 7/7/1974; H – 22, s/o
Donald C. Haynes and Jean Keach; W – 25, d/o Lovell
French and Daphyne Clogston
Harry F. of Pittsburg m. Angie **Brown** of Pittsburg 6/15/1916
Harry F. of Pittsburg m. Ella Hall **Maxum** of Colebrook
10/22/1923
Scott N. of Stewartstown m. Roxanne S. **Wheeler** of Pittsburg
7/23/1983
Stewart H. of Pittsburg m. Hazel E. **Danforth** of Pittsburg
12/16/1917
Terrance Owen m. Sandra Ann **Caron** 6/26/1971; H – 19, s/o
Bradley Haynes and Mona Hicks; W – 18, d/o Robert
Caron and Nancy Kois
Thomas H. m. Janet A. **Rodrique** 4/17/1971; H – 17, s/o Orville
Haynes and Frances Noyes; W – 17, d/o Roland Rodrique
Warren L. m. Beatrice E. **Knapp** 10/3/1942; H – 21, s/o Stewart
Haynes and Hazel E. Danforth; W – 17, d/o Raymond H.
Knapp and Verna M. Hall
Wayne Owen m. Donna Mae **Travers** 10/29/1960; H – 24, s/o
Stewart Harold Haynes and Hazel Elaine Danforth; W –
19, d/o John Joseph Travers, Jr. and Rose Mae Sweatt
Wilbur of Pittsburg m. May E. **Burgess** of Pittsburg 1/15/1921

HEATH,
Archie R. of Pittsburg m. Laura **Clogston** of Pittsburg 4/26/1910

HENDERSON,
Perley, Jr. m. Barbara Edith **Harmon** 2/20/1967; H – 35, s/o
Perley Henderson, Sr. and Elsie Hanson; W – 33, d/o
William A. Barnard and Florence Corson

HERMAN,
Paul Jules of Pittsburg m. Linda Lee **Cann** of Pittsburg
6/24/1988

HEWSON,
Thomas Patrick of Pittsburg m. Linda Dianne **Houle** of Pittsburg 4/29/1989

HIBBARD,
George E. m. Irene M. **Young** 3/1/1951; H – 20, s/o Ellis Hibbard and Carrie Gardner; W – 22, d/o Hazen Young and Muriel Laberee
George S. of Pittsburg m. Nellie G. **McLain** of Brunswick, VT 11/25/1914
Maurice E. m. Mary Jane **Dorman** 7/31/1932 in Pittsburg; H – 28; W – 20
Maurice E. m. Jennie A. **Howe** 4/24/1951; H – 47, s/o Edward G. Hibbard and Laura Roby; W – 30, d/o Tillie Howe and Bessie Roby

HICKS,
Alby E. m. Freda M. **Howe** 9/4/1943; H – 41, s/o Irving Hicks and Ella Holden; W – 25, d/o Tillie Howe and Bessie Robie
Irving Alba m. Rose Marie **Gray** 10/4/1969; H – 25, s/o Alba Hicks and Freda Howe; W – 18, d/o Tabor Gray and Eunice Jeffers

HILLIARD,
Frank M. of Pittsburg m. Lois M. **Gray** of Pittsburg 4/9/1921
George L. of Pittsburg m. Ada L. **Cole** of Pittsburg 6/30/1928
Merton L. of Pittsburg m. Stella A. **Hibbard** of Colebrook 11/29/1908
Wilber of Pittsburg m. Glen B. **French** of Pittsburg 11/30/1916

HOAG,
Roland Boyden, Jr. m. Susan Adele **Chappell** 8/10/1968; H – 22, s/o Roland Boyden Hoag, Sr. and Barbara Simonds; W – 20, d/o Colon Chappell and Doris Prescott

HODGMAN,
Ervin Wyatt m. June Ann **Brotherston** 7/29/1977; H – 24, s/o Wyatt Hodgman and Hazel Berg; W – 23, d/o John Brotherston and Helen Hobbs
Wyatt E. m. Hazel A. **Berg** 6/23/1951; H – 35, s/o Ervin Hodgman and Jessie Lebourbreau; W – 22, d/o George Berg, Sr. and Doris Gould

HOLDEN,
Fred H. m. Lucinda Eva **Noe** 11/11/1934 in Stratford; H – 44, s/o Hannibal Holden and Annie Magee; W – 35, d/o Frank Kinney and Jessie Hoadley
Willie J. of Pittsburg m. Louise D. **Foster** of Pittsburg 10/30/1928

HOLMES,
David Robert of Shutesbury, MA m. Lydia Rose **Elison** of Shutesbury, MA 8/13/1994
Shirley A. m. Muriel L. **Swain** 9/14/1935 in Pittsburg; H – 21, s/o Andrew Holmes and Ida M. Woodard; W – 21, d/o Louis Swain and Jennie Heath

HOWARD,
Roger Craig of San Diego, CA m. Marcia Ann **Mochrie** of Ramona, CA 9/29/1988

HOWE,
Jonathan K. of Pittsburg m. Cynthia A. **Sullivan** of Pittsburg 4/18/2002
Larry A. of Pittsburg m. Roberta J. **Fotheringham** of Portsmouth 9/25/1982
Tillie of Pittsburg m. Bessie **Roby** of Pittsburg 8/17/1911
Wayne Anthony of Pittsburg m. Cheryl Marie **Battersby** of Pittsburg 9/18/1992

HOWLAND,
Bernard Ralph m. Margaret Lucille **Ouellette** 9/28/1940; H – 23, s/o Roscoe E. Howland and Mercy T. Day; W – 17, d/o George D. Ouellette and Mary Rose Maheu
David R. of Pittsburg m. Corinne M. **Paquette** of Pittsburg 8/20/1983
Richard R. m. Barbara **Osiensky** 10/6/1962; H – 21, s/o Bernard R. Howland and Margaret L. Ouellette; W – 16, d/o Michael Osiensky and Stella Bien

HUBBARD,
Sterling Lance m. Donna Mae **Stuart** 8/9/1969; H – 21, s/o Winston Hubbard and Marjorie Londerville; W – 20, d/o Raymond Stuart and Muriel Rogers

HUGGINS,
Billie of Pittsburg m. Celia **Masters** of Pittsburg 7/12/1923
Chris W. of Pittsburg m. Debra A. **Martineau** of Canaan, VT 2/9/1987
Chris Wayne m. JoAnne **Griffin** 11/25/1978; H -21, s/o Gerald Hann and Eva Huggins; W – 19, d/o Albert Griffin and Joyce Burns
Harry C. of Pittsburg m. Althea I. **Hulrburt** of Clarksville 6/19/1926
Ralph m. Ruth E. **Osgood** 6/5/1934 in Pittsburg; H – 23, s/o Frank H. Huggins and Elnora Crawford; W – 20, d/o William H. Osgood and Eva L. Osgood

HUNT,
Elroy W. m. Leone J. **Lawton** 5/21/1951; H – 34, s/o Harry H. Hunt and Mary I. Heath; W – 18, d/o Herbert C. Lawton and Annie Bacon

HURLBERT,
Lawrence M. of Canaan, VT m. Helen M. **Day** of Pittsburg 7/24/1982

HURLBURT,
Burnham m. Gertrude **Nason** 2/10/1936 in Pittsburg; H – 23, s/o John Hurlbert and Rita Pearson; W – 18, d/o Vern Nason and Nellie King

HURLEY,
J. Daryl of Canada m. Diane Joan **Gavin** of Canada 12/7/1999
Kevin Thomas m. Sharon Anne **Young** 6/15/1974; H – 18, s/o Thomas Hurley and Virginia Wheeler; W – 19, d/o Arnold Young and Lou Young

INKELL,
Denis Gerard m. Pauline Yvette **Marquis** 9/27/1969; H – 23, s/o Mederick Inkell and Lucie Dionne; W – 19, d/o Leon Marquis and Edith Maurais

JAHODA,
John Curtis of Attleboro, MA m. Pamela Jane **Bellavance** of Attleboro, VT 7/4/1997

JAMESON,
Michael S. of Plymouth, MA m. Laura J. **Judkins** of Pittsburg 6/20/1987

JEWELL,
John K. m. Linda J. **McKearney** 8/20/1961; H – 22, s/o Arthur G. Jewell and Emily Swenk Markley; W – 21, d/o Clarence McKearney and Mary Rancloes

JOCK,
Brett Michael of Pittsburg m. Mary Ann **Blake** of Pittsburg 6/6/1998

JOHNSON,
Arthur of Pittsburg m. Christie M. **Shallow** of Colebrook 10/11/1918
Craig R. m. Nicole M. **Lambert** 7/24/1976; H – 21, s/o Rodney Johnson and Betty Masters; W – 18, d/o Aubert Lambert and Beatrice Labrecque
Danno D. of Pittsburg m. Mary A. **Crawford** of Pittsburg 12/22/1906
Embert Alton m. Ida Beryl **Locke** 6/14/1958; H – 29, s/o William Johnson and Marguerite Terrill; W – 23, d/o Guy Locke and Rena Harrison
Leonard W. of Columbia m. Lisa A. **Prehemo** of Pittsburg 8/23/1987
Rodney B. m. Betty J. **Masters** 7/12/1952; H – 26, s/o William Johnson and Marguerite Terrill; W – 18, d/o Weldon Masters and Evelyn Foster
William E. of Pittsburg m. Marguerite **Terrill** of Pittsburg 12/10/1927
William Harold of Pittsburg m. Deborah Jean **Cilley** of Pittsburg 12/3/2000

JOHNSTON,
Kelly Michael of Lemington, VT m. Marion Cook **Grantham** of Lemington, VT 8/9/1997

JORDAN,
Carl W. of Pittsburg m. Susie S. **Danforth** of Pittsburg 7/9/1919
Frederick Pushee m. Paula Robin **Hibbard** 7/8/1978; H – 26, s/o Frederick S. Jordan and Ellen Pushee; W – 21, d/o George Hibbard and Irene M. Young

JOYCE,
Robert Dean m. Kim Rhonda **Johnson** 9/2/1977; H – 23, s/o Roger Joyce and Marie Baillargeon; W – 18, d/o Rodney Johnson and Betty Masters

JUDD,
Archie N. m. Hazel B. **Hodgman** 3/5/1956; H – 20, s/o Burnham A. Judd and Alta Heath; W – 27, d/o George A. Berg, Sr. and Doris Gould
Archie N., Sr. of Pittsburg m. Barbara L. **Clement** of Pittsburg 7/18/1994
Archie Nathan, Jr. m. Jhody Lynn **Straw** 10/29/1977; H – 20, s/o Archie N. Judd, Sr. and Hazel Berg; W – 18, d/o Bernard Straw and Marjorie Huggins
Arthur S. of Pittsburg m. Ethel M. **Terrill** of Canaan, VT 6/29/1927
Burnham Alton m. Madelene **Stohl** 10/2/1954; H – 21, s/o Burnham R. Judd and Olive A. Heath; W – 27, d/o Harry F. Huggins and Althea I. Hurlburt
Burnham R. m. Olive A. **Heath** 6/29/1932 in W. Stewartstown; H – 22; W – 19
Kevin D. of Pittsburg m. Ruth S. **Lincoln** of Pittsburg 9/28/1985
Richard A. of Pittsburg m. Sheli M. **Machos** of Pittsburg 7/8/1989
Vincent V. of Pittsburg m. Christine **Windhurst** of Pittsburg 7/2/2005 in Pittsburg
Vincent Vaughn of Pittsburg m. Holly Jean **Cross** of Pittsburg 9/15/2001
Willie Dennison m. Janice Irene **Straw** 6/14/1955; H – 18, s/o Burnham R. Judd and Olive A. Heath; W – 17, d/o Merton V. Straw and Irene Pearl Ham

KEACH,
Garvin H. m. Lois A. **Heath** 9/14/1943; H – 33, s/o Herman W. Keach and Grace Hibbard; W – 22, d/o Archie R. Heath and Laura A. Wood

Harry R. of Pittsburg m. Bessie **Heath** of Pittsburg 12/15/1908
Harry R. of Pittsburg m. Mary L. **Johnson** of Pittsburg 7/29/1916

KEENAN,
Kevin P. of Rindge m. Kim M. **Kelley** of Rindge 5/24/1998

KELLY,
Sean Patrick of Pittsburg m. Donna Karen **Carrien** of Pittsburg 6/15/1996

KENEY,
Jason of Columbia m. Bertha **Towle** of Pittsburg 10/14/1904

KEYSER,
Peter A. of Pittsburg m. Loni M. **Crawford** of Pittsburg 7/19/2003

KIDDER,
Keith Davis m. Judith Ervena **Merrill** 12/23/1970; H – 27, s/o Arthur Kidder and Doris Montambault; W – 21, d/o Wilfred Frizzell and Natalie Whitehill

KIMBALL,
Milton W. of Derry m. Terrie L. **Judkins** of Pittsburg 7/12/1987

KING,
Karl Emile of Pittsburg m. Eleanor Gay **Barry** of Pittsburg 11/13/1990
Randall J. of Bloomfield, VT m. Constance V. **Haynes** of Pittsburg 10/31/1981

KITTREDGE,
Winston, Jr. of Pittsburg m. Judith Sandra **Aveni** of Pittsburg 9/23/1995

KNAPP,
Jarrod Ethan of Pittsburg m. Ok Kyong **Kim** of Pittsburg 3/20/1999
Ralph Morton m. Anita Marie **Hikel** 4/15/1973; H – 59, s/o Alfred Knapp and Joyce Forbes; W – 52, d/o Adelard Bedard and Dorilla Charron

KOSLOWSKY,
Alexander Paul of Pittsburg m. Rita Faye **Turner** of Pittsburg 8/14/1999

LACHANCE,
Alva Joseph m. Marguerite Cecilia **Revoir** 10/28/1939; H – 22, s/o Zephir Joseph LaChance and Mary Marie Thibeault; W – 17, d/o Emile Revoir and Doris Fox
Henry Joseph m. Sylvia Marion **LeVesque** 9/6/1947; H – 36, s/o Homer LaChance and Mary Paquette; W – 28, d/o Norman Robie and Alice Washburn

LADUCER,
Arthur of Windsor Mills, PQ m. Elizabeth **Cane** of Liverpool, England 10/22/1921

LAFLAMME,
Gaetan Ernie m. Paula Lee **Harwood** 2/16/1974; H – 20, s/o Gaston Laflamme and Pauline Lemay; W – 14, d/o Leland Harwood and Theo Parker

LAKIN,
Wendall Ward m. Margaret Pearl **Merrill** 6/28/1946; H – 28, s/o Walter Lakin and Mildred Heath; W – 23, d/o Willie Merrill and Margaret Berry

LAMPRON,
Ronald R. of Pittsburg m. Linda A. **Morissette** of Pittsburg 9/1/1980

LANCTOT,
Roger m. Brenda Lee **Uran** 7/18/1975; H – 17, s/o Edward Lanctot and Raymonde Lanctot; W – 18, d/o Frank Uran and Zelma Foster
Roger of Pittsburg m. Sara R. **Maurais** of Pittsburg 9/24/2005 in Pittsburg

LAPOINT,
George of Pittsburg m. Mabel S. **Crawford** of Pittsburg 2/6/1909
Richard E. of Pittsburg m. Rachel M. **Whiting** of Atkinson 6/19/2004
Richard Ernest m. Cathy Ann **DeLong** 8/7/1971; H – 21, s/o Richard Edward Lapoint and Mary Bullens; W – 18, d/o George DeLong and Doris Stanton
Richard Ernest of Pittsburg m. Christine Kay **Pinckney** of Pittsburg 7/21/1990

LAPOINTE,
Andre m. Claudette **Robinson** 7/1/1967; H – 22, s/o Albert LaPointe and Laurette Dodier; W – 20, d/o Eric Robinson and Evelyne Bacon

LASSONDE,
Kevin Donald of Pittsburg m. Stephanie Nicole **Lavoie** of Pittsburg 9/30/2000

LAUZON,
Henri m. Louise **Couture** 5/15/1945; H – 30, s/o Edmund Lauzon and Corine Gregoire; W – 18, d/o Wilfred Couture and Cora Gagnon

LAVOIE,
Rock Thadee m. Pauline Marie **Robinson** 8/7/1971; H – 29, s/o Telesphore Lavoie and Claire Brouillard; W – 21, d/o Eric Robinson and Evelyn Beloin

LAWRENCE,
Joseph D. of Franklin m. Rebecca L. **Trask** of Pittsburg 4/2/2005 in Tilton

LEA,
Herbert J. of Pittsburg m. Hazel M. **Shetney** of Stewartstown 9/8/1911

LECLERCQ,
Michael J. of Pittsburg m. Robin A. **Boissonneault** of Pittsburg 9/27/1980

LEDUC,
Jeremy Arthur of Pittsburg m. Janet Rae **Rice** of Pittsburg 5/4/1991

LEE,
Ernest of Pittsburg m. Minnie E. **Rowell** of Pittsburg 3/21/1905

LEIGH,
Edward, Jr. m. Nancy **Crawford** 1/31/1959; H – 22, s/o Edward F. Leigh and Ada Cross; W – 16, d/o Carroll Crawford and Caroline Dorman

Lester R. m. Virginia M. **Covill** 11/25/1950; H – 21, s/o Edward Leigh and Ada Cross; W – 22, d/o Shirley Covill and Elaine Dearth

LEMAY,
Benoit J-G. of Canaan, VT m. Carole N. **Fuller** of Canaan, VT 10/10/1981

Raymond F. m. Eva Elnora **Hann** 1/4/1970; H – 37, s/o Arthur Lemay and Eva Beaudoin; W – 34, d/o Ralph Huggins and Ruth Osgood

LEMIEUX,
Alva of Pittsburg m. Avis **Briggs** of Stewartstown 6/21/1925

LESSARD,
Ronald George m. Lise Alma **Marquis** 5/17/1969; H – 23, s/o Adelbert Lessard and Evelyn Breault; W – 22, d/o Leon Marquis and Edith Maurais

LITTLE,
William Bennett m. JoAnne Marie **White** 2/1/1975; H – 21, s/o William Little and Beatrice Currier; W – 16, d/o Robert White and Ann E. Riley
William Bilney m. Betsy Elizabeth **Jewell** 1/14/1969; H – 37, s/o Oscar P. Little and Lucy Bilney; W – 27, d/o Thomas Dorman, Sr. and Evelyn Haynes

LIZOTTE,
Patrick m. Laura Corina **Bernier** 12/24/1940; H – 39, s/o T. Paul Lizotte and Irene Libby; W – 19, d/o Adolph J. Bernier and Exiles Marie Nolin

LORD,
Austin P. of Pittsburg m. Mabel H. **Kane** of Pittsburg 1/2/1926
Corey Steven of Pittsburg m. Theresa Marie **Little** of Pittsburg 8/12/2000
Henry of Pittsburg m. Ella **Currier** of Pittsburg 4/26/1911
Irving of Pittsburg m. Ida M. **Booth** of Clarksville 12/13/1910
Leslie George m. Beverly Jean **Frizzell** 1/16/1976; H – 24, s/o Lester Lord and Helen Cahill; W – 21, d/o Clarence Frizzell and Marilyn Adams

Perley Elmer m. Alice Evelyn **Treem** 10/12/1946; H – 20, s/o
    Austin Lord and Mabel Kane; W – 20, d/o Harry Treem
    and Marie Lavoie
Roger A. m. Jean M. **Day** 7/3/1954; H – 18, s/o Austin Lord and
    Mable Kane; W – 17, d/o deceased and Ramona Haynes
William Edwin m. Kate **Fuller** 9/20/1939; H – 27, s/o William
    Lord and Edith Edell Gray; W – 25, d/o Frank Fuller and
    Ella Ocrena Carlton

LUTHER,
Sidney of Pittsburg m. Bert **Parker** of Pittsburg 10/5/1904
Sidney W. of Pittsburg m. Persis **Condon** of Pittsburg 8/7/1917

LYNCH,
William Patrick m. Beatrice Rena **Fuller** 1/12/1946; H – 28, s/o
    William Lynch and Ethel Little; W – 26, d/o Alfred Fuller
    and Alice Clark

LYONS,
Alex Douglas m. Alice Louise **Bissonnette** 11/23/1974; H – 23,
    s/o Willard Lyons and Rita Masters; W – 28, d/o Louis
    Bissonnette and Louise Lanctot
Dana Harlow m. Marilyn Joy **Chappell** 6/21/1962; H – 38, s/o
    Frank E. Lyons and Ruth Hope Mitchell; W – 25, d/o Colon
    Chappell and Doris Prescott
Paul Mark of Pittsburg m. Kirsten Frances **Koch** of Rochester
    7/8/1995

MADORE,
Daniel T. of Pittsburg m. Cindy L. **Covill** of Pittsburg 10/20/1984
Eusebe m. Suzanne **Paquette** 6/28/1958; H – 26, s/o Thomas
    Madore and Agnes Pelletier; W – 19, d/o Antonio Paquette
    and Marie Rose Drouin

MAILLOUX,
Christian Roger of Pittsburg m. Ruth Ann **Tucker** of Pittsburg 11/3/1990

MANOSH,
Peter J. of E. Fairfield, VT m. Heidi L. **Johnson** of Pittsburg 8/28/1982
Tristan J. of Gorham, ME m. Brandi **Mazur-McLaughlin** of Pittsburg 8/26/2006 in Hampton

MANSFIELD,
Ralph Elliott m. Pauline Dorothy **Dehl** 6/16/1973; H – 21, s/o Warren F. Mansfield and Florence E. Gould; W – 21, d/o Stephen E. Dehl and Beatrice I. Beaudette

MARCINKIEVICZ,
John R. of Pittsburg m. Melissa R. **Pfaff** of Pittsburg 7/26/2004

MARQUIS,
Adelard m. Yvonne Delina **Chaloux** 9/25/1934 in Stewartstown; H – 24, s/o Emile Marquis and Esther Lemieux; W – 18, d/o Charles Chaloux and Victoria Benoit
Fred m. Annette **Chaloux** 5/7/1938 in Stewartstown; H – 26, s/o Joseph Marquis and Anna Beloin; W – 19, d/o Charles Chaloux and Victoria Benoit
Gilles Paul m. Claudette Anita **Drouin** 10/31/1964; H – 23, s/o Leon Marquis and Edith Maurais; W – 21, d/o Bernard Drouin and Bernadette Houle
Oscar D. m. Aurore E. **Chaloux** 9/17/1942; H – 32, s/o Joseph Marquis and Anna Beloin; W – 24, d/o Charles Chaloux and Victoria Benoit
Raymond Albert m. Leanna Jean **Johnson** 8/30/1975; H – 21, s/o Albert Marquis and Annonciade Fauteux; W – 18, d/o Rodney Johnson and Betty Masters

Ronald Leon m. Lise Marthe **Roy** 5/30/1970; H – 25, s/o Leon Marquis and Edith Maurais; W – 20, d/o Sylvio Roy and Antoinnette Cote
Ronald M. of Pittsburg m. Kara S. **Leigh** of Pittsburg 7/23/2005 in Stewartstown

MARSH,
Elwin J. of Pittsburg m. Lillian **Moore** of Toronto, PQ 1/29/1923
Elwin J. of Pittsburg m. Lillie **Moor** of Toronto, PQ 1/29/1923
Robert J. of Pittsburg m. Mildred **Davis** of W. Stewartstown 12/24/1914
Samuel of Pittsburg m. Ruby **Covell** of Clarksville 4/21/1909
Samuel L. of Pittsburg m. Mabel **Condon** of Pittsburg 2/14/1917
Walter Edwin m. Pauline Martha **Deschene** 9/5/1940; H – 19, s/o Samuel Marsh and Mable Congdon; W – 18, d/o John Deschene and Ada Bean
Waylon J. of Pittsburg m. Andrea O. **Leigh** of Pittsburg 7/29/2006 in Pittsburg

MASSON,
George m. Sally **Frizzell** 10/10/1964; H – 20, s/o Aime Masson and Annette Bergeron; W – 18, d/o Wilfred Frizzell and Natalie Whitehill

MASTERS,
Jeffrey Alan m. Dottie-Jean **Amey** 1/5/1974; H – 21, s/o Russell Masters and Verna Hall; W – 20, d/o Holman J. Amey and Dorothy Sprague
Larry Charles m. Norma Lea **Hodge** 9/9/1964; H – 22, s/o Weldon I. Masters and Florence Evelyn Foster; W – 18, d/o Celon George Hodge and Wilma Lottie Crawford
Randall Ray m. Judith G. **Washburn** 7/23/1960; H – 19, s/o Weldon Masters and Florence E. Foster; W – 17, d/o George Washburn and Gertrude Collins

Ray L. of Pittsburg m. Ann M. **Thibeault** of Pittsburg 2/1/2007 in Pittsburg

Ray Leland m. Lisette Terry **Crete** 11/9/1968; H – 23, s/o Leland Masters and Maude Foster; W – 18, d/o Rosario Crete and Rita D'Anjou

Russell m. Verna R. **Hall** 7/4/1951; H – 19, s/o Weldon Masters and Florence Foster; W – 19, d/o Vernon Hall and Christie Hawes

Weldon of Pittsburg m. Florence **Foster** of Sanford, ME 12/18/1922

Weldon I. m. Vena E. **McKeage** 10/15/1962; H – 65, s/o William H. Masters and Celia Noble; W – 57, d/o George H. Washburn and Ada L. Crawford

MATHIEU,

Nicholas J. of W. Stewartstown m. Jennifer S. **Clogston** of Pittsburg 7/26/2008 in W. Stewartstown

Roland m. Louisa **Giguere** 9/8/1956; H – 27, s/o Joseph N. Mathieu and Blanche Charland; W – 17, d/o Joseph Giguere and Hirma Huard

MATTHEWS,

Donald H. m. Edna R. **Currier** 8/24/1942; H – 20, s/o John Matthews and Pauline Harwood; W – 23, d/o Andrew H. Currier and Nettie Witherell

MAXFIELD,

John R. m. Ruth E. **Taylor** 7/25/1935 in Pittsburg; H – 24, s/o Abner R. Maxfield and Nellie S. Hussey; W – 26, d/o William A. Taylor and Bertha A. Patterson

McCOMISKEY,

Walter G. m. Catherine E. **Frizzell** 12/18/1965; H – 20, s/o Walter D. McComiskey and Pauline Gilbert; W – 18, d/o Wilfred Frizzell and Natalie Whitehill

McKEAGE,
Brendon Dale m. Crystal Ann **Clogston** 1/23/1965; H – 16, s/o Willard McKeage and Irene Hicks; W – 17, d/o Keith Clogston and Dorothy Dalton
Brendon Keith of Pittsburg m. Wanda L. **Johnson** of Pittsburg 5/21/1994
Ivo R. of Pittsburg m. Vena A. **Washburn** of Pittsburg 6/25/1924
Rick D. of Pittsburg m. Tanya-Marie **Gervais** of Pittsburg 7/20/1996
Robert of Pittsburg m. Meade **Roby** of Pittsburg 9/8/1911
Willard m. Irene E. **Hicks** 8/21/1946; H – 31, s/o Robert McKeage and Mabel Harding; W – 17, d/o Carmi Hicks and Marion Day
William H. of Pittsburg m. Rebecca Moore **Reading** of Ottawa, Canada 11/5/1922

McKIBBEN,
Scott W. of Pittsburg m. Martha W. **Allen** of Isle La Motte, VT 3/2/1985

McKINNON,
Richard Carl of Pittsburg m. Holli Lynn **Estes** of Pittsburg 10/1/1994
Robert F. of Campton m. Priscilla Mary **Downing** of Thornton 8/12/1980

MERRILL,
Arthur of Pittsburg m. Jennie E. **Piersons** of Pittsburg 8/27/1904
Chauncey A. of Pittsburg m. Carrie F. **Cody** of Pittsburg 4/4/1908
Clyde E. of Pittsburg m. Madelene G. **Corkum** of Milan 7/18/1926
Edward G. of Pittsburg m. Clareson **Pike** of Pittsburg 1/21/1921
Fay of Pittsburg m. Hortense Q. **Masters** of Pittsburg 11/14/1916

Gerald Patrick m. Venessa Margaret **Young** 10/26/1946; H – 20, s/o Willie Merrill and Margaret Berry; W – 19, d/o Stewart Young and Hilda Brown

Glen P. of Pittsburg m. Wanda J. **Wright** of Pittsburg 7/24/1982

Glenford Charles m. Geraldine Mae **Young** 4/2/1949; H – 20, s/o Willie G. Merrill and Margaret S. Berry; W – 24, d/o Stewart H. Young and Hilda F. Brown

Hugh Stewart m. Judith Ervena **Frizzell** 7/1/1967; H – 19, s/o Gerald P. Merrill and Venessa Young; W – 18, d/o Wilfred C. Frizzell and Nathalie E. Whitehill

John m. Helen **Sanborn** 2/9/1957; H – 18, s/o Willie G. Merrill and Margaret Berry; W – 17, d/o Everett Stanton and Eva Sharon

Scott Patrick m. Diane Ann **Brooks** 5/3/1975; H – 23, s/o Gerald P. Merrill and Vanessa Young; W – 18, d/o Darwin Brooks, Jr. and Agnes Benoit

MIELNICKI,
Robert D. m. Carol Ann **Covey** 12/15/1967; H – 21, s/o Wallace J. Mielnicki and Mary F. Rowen; W – 18, d/o Charles A. Covey and Sophia Makarowicz

MILLER,
C. R. of Pittsburg m. Estella **Reynolds** of Pittsburg 3/7/1906

MISIASZEK,
Jack Nelson of Deerfield m. Nina Rae **Devarney** of Fremont 9/1/2000

MOORE,
Carl W. m. Marion E. **Fellows** 10/14/1937 in Pittsburg; H – 35, s/o William C. Moore and Stella Withrow; W – 33, d/o Herbert Bunnell and Gertrude Carter

MORAN,
Thimothy Gerard m. Nadine Ellen **Taylor** 8/7/1976; H – 23, s/o Thomas Moran and Pauline White; W – 22, d/o Roland H. Taylor, Sr. and Mary Ellen Decott

MORIN,
Vernon Joseph of North Port, FL m. Cynthia Charlotte **Moody** of Pittsburg 1/21/1995

MORRISSEY,
Roger William of Pittsburg m. Christine **Bertrand**of Sherbrooke, PQ 6/4/1991

MOUSSEAU,
Atlee B. of Pittsburg m. Fern M. **Covell** of Pittsburg 6/24/1916
Keane Atlee m. Katherine Alice **Smith** 8/20/1940; H – 18, s/o Atlee Burpee Mousseau and Fern Covell; W – 23, d/o Karl Beakington Smith and Alice Frances Keysar

NICHOLSON,
Angus Nichol m. Anne Althea **Therrien** 6/21/1952; H – 44, s/o Malcolm N. Nicholson and Christie Ann McDonald; W – 34, d/o Ned Smith and Eva Greenwood

NOYES,
Alan I. of Pittsburg m. Sherry L. **Goodwin** of Stewartstown 6/30/1979
George, III m. Carole **Labbe** 4/29/1972; H – b. 4/20/1948, s/o George Noyes and Alice Pariseau; W – b. 3/27/1947, d/o John Labbe and Marcelle Roy
Howard G. m. Margaret N. **Brooks** 8/31/1940; H – 34, s/o Ira A. Noyes and Bessie L. Gould; W – 25, d/o Harry S. Allen and Angie E. Roby

Howard Gould m. Margaret N. **Lawrence** 7/20/1967; H – 61, s/o Ira Noyes and Bessie Gould; W – 52, d/o Harry Allen and Angie Robie

Lawrence R. m. Theresa D. **Chaloux** 6/24/1950; H – 22, s/o George Noyes and Lela Bradley; W – 18, d/o Joseph Chaloux and Celanire Benoit

Timothy J. of Beecher Falls, VT m. Nicole L. **Madore** of Pittsburg 7/20/1985

OAKES,
Gordon Howard m. Pauline Laura **Clogston** 5/22/1948; H – 23, s/o Lovell Oakes and Myrtie Annis; W – 20, d/o Paul W. Clogston and Alta Wheeler

OLSEN,
George W., Jr. m. Mary E. **Mountain** 7/17/1942; H – 22, s/o George W. Olsen, Sr. and Mary Caldbeck; W – 19, d/o Benjamin Mountain and Mary E. Brander

OLSZANOWSKI,
Walter m. Stefania **Dziodzic** 1/1/1952; H – 53, s/o Alexander Olszanowski and Lucy Topolski; W – 40, d/o Jacob Dziedzic and Mary Salva

ORMSBEE,
Forrest C. of Colebrook m. Nina E. **Aldrich** of Pittsburg 11/23/1914

Willard D. of Pittsburg m. Regina L. **Burnham** of Penacook 1/23/1993

OSGOOD,
William H. of Newport, VT m. Minnie B. **Day** of Pittsburg 9/5/1931

OUELLETTE,
Eugene Frederick m. Nancy Elizabeth **Amey** 6/19/1954; H – 24, s/o George D. Ouellette and Mary R. Maheux; W – 25, d/o Holman J. Amey and Mary H. Somers

OWEN,
Edward G. of Pittsburg m. Elsie C. **Smith** of Pittsburg 6/28/1985
Edward Grant m. Hallie Ruth **Huggins** 6/27/1959; H – 21, s/o James Munn Owen and Gladys Bolton; W – 17, d/o Ralph Huggins and Ruth Esther Osgoode
Jeffrey Greenleaf m. Carol Muriel **Hibbard** 7/28/1973; H – 21, s/o Frank H. Owen and Claire Greenleaf; W – 19, d/o George Hibbard and Irene Young
Johnny M. of Pittsburg m. Paula N. **McCormack** of E. Hampstead 10/27/1984

PAGE,
John W. of Pittsburg m. Deborah A. **Brooks** of Stewartstown 3/2/2000

PAQUETTE,
Andrew m. Solange **Rouleau** 6/18/1960; H – 19, s/o Antonio Paquette and Rose Drouin; W – 18, d/o Armand Rouleau and Magella Labbe
Paul G. of Manchester m. Wanda M. **Riley** of Pittsburg 6/24/2000
Ronald A. of Pittsburg m. Gina M. **Saari** of Pittsburg 6/28/2002

PARISEAU,
David Leo m. Deborah Margaret **Covill** 8/14/1976; H – 25, s/o Theodore Pariseau and Denise Laperle; W – 25, d/o Lindsey Covill and Roberta Merrill

PARKER,
David C. m. Sylvie D. **Lamontagne** 9/30/1978; H – 28, s/o Harley Parker, Sr. and Geraldine Curtis; W – 21, d/o Simone Lamontagne and Rose Rene
David Curtis m. Veronica Jean **Grover** 6/17/1972; H – 7/9/1950, s/o Harley Parker, Sr. and Geraldine Curtis; W – b. 9/29/1953, d/o Brendon Grover and Joan Day
Reginald E. of Colebrook m. Jacquelyn R. **Straw** of Pittsburg 8/22/1987
Reuben Robert m. Christine Kay **Pinckney** 5/10/1975; H – 25, s/o George Parker and Lorette Cote; W – 18, d/o Richard Pinckney and Mary Ann Thompson

PARKHURST,
Erwin L. of Columbia m. Mildred D. **Gibson** of Pittsburg 11/25/1980

PATNAUDE,
Steven J. of N. Stratford m. Wanda J. **Dorman** of Pittsburg 8/22/1981

PEARSON,
Burwood G. m. Leona M. **Jacques** 3/13/1943; H – 19, s/o Samuel Pearson and Helen Gray; W – 35, d/o Leon C. Jacques and Lena M. Gardie

PEARSONS,
Fay W. of Pittsburg m. Hannah **Day** of Pittsburg 9/27/1910
Samuel E. of Pittsburg m. Hattie M. **Day** of Pittsburg 6/28/1905
Samuel E. of Pittsburg m. Helen B. **Gray** of Northumberland 8/13/1910

PERRIGO,
Paul Alan of Keene m. Susan Jayne **Bottomley** of Keene 10/27/2000

PHILBROOK,
Clement E. of Pittsburg m. Millicent Ann **Lomax** of Pittsburg 9/24/1988

PHILLIPS,
Clyde Erwin m. Jenness Holbrook **Carleton** 1/29/1949; H – 33, s/o Holman Phillips and Lena Erwin; W – 33, d/o Mark H. Carleton and Sadie J. Dodge

Clyde L. m. Lurlene **Shallow** 7/5/1940; H – 27, s/o Homer Phillips and Lina Irwin; W – 23, d/o James Shallow and Elizabeth Day

PIERCE,
Dale Alan m. Tammy Jean **Carlson** 1/14/1978; H – 19, s/o Robert Pierce and Constance Conery; W – 18, d/o Carl Carlson and Joanne Jackson

PLACEY,
David Allen of Manchester m. Karen Lee **Gray** of Pittsburg 9/10/1988

POND,
Guy W. of Pittsburg m. Arline **Paridis** of Pittsburg 8/15/1925

PONZEK,
Edward J. m. Rhea M. **Pellerin** 8/24/1966; H – 56, s/o John Ponzek and Helen Zjadacz; W – 53, d/o Felix Henault and Albina Dutilly

POOLE,
Kenneth A. of Stoneham, MA m. Carole L. **Conrad** of Stoneham, MA 10/3/1987

POTTER,
John of Pittsburg m. Emma **Tirrill** of Pittsburg 8/23/1920

PREHEMO,
Jeffrey William of Pittsburg m. Megan Marie **Hurley** of Pittsburg 7/25/1998
Neil R. of Pittsburg m. Karen **Kidder** of Pittsburg 7/20/2002
Raymond A. m. Gale E. **French** 5/15/1965; H – 21, s/o William Prehemo and Rose Paquette; W – 20, d/o Lovell French and Daphyne Clogston
Raymond Arthur of Pittsburg m. Carleen Ann **Brooks** of Pittsburg 10/30/1993
Robert W. m. Carlene Carol **Straw** 3/11/1967; H – 18, s/o Willie C. Prehemo and Mary Rose Paquette; W – 18, d/o Merton Von Straw and Irene Pearl Hann

PRESTON,
Cedric E. of Pittsburg m. Sandra Lee **Davis** of Pittsburg 2/11/1996

PRICE,
Arthur George m. Martha Joyce **Dalton** 11/15/1946; H – 37, s/o John Price and Bertha Hennessey; W – 22, d/o Albert Dalton and Lois Gray

PUGLISI,
Louis Joseph, III of Pittsburg m. Brenda Kay **Foote** of Pittsburg 9/25/1993

QUIMBY,
Earl D. m. Mabel C. **Smith** 7/23/1952; H – 29, s/o Walter Quimby and Almeda Roby; W – 38, d/o Gabe N. Lewis and Margarite Burger

RADUN,
David Robert of Bristol, CT m. Jennifer Lynn **Scoville** of Bristol, CT 8/5/2000

RAINVILLE,
Stewart A. m. Winnie L. **Hibbard** 3/28/1950; H – 18, s/o Albert Rainville and Evelyn Grapes; W – 16, d/o Maurice Hibbard and Mary Dorman

RANCLOES,
Francis G. of Pittsburg m. Lottie M. **Young** of Hall Stream, PQ 8/25/1919
Frank Oliver m. Glenna Delia **Knapp** 2/16/1947; H – 22, s/o Francis Rancloes and Lottie Young; W – 22, d/o Alfred Knapp and Joyce Forbes

RANCOURT,
Jules V. of Stewartstown m. Judy L. **Straw** of Pittsburg 6/23/1984
Richard Reginald of Colebrook m. Penny L. **Cross** of Colebrook 2/21/1998

RANSOM,
Arthur of Pittsburg m. Rose E. **Covell** of Pittsburg 4/28/1920

RATHBUN,
H. Lloyd m. Bessie Manning **Hill** 4/29/1955; H – 52, s/o George W. Rathbun and Nellie M. Beaulec; W – 45, d/o Phillip B. Whaley and Elizabeth W. Manning

REMICK,
Michael Howard of Pittsburg m. Kimberly Marie **Young** of Pittsburg 6/19/1993

REYNOLDS,
Daniel Joseph m. Linda Faye **Bunnell** 8/24/1972; H – b. 8/10/1951, s/o Martin Reynolds and Marion Kiser; W – b. 3/14/1954, d/o Kenneth Bunnell and Wilma Haynes

Maynard Wilson m. Hortense Violet **Merrill** 3/3/1947; H – 64, s/o James Reynolds and Eliza Gault; W – 47, d/o William Masters and Celia Noble

RICHARD,
Clovis m. Armoza **Paradis** 6/15/1936 in Stewartstown; H – 38, s/o Joseph Richard and Obline LeBlanc; W – 27, d/o Antoine Paradis and Henrianna Rovert

RICHARDS,
Arthur Emerson m. Arlene Maude **Young** 10/10/1946; H – 25, s/o George Richards and Christina Smith; W – 25, d/o Jesse Young and Florence Whitney

Roland R. m. Winona I. **Clark** 9/10/1947; H – 23, s/o Perley Richards and Ardes Heath; W – 18, d/o Raymond Clark and Iva Bunnell

RICKER,
Jimmie Eldwin m. Reva Sylvia **Brooks** 10/7/1944; H – 24, s/o George E. Ricker and Annie M. Hardy; W – 33, d/o Francis Brooks and Rena Bell Porter

RIENDEAU,
Robert Joseph m. Shirley Faye **McKearney** 12/12/1958; H – 18, s/o Philip Riendeau and Leonie Beloin; W – 16, d/o Clarence McKearney and Mary Rancloss

Yvon Moses of Pittsburg m. Arlene Evelyn **Richards** of Stewartstown 10/6/1979

RIPLEY,
Butler L. m. Reita W. **Reid** 8/19/1978; H – 59, s/o Charles W. Ripley and Althea H. Butler; W – 49, d/o Joseph Coy Reid and Dorothy Whitney

ROBBINS,
Robert Kenneth of Pittsburg m. Julie Anne **Haley** of Pittsburg 9/29/1988

ROBIE,
Chester L. m. Ruth **Fitzgerald** 7/2/1936 in Stewartstown; H – 26, s/o Norman Robie and Alice M. Washburn; W – 26, d/o Irving Flanders and Nellie Colby
Edwin M. m. Wilma J. **Ormsbee** 8/26/1950; H – 24, s/o Myron Robie and Mable Hawes; W – 32, d/o George Hawes and Geneva Farnsworth
Moses S. m. Bertha K. **Merrill** 8/11/1934 in Colebrook; H – 27, s/o Norman Roby and Alice Washburn; W – 23, d/o Chauncey Merrill and Carrie Cody

ROBINSON,
Craig Richard of Cambridge, MA m. Janice Marie **Santos** of Cambridge, MA 4/15/1989
Keith J. of Pittsburg m. Rebecca E. **Dotson** of Pittsburg 8/23/2008 in Colebrook

ROBIT,
Ezra of Pittsburg m. Lena **Leadbetter** of Pittsburg 9/1/1927

ROBY,
Edgar of Pittsburg m. Linnie **French** of Canaan, VT 9/9/1908
Edwin L. of Clarksville m. Alma L. **Hawes** 11/3/1908
Fred W. of Pittsburg m. Beddie **Harriman** of Pittsburg 8/19/1915
Gerald of Pittsburg m. Mildred **Brown** of Pittsburg 7/15/1923

RODRIQUE,
Henry m. Regina M. **Hicks** 11/12/1947; H – 27, s/o Mathias Roderique and Mary Roderique; W – 16, d/o Carmi Hicks and Marion Day
Sheridan Joseph m. Sharon Hilda **Chase** 3/21/1970; H – 21, s/o Henry Rodrique and Regina Hicks; W – 19, d/o Gordon Chase and Ernestine Lapoint

ROGERS,
Rene Reginald m. Gloria Isabelle **Washburn** 8/21/1960; H – 49, s/o Robert A. Rogers and Mabel I. Duncan; W – 41, d/o Samuel J. Washburn and Edith M. Brown

RONDEAU,
Leo Roland of Pittsburg m. Faith Kelley **Lapoint** of Pittsburg 9/11/1993

ROPPEL,
Norman J. m. Arlene H. **French** 12/22/1936 in Keene; H – 29, s/o George Roppel and Elizabeth Miller; W – 19, d/o Azel H. French and Leone Lapoint
Norman J. m. Edna B. **Kelly** 8/26/1957; H – 50, s/o George A. Roppel and Elizabeth Miller; W – 58, d/o James Kelly and Charlotte Butler

ROUGEAU,
Richard M. of Pittsburg m. Carmen R. **Harding** of Canaan, VT 9/16/2000

ROWAN,
Donald C. of Colebrook m. Grace **Masters** of Pittsburg 11/24/1928

ROWELL,
Walter of Pittsburg m. Lucy **Russell** of Pittsburg 12/17/1918

ROY,
Kenneth R. of Pittsburg m. Julie Ann **Ricker** of Pittsburg 3/23/1991
Kenneth R. of Pittsburg m. Naomi M. **Stone** of New Ipswich 7/29/2001
Maurice Yvon of Norton, VT m. Joanne Louise **Gagnon** of Norton, VT 8/14/1999

RUPP,
Edward Robert of Pittsburg m. Patricia-Ann **Lampman** of Pittsburg 9/23/1989

RUTTLE,
Douglas Ashton of Lockwood, NY m. Jacquelyn Lee **Parker** of Canaan, VT 9/22/1990

RYAN,
Leo Thomas m. Lorraine Doris **Samuels** 6/14/1956; H – 41, s/o Leo T. Ryan and Mary E. Brennan; W – 41, d/o Jacob R. Joseph and Eva Mannheim

SAARI,
Randall Alan of Pittsburg m. Gina Marie **Prehemo** of Pittsburg 9/24/1994

SAVARD,
Timothy Rowland of Pittsburg m. Lisa Marie **Wheeler** of Pittsburg 11/29/1997

SAWYER,
Robert R. of Pittsburg m. Harriet Y. **Welcome** of Boscawen 6/5/1993

SCHOFF,
Coleman Dean m. Eleanor Elvera **Gleason** 12/14/1946; H – 27, s/o Perley Schoff and Lizzie Johnson; W – 27, d/o Charles White and Beatrice Doak

Ray E. of Pittsburg m. Winifred L. **Bumford** of Colebrook 11/11/1918

SCHOPPE,
Herman H. of Pittsburg m. Lillian M. **Scott** of Clarksville 3/28/1904

SCOTT,
Arthur of Pittsburg m. Iva E. **Day** 1/7/1918

Fred T. of Pittsburg m. Lena **Danforth** of Pittsburg 9/29/1919

Fred T. m. Eva S. **Schoff** 12/27/1950; H – 58, s/o Gilbert Scott and Rachel Carnes; W – 40, d/o Harley Smith and Maud Greenwood

George C. of Pittsburg m. Laura B. **Harriman** of Canaan, VT 11/19/1918

George C. m. Elgie E. **Johnson** 8/26/1935 in Manchester; H – 39, s/o Robert Scott and Mary E. King; W – 45, d/o Alton B. Johnson and Sarah M. Taft

Harry F. of Pittsburg m. Rena **Danforth** of Pittsburg 10/10/1928

Karl Silsbury m. Ernestine **Clogston** 6/20/1948; H – 23, s/o Arthur Scott and Iva E. Day; W – 23, d/o Paul W. Clogston and Alta Wheeler

Marshall Millard m. Barbara Janice **Brown** 8/3/1961; H – 24, s/o Millard Scott and Arlene Marshall; W – 20, d/o Allen W. Brown and Harriet Fuller

Porter J. m. Eva M. **Smith** 6/15/1933 in Tilton; H – 27, b. Pittsburg, s/o Perley R. Schoff and Lizzie A. Johnson; W – 22, b. Jefferson, d/o Harlie A. Smith and Maude S. Greenwood

Willard C. m. Florence **Shatney** 7/20/1967; H – 62, s/o Roderick Scott and Mary Cairns; W – 42, d/o David Shatney and Avis Terrill

Willard Charles m. Emma Gladys **Stover** 11/5/1937 in Lancaster; H – 33, s/o Roderick Scott and Mary E. King; W – 33, d/o Lemuel Stover and Lydia Nelson

SHALLOW,
James M. of Pittsburg m. Lizzie P. **Day** of Pittsburg 9/29/1909

SHANNON,
Vern K. of Pittsburg m. Laura J. **Jameson** of Pittsburg 5/14/2005 in Pittsburg

SHERMAN,
Steven Lewis of Pittsburg m. Jessica Lynn **Ruggles** of Unity 4/25/1998

SHIELDS,
John M. m. Arlene **Washburn** 8/29/1964; H – 49, s/o Charles A. Shields and Gertrude Thompson; W – 40, d/o George H. Hann and Abbie Wheeler

Larry Edward of Pittsburg m. Norma Jean **Dupuis** of Pittsburg 10/8/1988

SHIVICK,
Thomas Francis, Sr. of Charlton, MA m. Gayle Virginia **Drew** of Charlton, MA 7/1/2000

SILVESTRI,
Joseph D. of Bellingham, MA m. Kerry L. **Fales** of Bellingham, MA 9/7/1991

SMITH,
Oliver O. m. Patricia J. **Mousseau** 4/6/1942; H – 22, s/o Karl B. Smith and Alice Keysar; W – 16, d/o Atlee B. Mousseau and M. Fern Mousseau

SPERRY,
James Arthur m. Sheila Margaret **Harris** 1/17/1978; H – 36, s/o Wilbur Sperry and Hazel Miller; W – 34, d/o Bernard Howland and Margaret Ouellette

STOHL,
Bruce Wayne m. Kristina Gale **Anderson** 11/8/1969; H – 22, s/o Delmar O. Stohl and Madelene Huggins; W – 22, d/o Mallet Anderson and Dorothy Hawes
Don Sterling m. Jocelyn Roberta **Mongeau** 6/27/1975; H – 24, s/o Delmar Stohl and Madelene Huggins; W – 19, d/o Roger Mongeau and Sandra Keller
Eric Gene m. Lois **Whitehill** 2/26/1972; H – b. 6/26/1949, s/o Delmar Stohl and Madelene Huggins; W – b. 8/14/1950, d/o Gordon Whitehill and Ruth Jeffers

STONE,
Norman E. m. Mary E. **Lord** 7/6/1941; H – 27, s/o Charles N. Stone and Florence Edgecomb; W – 21, d/o Henry C. Lord and Ella M. Currier

STOVER,
Ernest m. Marion E. **Jeffers** 8/29/1951; H – 23, s/o Willard Scott and Emma Stover; W – 21, d/o Eddie Beauchemin and Helen Forrest

STRAW,
Bernard Austin m. Marjorie **Huggins** 10/18/1958; H – 21, s/o Merton Vaughn Straw and Irene Hann; W – 20, d/o Ralph Huggins and Ruth Osgoods

SWEATT,
Alonzo of Pittsburg m. Eva **French** of Canada 6/1/1909

TABOR,
Parker W. m. Nina **Williams** 2/3/1932 in Boston, MA; H – 47; W – 40

TERRILL,
Harry E. of Pittsburg m. Gladys **Lea** of Pittsburg 3/24/1908
Perley A. of Pittsburg m. Antoinette N. **Booth** of Manchester 4/24/1929

THIBAULT,
Gerard m. Waneta A. **Haynes** 3/9/1943; H – 21, s/o Hector Thibault and Clara Pevin; W – 19, d/o Stewart Haynes and Hazel Danforth

THIBEAULT,
Adrien R. m. Hugeutte C. **Riendeau** 5/10/1950; H – 21, s/o Joseph Thibeault and Rose Marquis; W – 21, d/o George Riendeau and Ariana Gagner
George R. m. Bertina **Paradis** 7/26/1936 in Stewartstown; H – 27, s/o Camille Thibeault and Hermenise Champeau; W – 19, d/o Antoine Paradis and Marianne Robert
Leonard A. m. Wando **Zesut** 6/16/1941; H – 20, s/o Amede Thibeault and Exelia Chaloux; W – 21, d/o Anthony Zesut and Victoria Pescena
Paul A. m. May **Fuller** 10/23/1949; H – 29, s/o Hector Thibeault and Clara Pevin; W – 33, d/o Frank Fuller and Ella O. Corkum
Raymond Gilles m. Louisette Gaetane **Marchand** 10/17/1959; H – 20, s/o Joseph Thibeault and Rose Ida Marquis; W – 20, d/o Ovide Marchand and Jeanne Champagne

Richard P. of Pittsburg m. Pauline K. **Noyes** of Pittsburg 8/18/1984

THISTLE,
Daniel N. of Pittsburg m. Carol B. **Sackett** of Pittsburg 12/24/2001

TILTON,
Curtis Edward m. Suzanne Grace **Gross** 12/24/1965; H – 17, s/o Edward Tilton and Addie Young; W – 18, d/o Harry Gross and Betty Gouderman
Edward Earl m. Addie Cora **Young** 4/21/1946; H – 36, s/o Curtis Tilton and Lucy Staples; W – 21, d/o Hollis Young and Melvina Young

TINIOS,
Peter J. of Hampton m. Lynne C. **Scheurich** of Farmington, NY 7/4/2000

TOWLE,
Edgar A. of Pittsburg m. Inez **Gorden** of Pittsburg 10/25/1916
Edwin A. of Pittsburg m. Alice L. **Gordon** of Lancaster 8/10/1911
Edwin A. of Pittsburg m. Ethel L. **Stanton** of Colebrook 11/17/1923
Ernie Arthur m. Shirley Ann **Sweeney** 11/20/1965; H – 20, s/o Fred Towle and Barbara Woods; W – 21, d/o Julius Sweeney and Dorothy Lounderville
Gordon E. m. Marie L. **Reynolds** 1/18/1942; H – 18, s/o Edgar Towle and Inez Gordan; W – 18, d/o Carl Reynolds and Pauline Dussault
John M. m. Leora M. **Heath** 10/13/1942; H – 29, s/o Charles W. Towle and Lucy Waldron; W – 25, d/o Archie R. Heath and Laura A. Wood

John Manning m. Celia Mae **Bruce** 11/4/1948; H – 35, s/o Charles W. Towle and Lucy Waldron; W – 29, d/o Harry G. Bruce and Elmira Picard

King E. of Pittsburg m. Sibyl **Haviland** of Concord, VT 3/9/1927

King E. m. Mildred C. **Manseau** 6/17/1933 in Jefferson; H – 25, b. Pittsburg, s/o Charles Towle and Lucy Waldron; W – 26, b. Bury, PQ, d/o Horace Manseau and Rebecca Goodnough

Lee R. m. Bette F. **Drummond** 6/25/1960; H – 25, s/o King Towle and Mildred Manseau; W – 17, d/o Orbie Drummond and Mable Sorock

TROMBLY,

James J. of Pittsburg m. Denise M. P. **Plourde** of Pittsburg 8/28/1985

TRYBULSKI,

Walter A. of Pittsburg m. Marie R. **Menard** of Pittsburg 6/30/2001

UNDERHILL,

Bret Stephen of Pittsburg m. Norma Ada **Keezer** of Clarksville 7/20/1996

URAN,

Harold Frederick m. Ruth Lillian **Marsh** 8/3/1940; H – 30, s/o Frank Uran and Jessie Page; W – 17, d/o Samuel Marsh and Mable Congdon

John Michael m. Alice Jean **Dresser** 12/19/1971; H – 22, s/o Frank Uran and Zelma Foster; W – 20, d/o Raymond Newton and Sarah Tippitt

Paul Dennis m. Mary Ellen **Nason** 9/3/1966; H – 22, s/o Frank E. Uran and Zelma E. Foster; W – 17, d/o Clark Nason and Dora J. McKee

Stephen Charles m. Barbara Jean **Ricker** 10/12/1975; H – 25, s/o Frank Uran, Sr. and Zelma Foster; W – 18, d/o Raymond Ricker and Gladys Brooks

VARNEY,
Arthur L. m. Freda S. **Fuller** 7/8/1933 in Old Orchard, ME; H – 44, b. Bowdoinham, ME, s/o Edward D. Varney and Rachel M. Curtis; W – 36, b. Pittsburg, d/o Will H. Bacon and Nellie E. Perry
Edward D. m. Alberta G. **Hall** 11/14/1953; H – 19, s/o Arthur L. Varney and Freda S. Bacon; W – 17, d/o Vernon H. Hall and Christie R. Hawes
Harold E. of Pittsburg m. Ina M. **Fisk** of Groveton 7/25/1915
Leslie A. of Pittsburg m. Regina G. **McKeage** of Pittsburg 3/12/2005 in Pittsburg

VASHAW,
Frank D., Jr. m. Shirley M. **Stover** 6/23/1952; H – 24, s/o Frank Vashaw and Ethelyn Dudley; W – 27, d/o Willard Scott and Emma Stover

VEILLEUX,
Denis L. m. Armande H. **Robinson** 9/2/1967; H – 20, s/o Leo Veilleux and Marie Irene Drouin; W – 20, d/o Eric Robinson and Evelyn Beloin

WALRAVEN,
Morris Perry m. Sandra Edith **Washburn** 6/22/1973; H – 24, s/o Robert L. Walraven and Faye Gilreath; W – 22, d/o Kenneth Washburn and Elizabeth Heath

WARD,
Lloyd Paul m. Lena Mary **Scott** 10/12/1940; H – 21, s/o Leo Parl Ward and Odetta Ward; W – 28, d/o Chauncey Merrill and Carrie F. Cody

WASHBURN,
Charles of Pittsburg m. Mary **Forest** of Stewartstown 3/13/1905
Kenneth Roger m. Elizabeth **Heath** 8/30/1940; H – 20, s/o Samuel Washburn and Edith May Brown; W – 20, d/o Archie R. Heath and Laura A. Wood
Samuel J. of Pittsburg m. Edith M. **Brown** of Pittsburg 3/20/1908
William H. m. Arlene R. **Hann** 8/7/1942; H – 25, s/o Samuel Washburn and Edith Brown; W – 18, d/o George Hann and Abbie Wheeler
Willis E. m. Alice R. **Hilliard** 2/7/1943; H – 31, s/o Samuel Washburn and Edith Brown; W – 23, d/o Wilbur L. Hilliard and Glen French

WEBSTER,
Harold A., Jr. of Pittsburg m. Joy C. **Dobens** of Clarksville 10/6/1987
Harold Adams, Jr. m. Barbara Ruth **Brown** 6/10/1970; H – 51, s/o Harold Webster, Sr. and Charlotte White; W – 52, d/o Ernest Lapoint and Edith Terrill

WHAREM,
William David, Jr. of Pittsburg m. Ginger Beth **Estes** of Pittsburg 3/3/2001

WHEELER,
Claude Arthur m. Alberta Annette **Gagne** 12/20/1958; H – 23, s/o Raymond Wheeler and Doris Francis Chandler; W – 18, d/o Albert Gagne and Cecile Boudreau
Dennis D. of Pittsburg m. Allison J. **Goulette** of Pittsburg 12/27/1980
Dennis Donald of Pittsburg m. Deanna Lea **Cameron** of Pittsburg 2/14/2000

Donald R. m. Sheila M. **Howland** 6/24/1961; H – 21, s/o
    Raymond Wheeler and Doris Chandler; W – 17, d/o
    Bernard Howland and Margaret Ouellette
Elwin of Lancaster m. Lucie M. **Baldwin** of Pittsburg 6/11/1915
Kendall B. of Clarksville m. Lisa M. **Howe** of Pittsburg 8/7/1982
Raymond A. m. Doris F. **Chandler** 9/15/1932 in Alton; H – 24; W
    – 19
Walter m. Leora M. **Willis** 7/26/1967; H – 56, s/o Walter J.
    Wheeler and Celia Harriman; W – 50, d/o Archie Heath
    and Laura Wood

WHITAKER,
Paul Bowen, Jr. of Somers, CT m. Barbara Ann **Boucher** of
    Somers, CT 8/14/1993

WIEGAND,
Martin Emil of Bridgewater, CT m. Ann Beth **Rodgers** of
    Bridgewater, CT 9/20/1996

WILLIS,
Leslie Joseph m. Leora Martha **Tuttle** 10/5/1946; H – 37, s/o A.
    C. Willis and Alice McLeod; W – 29, d/o Archie Heath and
    Laura Wood

WOOD,
Charles A. of Bangor, ME m. Cora **Condon** of Pittsburg 7/3/1910

WOODARD,
Daniel P. of Pittsburg m. Ellen E. **Furbush** of Pittsburg
    7/26/1920

WOODBURY,
Robert M. of Pittsburg m. Pauline M. **Kwapniewski** of
    Londonderry 5/26/2005 in Manchester

WOODROW,
Carroll E. m. Francis E. **Bacon** 1/11/1936 in Pittsburg; H – 20, s/o D. W. Woodrow and Myrtle Woodrow; W – 18, d/o Ernest Bacon and Florence Weagle

WRIGHT,
Samuel of Pittsburg m. Flora **Bacon** of Pittsburg 9/18/1920
Steven Robert m. Roxanne Lee **Bryant** 6/28/1975; H – 21, s/o Robert Wright and Natalie Post; W – 18, d/o Ray Bryant and Jean Crawford

YOUNG,
Almon Josiah m. Arline Hedine **French** 8/8/1948; H – 24, s/o Merle Young and Bessie Thompson; W – 30, d/o Axel French and Leona Lapointe
Arnold S. m. Lou Alberta **Young** 4/5/1950; H – 20, s/o Stewart Young and Hilda Brown; W – 20, d/o Clayton Young and Alice Hall
Bryan Albert of Stewartstown m. Lisa Ann **Johnson** of Stewartstown 9/26/1998
Clayton F. of Pittsburg m. Alice L. **Hall** of Clarksville 7/3/1928
Duane Richard of Pittsburg m. Luanne Marie **Foss** of Pittsburg 2/6/1993
Hollis H. of Clarksville m. Melvina **Young** of Pittsburg 10/27/1919
Holman Hollis m. Lorene Nell **Scott** 10/1/1949; H – 28, s/o Hollis H. Young and Melvina I. Young; W – 27, d/o Fred T. Scott and Lena Danforth
Howard Clifton m. Ferne Arthur **Brown** 7/19/1963; H – 31, s/o Clayton F. Young and Alice L. Hall; W – 35, d/o Andrew J. W. Archer and Glenn Myra Kay
Jason L. of Pittsburg m. Tanya L. **Paquette** of Pittsburg 1/6/2007 in Pittsburg
Leonard William m. Marilyn Anne **White** 6/20/1970; H – 22, s/o Philip L. Young and Mildred Andrews; W - 20, d/o Robert R. White and Anne Riley

Phillip Leavitt m. Mildred Alida **Andrews** 8/10/1940; H – 22, s/o Ivan Delano Young and Linnie Hawes; W – 18, d/o George Andrews and Jennie Matson
Richard Wayne m. Sandra Lee **Haynes** 8/4/1973; H – 21, s/o Jesse Young and Margaret Beauchemin; W – 19, d/o Robert Pierce and Constance Conery
Roger Winton m. Beth Clara **Wallace** 10/1/1946; H – 21, s/o Jesse Young and Florence Whitney; W – 18, d/o Lew Wallace and Gladys Clark
Roy J. of Pittsburg m. Hannah **Pearsons** of Pittsburg 1/10/1921
Sanford W. of Pittsburg m. Jill E. **Frizzell** of Colebrook 9/8/1984
Sidney Arnold m. Denise Claire **Desrosiers** 8/27/1977; H – 24, s/o Arnold Young and Lou Young; W – 23, d/o Joseph Desrosiers and Cecile Labeau
Stewart of Pittsburg m. Hilda **Brown** of Canaan, VT 7/7/1923
William J. m. Lottie E. **Howe** 6/7/1937 in Colebrook; H - 23, s/o Roy Young and Lou Farnsworth; W – 21, d/o Tillie Howe and Bessie Roby
Winston John m. Andrea May **Lord** 7/15/1972; H – b. 10/8/1942, s/o Phillip Young and Mildred Andrews; W – b. 4/20/1952, d/o William E. Lord and Kate Fuller

YUSKAUSKAS,
Vincent Charles m. Evelyn Margaret **Wells** 12/22/1973; H – 52, s/o Frank Yuskauskas and Anna Simmons; W – 42, d/o Ernest Wells and Margaret Hughes

Aldrich, Florence – Farnsworth, Earl
Aldrich, Nina E. – Ormsbee, Forrest C.
Allen, Margaret N. – Brooks, Leo M.
Allen, Martha W. – McKibben, Scott W.
Alls, Blanche – Day, Edwin C.
Amey, Dottie-Jane – Masters, Jeffrey Alan
Amey, Nancy Elizabeth – Ouellette, Eugene Frederick
Anderson, Kristina Gale – Stohl, Bruce Wayne
Andrews, Mildred Alida – Young, Phillip Leavitt
Aveni, Judith Sandra – Kittredge, Winston, Jr.

Bacon, Flora – Wright, Samuel
Bacon, Francis E. – Woodrow, Carroll E.
Bacon, Freda – Fuller, Andrew C.
Baird, Linda Susan – Chase, Christopher James
Baldwin, Lucie M. – Wheeler, Elwin
Banks, Catherine M. – Covill, Bernard A.
Barry, Eleanor Gay – King, Karl Emile
Barton, Brenda Emily – Dorman, Walter Douglas
Battersby, Cheryl Marie – Howe, Wayne Anthony
Beauchemin, Rosalie E. – Bauer, August L.
Bedard, Barbara Jean – Dorman, Wendell Lyndon
Belanger, Catherine Ann – Boutin, Gerald G.
Bellavance, Pamela Jane – Jahoda, John Curtis
Beloin, Colette M. – Bellows, Carl W.
Beloin, Suzanne M. – Carrier, Bernard P.
Bennett, Florence – Davis, Ora M.
Bennett, Mellissa Lynn – Anderson, Raymond J. M.
Bennett, Mildred – Davis, Frank H.
Berg, Hazel A. – Hodgman, Wyatt E.
Bernier, Laura Corina – Lizotte, Patrick
Bertrand, Christine – Morrissey, Roger William
Bishop, Katharyn Margaret – Fuller, David James
Bissonnette, Alice Louise – Lyons, Alex Douglas

Blake, Mary Ann – Jock, Brett Michael
Blanchard, Pearl M. – Blanchard, Jesse A.
Blanchard, Suzanne Elaine – Gibson, George Arthur
Blank, Mary – Aldrich, Henry W.
Blodgett, Nettie N. – Baldwin, George W.
Boissonneault, Robin A. – Leclercq, Michael J.
Booth, Antoinette N. – Terrill, Perley A.
Booth, Ida M. – Lord, Irving
Bottomley, Susan Jayne – Perrigo, Paul Alan
Boucher, Barbara Ann – Whitaker, Paul Bowen, Jr.
Bourassa, Aline Beulah (Pond) – Burtchnell, William Edward
Bourassa, Kathy Ann – Bolduc, Michael Leslie
Briggs, Avis – Lemieux, Alva
Brooks, Barbara Elaine – Hann, Bradley
Brooks, Carleen Ann – Prehemo, Raymond Arthur
Brooks, Deborah A. – Page, John W.
Brooks, Diane Ann – Merrill, Scott Patrick
Brooks, Margaret N. (Allen) – Noyes, Howard G.
Brooks, Nora Leone – Goodreau, Archie W.
Brooks, Reva Sylvia – Ricker, Jimmie Eldwin
Brotherston, June Ann – Hodgman, Ervin Wyatt
Brown, Angie – Haynes, Harry F.
Brown, Annie E. – Clark, Willie P.
Brown, Barbara Janice – Scott, Marshall Millard
Brown, Barbara Ruth (Lapoint) – Webster, Harold Adams, Jr.
Brown, Corinne – Cameron, George A.
Brown, Edith M. – Washburn, Samuel J.
Brown, Ferne (Arthur) – Young, Howard Clayton
Brown, Hannah Eile – Fox, Kenneth Howard
Brown, Hilda – Young, Stewart
Brown, Hilda Francese – Covell, Gary Winston
Brown, Jennifer Lee – French, Brian Azel
Brown, Maureen Evelyn – Brown, William Dean
Brown, Mildred – Roby, Gerald
Brown, Phyllis Louise – Castonguay, Donald O.

Brown, Virginia (Clogston) – Brown, Alfred
Bruce, Celia Mae – Towle, John Manning
Brungot, Jacqueline M. – Blakely, Lawrence F., Jr.
Bruno, Anna Marie – Day, Gerald Alfred
Bryant, Jean (Crawford) – Chaloux, Lionel G.
Bryant, Raelene M. – Biron, Michael A.
Bryant, Roxanne Lee – Wright, Steven Robert
Bryant, Sherry Lynn – Dorman, Winston Arnold
Bumford, Beverly Jane – Brown, George Franklin, Jr.
Bumford, Donna A. – Gray, Robert N.
Bumford, Jacquelyn Ethyl – Flanders, Walter Wilfred
Bumford, Winifred L. – Schoff, Ray E.
Bunnell, Linda Faye – Reynolds, Daniel Joseph
Burgess, May E. – Haynes, Wilbur
Burnham, Regina L. – Ormsbee, Willard D.
Burrill, Joanne Marie – Cilley, Clifton Cleve, Jr.

Cameron, Deanna Lea – Wheeler, Dennis Donald
Cameron, Michelle Ann – Covell, Dwayne Otis
Campbell, Nancy E. (Cross) – Frizzell, Roy W.
Cane, Elizabeth – Laducer, Arthur
Cann, Linda Lee – Herman, Paul Jules
Carleton, Jenness Holbrook – Phillips, Clyde Erwin
Carlson, Tammy Jean – Pierce, Dale Alan
Caron, Sandra Ann – Haynes, Terrance Owen
Carrien, Donna Karen – Kelly, Sean Patrick
Carroll, Riana Frost – Couture, Rick Paul
Carter, Constance V. – Butler, Rick E.
Chaloux, Annette – Marquis, Fred
Chaloux, Arlene Cecile – Elemond, Jean-Paul
Chaloux, Aurore E. – Marquis, Oscar D.
Chaloux, Marie Claire – Gagne, Rene
Chaloux, Theresa D. – Noyes, Laurence R.
Chaloux, Yvonne Delina – Marquis, Adelard
Chamberlain, Ramona J. – Cameron, Warren J.

Champagne, Elaine A. – Hall, Donald C.
Chandler, Doris F. – Wheeler, Raymond A.
Chappell, Alice J. – Covill, Clesson
Chappell, Marilyn Joy – Lyons, Dana Harlow
Chappell, Susan Adele – Hoag, Roland Boyden, Jr.
Chaquet, Maria – Dragon, Alfred
Chase, Ernestine Helen (Lapoint) – Colcord, Charles Foster
Chase, Sharon Hilda – Rodrique, Sheridan Joseph
Cilley, Deborah Jean – Johnson, William Harold
Clark, Evelyn Ruby – Grover, Glen H.
Clark, Hallie Eliza – Day, Wendall Waide
Clark, Lisa R. – Boutin, Ivon J.
Clark, Winona I. – Richards, Roland R.
Clement, Barbara L. – Judd, Archie N., Sr.
Clogston, Crystal Ann – McKeage, Brendon Dale
Clogston, Daphyne W. – French, Lovell L.
Clogston, Ernestine – Scott, Karl Silsbury
Clogston, Janice Hope – Dobson, Brandon James
Clogston, Jennifer S. – Mathieu, Nicholas J.
Clogston, Laura – Heath, Archie R.
Clogston, Pauline Laura – Oakes, Gordon Howard
Clogston, Virginia L. – Brown, Alfred P.
Codey, Birdie M. – Covell, Everett H.
Cody, Carrie F. – Merrill, Chauncey A.
Cole, Ada L. – Hilliard, George L.
Coleman, Rita M. – Griffin, Wayne R.
Condon, Cora – Wood, Charles A.
Condon, Mabel – Marsh, Samuel L.
Condon, Persis – Luther, Sidney W.
Connary, April L. – Hand, Jonathan M.
Conrad, Carole L. – Poole, Kenneth A.
Cook, Bertha M. – Barry, Alton Charles
Corkum, Ella O. – Fuller, Frank
Corkum, Madelene G. – Merrill, Clyde E.
Correll, Dianna M. – Bolton, William E.

Cote, Cecile A. – Fuller, William E.
Coutts, Judith A. – Grover, William A.
Couture, Louise – Lauzon, Henri
Couture, Nathalie Chantale – Desrochers, Michael Alan
Covell, Diane Ruth – Haynes, Eldon Stewart
Covell, Fern M. – Mousseau, Atlee B.
Covell, Joanne Elaine – Foote, Frederick James
Covell, Rose E. – Ransom, Arthur
Covell, Ruby – Marsh, Samuel
Covell, Ruth M. – Clark, Kenneth R.
Covey, Carol Ann – Mielnicki, Robert D.
Covey, Jacqueline M. – Brungot, Norman S., Jr.
Covill, Cindy L. – Madore, Daniel T.
Covill, Deborah Margaret – Pariseau, David Leo
Covill, Geneva Maude – Clogston, Edmund Linden
Covill, Irma J. – French, Wayland W.
Covill, Madeline M. – Dion, Charles J.
Covill, Mertie – Crawford, Orrie
Covill, Robin L. – Fosher, Thomas J.
Covill, Virginia M. – Leigh, Lester R.
Crawford, Linda Ann – French, Melvin Otis
Crawford, Loni M. – Keyser, Peter A.
Crawford, Mabel S. – Lapoint, George
Crawford, Margaret – Covill, Robert D.
Crawford, Mary A. – Johnson, Danno D.
Crawford, Nancy – Leigh, Edward, Jr.
Crawford, Nettie W. – Brooks, Glen C.
Creon, Ethel May (Gable) – Davis, James A.
Crete, Lisette Terry – Masters, Ray Leland
Cross, Holly Jean – Judd, Vincent Vaughn
Cross, Penny L. – Rancourt, Richard Reginald
Currier, Edna R. – Matthews, Donald H.
Currier, Ella – Lord, Henry
Currier, Nettie A. (Witherall) – Brown, Herbert L.
Currier, Ruth Martha – Bagley, Guy Andrew

Curtis, Heidi L. – Frizzell, Bradley Alan

D'Anjou, Bibiane Emily – Brunelle, Lawrence Albert
Daggett, Gladys Flagg (Carbee) – Dobson, Charles Thomas
Dalton, Dorothy E. – Clogston, Keith W.
Dalton, Margaret Joyce – Price, Arthur George
Danforth, Hazel E. – Haynes, Stewart H.
Danforth, Lena – Scott, Fred T.
Danforth, Rena – Scott, Harry F.
Danforth, Susie S. – Jordan, Carl W.
Daubenschmidt, Janelle Elizabeth Brown – Dunklee, Alan Edward, Jr.
Davis, Jennifer Lee – Brungot, Norman S., III
Davis, Laura Bell – Foster, Lawrence Bartlett
Davis, Mildred – Marsh, Robert J.
Davis, Sandra Lee – Preston, Cedric E.
Day, Evelyn B. – Clogston, Clifton W.
Day, Geraldine M. – DesChene, George O.
Day, Hannah – Pearsons, Fay W.
Day, Hattie M. – Pearsons, Samuel E.
Day, Helen M. – Hurlbert, Lawrence M.
Day, Iva E. – Scott, Arthur
Day, Jean M. – Lord, Roger A.
Day, Joan – Grover, Brendon
Day, Leone D. – Covell, Garlond T.
Day, Lizzie P. – Shallow, James M.
Day, Mercy T. – Baswell, Harry W.
Day, Minnie B. – Osgood, William H.
Dearth, Elaine – Covell, Shirley J.
Dearth, Hilda – Covell, Forest A.
Dehl, Deborah Ann – Dionne, Serge Armand
Dehl, Pauline Dorothy – Mansfield, Ralph Elliott
DeLong, Cathy Ann – Lapoint, Richard Ernest
Deschene, Dorothy Shatford (Greenwood) – Descene, George Oliver

Deschene, Martha – Hawkins, Everett
Deschene, Pauline Martha – Marsh, Walter Edwin
Desrosiers, Denise Claire – Young, Sidney Arnold
Devarney, Nina Rae – Misiaszek, Jack Nelson
Dion, Marion Angeline – Bouchard, Aurele William
Dionne, Helen M. R. – Flanders, Gordon M.
Dobens, Joy C. – Webster, Harold A., Jr.
Dobson, Julia M. – French, Otis E.
Dobson, Rebecca E. – Robinson, Keith J.
Dorman, Caroline – Crawford, Carrol
Dorman, Emily M. – Bernhardt, William F.
Dorman, Mary Jane – Hibbard, Maurice E.
Dorman, Wanda J. – Patnaude, Steven J.
Downing, Priscilla Mary – McKinnon, Robert F.
Dresser, Alice Jean (Newton) – Uran, John Michael
Drew, Gayle Virginia – Shivik, Thomas Francis, Sr.
Drouin, Claudette Anita – Marquis, Gilles Paul
Drummond, Bette F. – Towle, Lee R.
Dube, Therese Noella – Chaloux, Leo N.
Duffy, Gloria D. – Dwyer, Michael K.
Dupuis, Norma Jean – Shields, Larry Edward
Duquette, Laura M. – Cross, Harold W.
Duquette, Mary Rose – Guay, Nelson
Dziodzic, Stefania – Olszanowski, Walter

Eames, Elsie June – Hall, David George
Earle, Janice L. – Earle, Charles G.
Edes, Leona Effie – Blais, Rowland Roy
Eldridge, Karen B. – Eldridge, Timothy W.
Elison, Lydia Rose – Holmes, David Robert
Elliott, Donna Susan – Harding, Michael Richard
Emmons, Vivian Carleton (Bemis) – Danforth, Robert Henry
Estes, Brandy L. – Bolens, William F.
Estes, Ginger Beth – Wharem, William David, Jr.
Estes, Holli Lynn – McKinnon, Richard Carl

Evans, Monica C. – Gleason, Michael F.

Fales, Kerry L. – Silvestri, Joseph D.
Farnsworth, Geneva – Hawes, George W.
Fellows, Grace – Gathercole, Roy C.
Fellows, Marion E. (Bunnell) – Moore, Carl W.
Firda, Holly A. – Bennett, Anthony F.
Fisk, Ina M. – Varney, Harold E.
Fissette, Doris (Gray) – Cook, Roland Simpson
Fitzgerald, Ruth (Flanders) – Robie, Chester L.
Fluet, Jo-Anne M. – Bergeron, Paul A.
Fogg, Muriel Lee – Dobson, Jerry Earl
Fogg, Thelma Beatrice – Bacon, James H.
Foote, Brenda Kay – Puglisi, Louis Joseph, III
Foote, Ruth Helen – Covell, Leslie Lafe
Forbes, Geraldine Marvis – Day, Alfred Edwin
Forest, Mary – Washburn, Charles
Fortier, Christine Alice – Caron, Leo Paul
Foss, Luanne Marie – Young, Duane Richard
Foster, Florence – Masters, Weldon
Foster, Louise D. – Holden, Willie J.
Fotheringham, Roberta J. – Howe, Larry A.
Fraser, Mary Ange (Venne) – Barton, John Allen, Sr.
French, Ann Marie – Guilmette, Jeremy Ramon
French, Arcia A. – Amey, Paul R.
French, Arlene H. – Roppel, Norman J.
French, Arline Hedine – Young, Almon Josiah
French, Cheryl Lynn – Haynes, Gary Charles
French, Darlene K. – Dumais, John R.
French, Elinor Ruth – Camarda, Phillip
French, Eva – Sweatt, Alonzo
French, Gale E. – Prehemo, Raymond A.
French, Glen B. – Hilliard, Wilber
French, Linnie – Roby, Edgar
Frey, M. J. – George, Bertram E.

Frizzell, Beverly Jean – Lord, Leslie George
Frizzell, Catherine E. – McComiskey, Walter G.
Frizzell, Jill E. – Young, Sanford W.
Frizzell, Judith Ervena – Merrill, Hugh Stewart
Frizzell, Sally – Masson, George
Fuller, Beatrice Rena – Lynch, William Patrick
Fuller, Carole N. – Lemay, Benoit J-G.
Fuller, Freda S. (Bacon) – Varney, Arthur L.
Fuller, Harriet – Brown, Allen
Fuller, Hattie – Hawes, L. A.
Fuller, Hazle – Fissett, George
Fuller, Kate – Lord, William Edwin
Fuller, May – Thibeault, Paul A.
Furbush, Ellen E. – Woodard, Daniel P.

Gadwah, Beverly Jean – Dorman, Wayne Edward
Gadwah, Kimberly – Gray, Harold
Gagne, Alberta Annette – Wheeler, Claude Arthur
Gagnon, Joanne Louise – Roy, Maurice Yvon
Gamsby, Susan O. – Gosselin, Bernard M.
Gauvin, Catherine Marie – Dupuis, Romeo Gaston, Jr.
Gavin, Diane Joan – Hurley, J. Daryl
Gervais, Tanya-Marie – McKeage, Rick D.
Getchell, Ann M. – Gray, Lindsey R.
Gibson, Mildred D. – Parkhurst, Erwin L.
Giguere, Louisa – Mathieu, Roland
Gleason, Eleanor Elvera (White) – Schoff, Coleman Dean
Goerson, Myrtle – Bacon, George A.
Goodwin, Constance Violet (Haynes) – Goodwin, Harry Alton, Jr.
Goodwin, Sherry L. – Noyes, Alan I.
Gorden, Inez – Towle, Edgar A.
Gordon, Alice L. – Towle, Edwin A.
Gosselin, Rosie – Dorman, Thomas E.
Gould, Kelly – Boutin, Gerald
Goulet, Christine McCaffrey – Anderson, Jon R. G.

Goulette, Allison J. – Wheeler, Dennis D.
Goulette, Brenda Hazel – Green, Frank Edward
Grantham, Marion Cook – Johnston, Kelly Michael
Gray, Doris E. – Fissette, Roger C.
Gray, Heather – Caron, Charles Robert
Gray, Helen B. – Pearsons, Samuel E.
Gray, Karen Lee – Placey, David Allen
Gray, Laurel Joyce – Amey, Roy Edward
Gray, Lois M. – Hilliard, Frank M.
Gray, Rose Marie – Hicks, Irving Alba
Griffin, JoAnne – Huggins, Chris Wayne
Grinell, Mishawn C. – Hann, David E.
Gross, Suzanne Grace – Tilton, Curtis Edward
Grover, Veronica Jean – Parker, David Curtis

Haley, Julie Anne – Robbins, Robert Kenneth
Hall, Alberta G. – Varney, Edward D.
Hall, Alice L. – Young, Clayton F.
Hall, Rebecca Helen – Dearth, Warren William
Hall, Verna R. – Masters, Russell
Hann, Arlene R. – Washburn, William H.
Hann, Eva Elnora (Huggins) – Lemay, Raymond F.
Harding, Carmen R. – Rougeau, Richard M.
Harding, Winifred Lucille – Brooks, Leo Manfred
Harmon, Barbara Edith (Barnard) – Henderson, Perley, Jr.
Harmon, Irene M. – Hann, Kenneth U.
Harper, Karin L. – Bartlett, Michael J.
Harriman, Beddie – Roby, Fred W.
Harriman, Laura B. – Scott, George C.
Harris, Alicia Anne – Bentley, Christopher Robert
Harris, Sheila Margaret (Howland) – Sperry, James Arthur
Harrison, Melisa A. – Connor, William Allan
Harwood, Paula Lee – Laflamme, Gaetan Ernie
Havalotti, Tammy L. – Gray, Leonard R.
Haviland, Sibyl – Towle, King E.

Hawes, Alma L. – Roby, Edwin L.
Hawes, Christie R. – Hall, Vernon R.
Hawes, Constance – Allen, George
Hawes, Dorothy F. – Anderson, Mallet A.
Haynes, Bertha S. – Dorman, Thomas E.
Haynes, Beverly Lee – Couture, Neil Paul
Haynes, Constance – Hawes, Frank B.
Haynes, Constance V. – King, Randall J.
Haynes, Constance Violet – Goodwin, Douglas Stewart
Haynes, Glendwen J. – Bunnell, Holman G.
Haynes, Majel Mae – Hawes, Russell V.
Haynes, Roena – Cote, Gerard
Haynes, Sandra Lee – Hall, Richard Burton
Haynes, Waneta A. – Thibault, Gerard
Haynes, Winnie – Dorman, Walter
Heath, Bessie – Keach, Harry R.
Heath, Elizabeth – Washburn, Kenneth Roger
Heath, Leora M. – Towle, John M.
Heath, Lois A. – Keach, Garvin H.
Heath, Nerine Mae – Fissette, Robert Arthur
Heath, Olive A. – Judd, Burnham R.
Hibbard, Carol Muriel – Owen, Jeffrey Greenleaf
Hibbard, Dorris – Brown, Herbert
Hibbard, Hattie – Farnsworth, Harry D.
Hibbard, Jean Anne – Covill, Dennis Lindsey
Hibbard, Paula Robin – Jordan, Frederick Pushee
Hibbard, Stella A. – Hilliard, Merton L.
Hibbard, Velma – Gray, Merrill A.
Hibbard, Winnie L. – Rainville, Stewart A.
Hicks, Bernadine Adelaide – Blanchard, Roy George
Hicks, Ervena M. – Dorman, Thomas, Jr.
Hicks, Irene E. – McKeage, Willard
Hicks, Mona Eileen – Haynes, Bradley Phil
Hicks, Regina M. – Rodrique, Henry J.
Hikel, Anita Marie (Bedard) – Knapp, Ralph Morton

Hill, Bessie Manning (Whaley) – Rathbun, H. Lloyd
Hilliard, Alice R. – Washburn, Willis E.
Hilliard, Audrey E. – Chamberlain, William A.
Hodge, Mhilia – Cross, Harlan
Hodge, Norma Lea – Masters, Larry Charles
Hodgman, Hazel (Berg) – Judd, Archie N.
Holbrook, Dorothy – Crawford, Jay J.
Holland, Elaine P. – Castine, Peter H.
Holt, Elaine C. – Brooks, Russell E.
Horkovich, Joan Marie Daly – Deneher, Michael
Houle, Linda Dianne – Hewson, Thomas Patrick
Howard, Bonnie Joyce – Ellis, George Colin, Jr.
Howe, Freda M. – Hicks, Alby E.
Howe, Jennie A. – Hibbard, Maurice E.
Howe, Lisa M. – Wheeler, Kendall B.
Howe, Lottie E. – Young, William J.
Howland, Brenda N. – Congdon, Robert N.
Howland, Sheila M. – Wheeler, Donald R.
Hufault, Theresa Marie – Carleton, David John
Huggins, Eva Eleanor – Hann, Gerald Edward
Huggins, Hallie Ruth – Owen, Edward Grant
Huggins, Jessie R. – Day, Lloyd D.
Huggins, Marjorie – Straw, Bernard Austin
Huggins, Norma Elnora – Burns, Robert John
Hurlburt, Althea I. – Huggins, Harry C.
Hurley, Megan Marie – Prehemo, Jeffrey William
Hutchinson, Patti Anne – Barr, Ronald Eugene

Jackson, Joanne I. – Carlson, Carl T.
Jackson, Matilda – Crawford, Alfred J.
Jacques, Leona M. – Pearson, Burwood G.
Jameson, July Ann – Begin, Richard Louis
Jameson, Laura J. – Shannon, Vern K.
Jeffers, Eunice E. – Gray, Tabor P.
Jeffers, Marion E. (Beauchemin) – Stover, Ernest

Jewell, Betsy Elizabeth (Dorman) – Little, William Bilney
Johnson, Elgie E. – Scott, George C.
Johnson, Emma M. – Hall, George D.
Johnson, Heidi L. – Manosh, Peter J.
Johnson, Kim Rhonda – Joyce, Robert Dean
Johnson, Leanna Jean – Marquis, Raymond Albert
Johnson, Lisa Ann – Young, Bryan Albert
Johnson, Mary L. – Keach, Harry R.
Johnson, Wanda L. – McKeage, Brendon Keith
Judd, Kim R. – Chase, Warren E.
Judkins, Laura J. – Jameson, Michael S.
Judkins, Terrie L. – Kimball, Milton W.

Kane, Florence Carleen – Aldrich, Cecil Orin
Kane, Mabel H. – Lord, Austin P.
Keach, Muriel V. – Currier, Andrew H.
Keezer, Linda Ellen (Adams) – Covill, Forrest Alfred
Keezer, Norma Ada – Underhill, Bret Stephen
Kelley, Kim M. – Keenan, Kevin P.
Kelley, Marian Theresa – Gray, Robert Edward
Kelly, Edna B. – Roppel, Norman J.
Kench, Paula Marie – Bilodeau, Raymond Joseph
Kidder, Karen – Prehemo, Neil R.
Kim, Ok Kyong – Knapp, Jarrod Ethan
Klebe, Janine C. – Frizzell, Roy W.
Knapp, Beatrice E. – Haynes, Warren L.
Knapp, Diana H. – Brsitol, Melvin L.
Knapp, Glenna Delia – Rancloes, Frank Oliver
Koch, Kirsten Frances – Lyons, Paul Mark
Kubosiak, Rebecca Lynn – Goodnow, Douglas Everett
Kwapniewski, Pauline M. – Woodbury, Robert M.

Labbe, Carole – Noyes, George, III
Labbe, Louise M. – Blais, Dennis G.
Lachance, Helen Sylvia – Dion, Peter Edward

Lacoy, Karen L. – Chandonnet, Eugene R.
Ladd, Grathia Janet – Bryant, Ray Allen
Ladd, Lorraine F. – Hann, Kelly S.
Ladd, Sherry Ann – Fish, Blaine Delma
Lagasce, Rosie – Coron, John
Lagoulis, Virginia – Beauchemin, Gene L.
Lambert, Nicole M. – Johnson, Craig R.
Lamontagne, Sylvie D. – Parker, David C.
Lampman, Patricia-Ann – Rupp, Edward Robert
Lang, Violet M. – Aldrich, Darwin L.
Langley, Marcia Louise – Beauchemin, Lawrence George
Lantagne, Leona (Waters) – Allen, Wilber
Laperle, Vivian – Fillion, Donald
LaPoint, Barbara R. – Brown, Otis J.
Lapoint, Faith Kelley – Rondeau, Leo Roland
Lavoie, Stephanie Nicole – Lassonde, Kevin Donald
Lawrence, Margaret N. (Allen) – Noyes, Howard Gould
Lawton, G. Beryl – Beecher, Leo
Lawton, Leone J. – Hunt, Elroy W.
Lea, Gladys – Terrill, Harry E.
Leadbetter, Lena – Robit, Ezra
Leigh, Andrea O. – Marsh, Waylon J.
Leigh, Kara S. – Marquis, Ronald M.
Lemanski, Laurie A. – Ekberg, Mark C.
LeVesque, Sylvia Marion (Robie) – LaChance, Henry Joseph
Lincoln, Ruth S. – Judd, Kevin D.
Little, Laurie Lee – Bacon, William Austin
Little, Theresa Marie – Lord, Corey Steven
Locke, Deborah Arline – Amey, John Holman
Locke, Fay Anita – Hall, Burton Hawes
Locke, Ida Beryl – Johnson, Embert Alton
Lomax, Millicent Anne – Philbrook, Clement E.
Lord, Andrea May – Young, Winston John
Lord, Edith E. – Buteau, Andre
Lord, Irma F. – Clogston, Clifton W., Jr.

Lord, Mary E. – Stone, Norman E.
Lord, Myra J. – Brooks, Lawrence H.
Lynch, Dorothy E. – Emmons, Merrill C.
Lynch, Norma E. – Covill, Gordon L.

Machos, Sheli M. – Judd, Richard A.
Mackey, Cheryl A. – Covill, David G.
MacLeod, Beverly Irene – Bergeron, Leopold Rosaire
Madore, Helene C. – Clogston, Ricky C.
Madore, Lucie A. – Gray, Arnold E.
Madore, Nicole L. – Noyes, Timothy J.
Malsbury, Amy Marie – Billings, Christopher Cooper
Mandigo, Mary E. – Berry, Kenneth W.
Manseau, Mildred C. – Towle, King E.
Marchand, Louisette Gaetane – Thibeault, Raymond Gilles
Marquis, Lise Alma – Lessard, Renald George
Marquis, Pauline Yvette – Inkell, Denis Gerard
Marsh, Leora – Buffington, Elmer E.
Marsh, Rilma – Bunnell, Everett M.
Marsh, Ruth Lillian – Uran, Harold Frederick
Martin, Pearl M. – Blanchard, Jesse A.
Martineau, Debra A. – Huggins, Chris W.
Masters, Betty J. – Johnson, Rodney B.
Masters, Celia – Huggins, Billie
Masters, Grace – Rowan, Donald C.
Masters, Hortense Q. – Merrill, Fay
Masters, Jane Harriet – Fish, Marshall Schoff
Masters, Lila – Hastings, James W.
Masters, Norma (Hodge) –Bacon, John H.
Masters, Patricia Ann – Gendon, Phillip Ovila
Maurais, Sara R. – Lanctot, Roger
Maxum, Ella Hall – Haynes, Harry F.
Mazur-McLaughlin, Brandi – Manosh, Tristan J.
McComiskey, Pauline Matilda (Gilbert) – Gilbert, Dean Coolidge
McCormack, Paula N. – Owen, Johnny M.

McKeage, Ivona Ada – Clogston, William Chester
McKeage, Ivona Ada – Hartshorn, Raymond V.
McKeage, Penny L. – Cross, Ricky D.
McKeage, Regina G. – Varney, Leslie A.
McKeage, Stephanie Jo – Dube, Richard N., II
McKeage, Vena E. (Washburn) – Masters, Weldon I.
McKeage, Violet – Blais, Roy
McKearney, Linda J. – Jewell, John K.
McKearney, Shirley Page – Riendeau, Robert Joseph
McLain, Nellie G. – Hibbard, George S.
McMaster, Arlene Helen – Edmond, Stuart Deane
Meiggs, Dorothy K. – Brooks, Clinton W.
Menard, Marie R. – Trybulski, Walter A.
Merrill, Bertha K. – Robie, Moses S.
Merrill, Blanch – Blodgett, Arthur
Merrill, Hortense Violet (Masters) – Reynolds, Maynard Wilson
Merrill, Judith Ervena (Frizzell) – Kidder, Keith Davis
Merrill, Margaret Pearl – Lakin, Wendall Ward
Merrill, Mebal R. – Brown, Isaac
Merrill, Roberta June – Covill, Lindsey Leroy
Merrill, Sharon – Bumford, Fredric S.
Mills, Maple – Brown, George L.
Mitchell, Heather Lyn – Amey, Mark Everett
Mochrie, Marcia Ann – Howard, Roger Craig
Mongeau, Jocelyn Roberta – Stohl, Don Sterling
Moody, Cynthia Charlotte – Morin, Vernon Joseph
Moor, Lillie – Marsh, Elwin J.
Morissette, Linda A. – Lampron, Ronald R.
Mountain, Mary E. – Olsen, George W., Jr.
Mousseau, Helen – Garcelon, David C.
Mousseau, Melissa Amelia – Fandrich, Edgar Jacob
Mousseau, Patricia J. – Smith, Oliver O.

Nason, Gertrude – Hurlburt, Burnham
Nason, Glee Adell – Day, Harry Lee

Nason, Mary Ellen – Uran, Paul Dennis
Newman, Nancy Lee (Cooper) – Bibbo, James Vincent, III
Nichols, Barbara A. – Clogston, Edmund L.
Noe, Lucinda Eva (Kinney) – Holden, Fred H.
Nolan, Delia – Fissette, Joseph H.
Norgoal, Gail Ellen – Goerke, Arthur Wayne
Noyes, Cheryl Ann – Cote, Paul A.
Noyes, Margaret (Allen) – Hawes, Herbert
Noyes, Pauline K. – Thibeault, Richard P.

Ormsbee, Wilma J. (Hawes) – Robie, Edwin M.
Osgood, Ruth E. – Huggins, Ralph
Osiensky, Barbara – Howland, Richard R.
Ouelette, Margaret Lucille – Howland, Bernard Ralph
Owen, Cheryl Elaine – Clogston, Bruce Wayne
Owen, Evelyn Grace – Dorman, Sherman Alson
Owen, Jamie N. – Gray, Seth P.

Paquette, Corinne M. – Howland, David K.
Paquette, Marie Jeanne – Flanders, Gordan M.
Paquette, Suzanne – Madore, Eusebe
Paquette, Tanya L. - Young, Jason L.
Paradis, Armoza – Richard, Clovis
Paradis, Bertina – Thibeault, George R.
Paridis, Arline – Pond, Guy W.
Pariseau, Deborah C. – Cross, Dennis E.
Parker, Bert – Luther, Sidney
Parker, Jacquelyn Lee – Ruttle, Douglas Ashton
Pearsons, Hannah – Young, Roy J.
Pellerin, Rhea M. (Henault) – Ponzek, Edward J.
Penn, Margaret – Covell, Roy E.
Pfaff, Melissa R. – Marcinkevicz, John R.
Philbrook, Irma – Bacon, Claude S.
Phillips, Dorothy Anne – Covey, Charles Arthur, Jr.
Pierce, Linda Jane – Young, Richard Wayne

Piersons, Jennie E. – Merrill, Arthur
Pike, Clareson – Merrill, Edward G.
Pinckney, Christine Kay – Lapoint, Richard Ernest
Pinckney, Christine Kay – Parker, Reuben Robert
Plante, Michele Marie – Daniels, Stephen Allen
Plourde, Denise M. P. – Trombly, James J.
Poillon, Christine Jon – Gallagher, Charles Thomas
Prehemo, Gina Marie – Saari, Randall Alan
Prehemo, Lisa A. – Johnson, Leonard W.
Purrington, Darcy Lynn – Anderson, Clint Edward

Rattigan, Deborah Agnes (White) – Gadwah, Bruce Edwin
Ray, Shirley A. – Bunnell, Clifford J.
Reading, Rebecca Moore – McKeag, William H.
Reid, Kim C. – Hammersley, James E.
Reid, Reita W. – Ripley, Butler L.
Revoir, Marguerite Cecilia – LaChance, Alva Joseph
Reynolds, Estella – Miller, C. R.
Reynolds, Marie L. – Towle, Gordon E.
Rice, Janet Rae – Leduc, Jeremy Arthur
Richards, Arlene Evelyn – Riendeau, Yvon Moses
Richards, Shirley A. – Brunelle, Billy
Ricker, Barbara Jean – Uran, Stephen Charles
Ricker, Julie Ann – Roy, Kenneth R.
Riendeau, Huguette C. – Thibeault, Adrien R.
Riley, Wanda M. – Paquette, Paul G.
Robertshaw, Thelma Iris – Gray, Patrick Hibbard
Robideau, Mary A. (Gadomski) – Cooney, Joseph J.
Robidoux, Patty Joe – Arsenault, Kenneth Paul
Robinson, Armande H. – Veilleux, Denis L.
Robinson, Claudette – LaPointe, Andre
Robinson, Mariette A. – Dagesse, Richard A.
Robinson, Monica Rita – Dagesse, Yvon Doris
Robinson, Pauline Marie – Lavoie, Rock Thadee
Roby, Angie – Allen, Harry S.

Roby, Bessie – Howe, Tilly
Roby, Meade – McKeage, Robert
Rockelin, Mary A. – Aldrich, Henry W.
Rodgers, Ann Beth – Wiegand, Martin Emil
Rodrique, Carleen Ann – Brooks, Ray Everett
Rodrique, Janet A. – Haynes, Thomas H.
Rodrique, Michelle Cheri – Bolens, William Fredrick
Ropple, Marie Leona – Conroy, Robert Edward
Rouleau, Solange – Paquette, Andrew
Rowell, Minnie E. – Lee, Ernest
Roy, Lise Marthe – Marquis, Ronald Leon
Ruggles, Jessica Lynn – Sherman, Steven Lewis
Russell, Lucy – Rowell, Walter

Saari, Gina M. – Paquette, Ronald A.
Sackett, Carol B. – Thistle, Daniel N.
Samuels, Lorraine Doris – Ryan, Leo Thomas
Sanborn, Helen (Stanton) – Merrill, John
Santos, Janice Marie – Robinson, Craig Richard
Sarazin, Wendy Sue – Hatch, John J.
Scheurich, Lynne C. – Tinios, Peter J.
Schoff, Bernice – Flanders, Gordan M.
Schoff, Eva S. (Smith) – Scott, Fred T.
Scott, Eva H. – Gallagher, Frank L.
Scott, Eva S. (Smith) – Gadwah, Mervyn Oliver
Scott, Kathleen Marie – Covell, Dwayne Otis
Scott, Lena Mary (Merrill) – Ward, Lloyd Paul
Scott, Lillian M. – Schoppe, Herman H.
Scott, Lorene Nell – Young, Holman Hollis
Scott, Terry Mae – Day, Howard Edwin
Scoville, Jennifer Lynn – Radun, David Robert
Shallow, Christie M. – Johnson, Arthur E.
Shallow, Katherine A. – Fogg, Leland
Shallow, Lurlene – Phillips, Clyde L.
Shatney, Florence – Scott, Willard C.

Shatney, Florence Eldora – DesChene, George Oliver
Shetney, Hazel M. – Lea, Herbert J.
Shuler, Lori Ann – Fogg, James David
Slack, Deborah M. – Covill, Roger G.
Smith, Alice – Fissette, George H.
Smith, Elsie C. – Owen, Edward G.
Smith, Eva M. – Schoff, Porter J.
Smith, Goldie – Fuller, Andrew C.
Smith, Katherine Alice – Mousseau, Keane Atlee
Smith, Mabel C. (Lewis) – Quimby, Earl D.
Smith, Marcia D. – Armstrong, David D.
Sommers, Mary H. – Amey, Holman J.
Spat, Anna C. – Goldrup, Robert C.
Sprague, Dorothy – Amey, Holman J.
Stanton, Ethel L. – Towle, Edwin A.
Statkum, Billie E. – Chaloux, Lionel G.
Stevens, Nora M. – Burges, Albert N.
Stewart, Carolyn M. – Hawes, Warren G.
Stohl, Madelene (Huggins) – Judd, Burnham Alton
Stone, Naomi M. – Roy, Kenneth R.
Stover, Emma Gladys – Scott, Willard Charles
Stover, Shirley M. – Vashaw, Frank D., Jr.
Straw, Carlene Carol – Prehemo, Robert W.
Straw, Jacquelyn R. – Parker, Reginald E.
Straw, Janice Irene – Judd, Willie Dennison
Straw, Jhody Lynn – Judd, Archie Nathan, Jr.
Straw, Judy L. – Rancourt, Jules V.
Stuart, Donna Mae – Hubbard, Sterling Lance
Sullivan, Cynthia A. – Howe, Jonathan K.
Swain, Muriel L. – Holmes, Shirley A.
Sweeney, Francese A. – Goulette, David Ralph
Sweeney, Shirley Ann – Towle, Ernie Arthur
Sweet, Pamela J. – Hadley, Chuck L.

Tabor, Sarah Jane – Cummings, William Elwin

Tame, June S. E. – Goldrup, William M.
Taylor, Nadine Ellen – Moran, Thimothy Gerard
Taylor, Ruth E. – Maxfield, John R.
Terrill, Ellen – Furbush, George M.
Terrill, Ethel M. – Judd, Arthur S.
Terrill, Marguerite – Johnson, William E.
Therrien, Anne Althea (Smith) – Nicholson, Angus Nichol
Thibeault, Ann M. – Master, Ray L.
Thurber, Sheila M. – Covill, Forrest A.
Tilton, Mrs. Lucy M. – Farnsworth, Harry D.
Tirrill, Emma – Potter, John
Towle, Alice Iona – Ball, Ernest James
Towle, Bertha – Keney, Jason
Towle, Leora Martha (Heath) – Willis, Leslie Joseph
Trask, Rebecca L. – Lawrence, Joseph D.
Travers, Donna Mae – Haynes, Wayne Owen
Treem, Alice Evelyn – Lord, Perley Elmer
Tucker, Ruth Ann – Mailloux, Christian Roger
Turner, Rita Faye – Koslowsky, Alexander Paul

Uran, Brenda Lee – Lanctot, Roger
Uran, Rose M. – Bernard, Peter L.

Varney, Freda S. (Bacon) – Brown, Herbert

Wade, Catherine – Day, Irving
Wake, Laurie A. – Bourgoine, Anthony E.
Wallace, Beth Clara – Young, Roger Winton
Washburn, Ada L. – Cole, Herman C.
Washburn, Arlene (Hann) – Shields, John M.
Washburn, Colleen A. – Brunelle, David A.
Washburn, Dallas Ann – Chase, Ronald Warren
Washburn, Gloria Isabelle – Rogers, Rene Reginald
Washburn, Judith G. – Masters, Randall Ray
Washburn, Linda J. – Clogston, Edmund L.

Washburn, Sandra Edith – Walraven, Morris Perry
Washburn, Vena A. – McKeage, Ivo R.
Waterhouse, Jane M. – Foote, Jarvis N.
Welcome, Harriet T. – Sawyer, Robert R.
Wells, Evelyn Margaret – Yuskauskas, Vincent Charles
Wheeler, Alta – Clogston, Paul W.
Wheeler, Laura M. – Cass, Earnest E.
Wheeler, Lena May – Berry, Arthur Merton
Wheeler, Lillian Ruth – Hann, Austin Carl
Wheeler, Lisa Marie – Savard, Timothy Rowland
Wheeler, Lizzie A. – Betts, Norman K.
Wheeler, Roxanne S. – Haynes, Scott N.
Wheeler, Sheila Margaret (Howland) – Harris, Ernest John
White, JoAnne Marie – Little, William Bassett
White, Marilyn Anne – Young, Leonard William
White, Wanda June – Burrill, Paul Kingman
Whitehill, Lois – Stohl, Eric Gene
Whiting, Rachel M. – Lapoint, Richard E.
Whitman, Rhoda Lyn (Blaney) – Anderson, Michael B.
Williams, Mildred Anna – Fuller, Andrew C.
Williams, Nina – Tabor, Parker W.
Willis, Esther Alena – Brousseau, Waldo Charles
Willis, Leora M. (Heath) – Wheeler, Walter
Windhurst, Christine – Judd, Vincent V.
Wiswell, Shelly J. – Francoeur, Clark Alan
Wolny, Lynn – Gilson, Daniel
Wright, Ann – Allison, Rupert Nash
Wright, Myrtle F. – Dore, Cleveland H.
Wright, Wanda J. – Merrill, Glen P.

Young, Addie Cora – Tilton, Edward Earl
Young, Arlene Maude – Richards, Arthur Emerson
Young, Carlene Alida – Fish, Jarvis Thurman
Young, Geraldine Mae – Merrill, Glenford Charles
Young, Irene M. – Hibbard, George E.

Young, Judith Eileen – Dalton, Merrill Albert
Young, Kimberly Marie – Remick, Michael Howard
Young, Linnie M. – Gray, Leroy E.
Young, Lorraine E. – Cameron, Donald A.
Young, Lottie M. – Rancloes, Francis G.
Young, Lou Alberta – Young, Arnold S.
Young, Lynn R. – Dysart, John E.
Young, Melvina – Young, Hollis H.
Young, Nancy Arleta – Covill, Earle Wilbur
Young, Sharon Anne – Hurley, Kevin Thomas
Young, Venessa Margaret – Merrill, Gerald Patrick

Zesut, Wando – Thibeault, Leonard A.
Zub, Deborah Anne – Clarke, Andrew Edward

DEATHS

ABBOTT,
William A., d. 3/20/1931

ADAM,
Conrad, d. 10/18/1918

AINSWORTH,
Timothy W., d. 12/29/2002 in Pittsburg; Donald Ainsworth and Joanna Whitcher

ALBERT,
Robert, d. 11/3/2007 in Colebrook; Armand Albert and Roberta Paradis

ALDRICH,
Addison Bedel, d. 1/1/1914 at 92/8
Alice, d. 1/8/1932
Burton Aaron, d. 7/8/1941 at 68/9/17 in W. Stewartstown; single
Ella, d. 5/18/1930
Elmer, d. 12/16/1934 at 64/3/5; single
Fred E., d. 1/21/1975 at 82 in N. Stonington, CT; divorced; b. NH
Georgia, d. 6/25/1964 at 53 in Laconia; single
Henry, d. 12/8/1942 at 68/0/7 in Pembroke; married
Junie, d. 9/5/1976 at 84 in Cumberland, RI; widow; b. NH
Melvina, Mrs., d. 5/23/1922
Merton, d. 4/11/1937 at 49/0/27 in Stewartstown; apoplexy; single
Violette, d. 5/7/1909 at 74
Willie, d. 8/1/1910 at 47

ALLEN,
Harry S., d. 12/1/1980 in Stewartstown

AMEY,
Alfred, d. 6/4/1987 in Stewartstown

Alfred E., d. 11/13/1951 at 85/2/7 in Pittsburg; widower
Dorothy G., d. 10/3/1994 in Colebrook; Leroy Sprague and Ruth
 Richardson
Emily, d. 10/3/1916
Eric John, d. 8/21/1994 in Lebanon; John Amey and Deborah
 Locke
Etta, d. 10/2/1925
Holman J., d. 6/25/1976 at 74 in Pittsburg; married; b. NH
Mary Helen, d. 2/11/1945 at 45/10/24 in Exeter; married

ANDERSON,
Dorothy F., d. 3/22/1986 in Colebrook
Mallet, d. 6/12/2008 in Pittsburg; Carleton Anderson and Kristina
 Swenson

ANDREWS,
George Gilbert, d. 12/14/1960 at 73 in W. Stewartstown; widower
Jennie Alida, d. 11/8/1955 at 63/5 in Pittsburg; married
Leslie A., d. 2/10/1958 at 38 in W. Stewartstown; single

ARMS,
Annie, d. 11/18/1939 at 73/19/22 in Pittsburg; apoplexy; single

ARSENAULT,
Frank, d. 10/24/1940 at 69 in Pittsburg
John R., d. 1/14/2000 in Pittsburg; John E. Arsenault and Gloria
 Cloutier

AUDIT,
Edgar, d. 8/9/1939 at 22/4/29 in Pittsburg; cerebral hemorrhage;
 single

AVENI,
Anthony, d. 6/30/1993 in Pittsburg; Joseph Aveni and Maria
 Abbadessa

BACON,
Archie, d. 3/28/1918
Ernest W., d. 6/6/1940 at 42/1/17 in Concord; married
J. H., d. 12/2/1911 at 68
Nellie Sanborn, d. 4/7/1956 at 83 in W. Stewartstown; widow
Thelma, d. 3/3/1967 at 48 in Concord; married
William H., d. 5/2/1942 at 71/6/8 in Pittsburg; married

BAKER,
Charles, d. 1/19/2004 in Colebrook; Edward Baker and Grace Tatro
Dorothy, d. 10/1/2006 in Colebrook; John Baker and Margaret Kelly

BALDUCE,
infant, d. 1/12/1924

BALDWIN,
Frank W., d. 12/22/1964 at 89 in Lancaster; divorced
Isabel, d. 1/10/1918
James W., d. 10/6/1932 at 86/4/4
Nettie N., d. 9/2/1919

BARDWELL,
Mary B., d. 5/21/1987 in Colebrook
Perry C., d. 7/5/1997 in Colebrook; Charles M. Bardwell and Annie Hall

BARNES,
Gwendolyn M., d. 9/9/2001 in Lebanon; George Caron and Rachel Goodale
Harry, d. 4/25/2006 in Pittsburg; Harry Barnes and Hazel Cowdry

BARRY,
Dayna H., d. 10/29/1988 in Colebrook
Marjorie E., d. 6/12/2000 in Columbia; Dana Holden and Mabel Walker

BARTSCH,
Andrew, d. 1/26/1997 in Pittsburg; Frederick Bartsch and Ingrid Steege

BASTIAN,
Arthur T., d. 10/3/1989 in Pittsburg

BEAUCHAMP,
Arthur, d. 9/9/2008 in Pittsburg; Arthur Beauchamp and Katherine Donahue

BEAUCHEMIN,
Louis, d. 5/22/1986 in Pittsburg
Una, d. 3/29/2004 in W. Stewartstown; Victor Furgerson and Elsie Kidder

BECKETT,
Kathryn Anne, d. 5/14/1995 in Colebrook; Eric Ewens, Sr. and Ellen -----

BEECHER,
Nathan W., d. 4/2/1942 at 75/0/16 in Pittsburg; married

BELANGER,
Leroy Arthur, d. 7/6/2001 in Pittsburg; Leroy Lawrence Belanger and Annette Fleury
Vinettie, d. 8/4/1972 at 63 in Colebrook; widow

BELOIN,
Annie, d. 9/2/1915 at 0/19

BELVILLE,
Abagail, d. 1/7/1905 at 74

BEMIS,
George Roosebrook, d. 7/26/1954 at 87 in Pittsburg; widower

BENNETT,
Edward B., d. 8/23/1980 in Pittsburg

BERRY,
Albert, d. 5/25/2004 in Meredith; Albert Berry and Edith Whitehouse

BERTHIAUME,
Lucien, d. 12/14/1944 at 33/9/7 in Pittsburg; married

BIBIGHAUS,
Stephen, d. 10/11/1977 at 67 in Colebrook; single; b. PA

BILSKI,
Adam F., d. 12/28/1990 in Colebrook

BIRON,
Amedee, d. 2/16/1952 at 83/3/6 in Pittsburg; married

BLACK,
Wallace G., d. 9/23/1995 in Colebrook; S. Bruce Black and Adele Bergner

BLAIS,
Howard, d. 8/2/1996 in Pittsburg; Roy Blais and Violet McKeage
Madeline, d. 4/23/2008 in Colebrook; George Tenney and Eva Frith
Roy, d. 7/2/1978 at 81 in Lancaster; widower; b. NH

Violet, d. 7/23/1927

BLANCHARD,
Dennis Roy, d. 2/28/1947 at 0/0/5 in W. Stewartstown
H. Augustus, d. 3/5/1926
Sarah, d. 4/17/1930

BLODGETT,
Lucy, d. 4/8/1918

BLOOD,
Irving, d. 7/27/1931

BOISVERT,
Anna, d. 5/4/2006 in W. Stewartstown; Walter Mehlhorn and Anna Anderson

BOLTON,
Florence L., d. 5/24/1993 in Colebrook; Arnold Cunningham and Lorence Bolton

BONENFANT,
Jason R., d. 9/12/1998 in Spofford; Raymond H. Bonenfant and Deborah J. Wilson

BOTSFORD,
Pauline L., d. 3/30/2002 in Lebanon; Lucien Letendre and Odena Bertrand

BOUCHARD,
Wilfred, d. 11/12/1918

BOUCHER,
Irigene, d. 11/8/1939 at 29/6/28 in Pittsburg; fractured skull; married

BOURASSA,
George J., d. 3/21/1979 in Quincy, MA; Edward Bourassa and Emma Lette

BOUTIN,
Henri, d. 5/6/2003 in Colebrook; Arthur Boutin and Lida Bouffard

BOWMAN,
Charles, d. 6/8/1936 at 74/4/5; chronic arthritis; married

BRACKETT,
Celia, Mrs., d. 5/21/1920

BRADY,
Frances Adele, d. 6/12/1992 in Attleboro, MA

BRESSETTE,
Frederick, d. 7/31/1977 at 18 in Lancaster; never married; b. NH
Hazel A., d. 1/13/1966 at 53 in W. Stewartstown; married

BRITT,
James Francis, d. 11/24/1996 in Framingham, MA; Patrick Britt and Kathleen Mullen

BROOKS,
infant, d. 8/25/1926
Dorothy W., d. 7/8/1973 at 64 in Colebrook; married; b. VT
Francis, d. 12/27/1963 at 79 in W. Stewartstown; widower
Fred Edward, d. 2/16/1961 at 83 in W. Stewartstown; widower
Lena Belle, d. 9/28/1927
Leon, d. 9/22/1933 at 43/1/9; single
Lula May, d. 3/18/1963 at 59 in W. Stewartstown; single
Rosa Bell, d. 3/16/1947 at 66/5/6 in Pittsburg; married
William Harvey, d. 12/13/1946 at 67/3/14 in Pittsburg; single

BROWN,
infant, d. 6/6/1920
infant, d.7/4/1924
Alfred P., d. 7/5/1991 in Pittsburg
Bruce E., d. 2/1/1951 at 1/9/27 in W. Stewartstown
Danny Lyle, d. 8/22/1969 at 19 in Stewartstown; never married
Edward, d. 12/15/1941 at 77/6/12 in Pittsburg; widower
Elwin, d. 9/4/1953 at 73 in W. Stewartstown; married
Eva D., d. 8/3/1941 at 68/11/8 in Pittsburg; married
Fred J., d. 12/1/1953 at 77/11/3 in W. Stewartstown; widower
Freda S., d. 10/30/1983 in Colebrook
Harold Scott, d. 5/18/1965 at 59 in Pittsburg; single
Herbert Lester, d. 3/26/1968 at 70 in W. Stewartstown; married
Isaac, d. 9/18/1987 in Pittsburg
James A., d. 4/6/1969 at 88 in W. Stewartstown; married
Kelly Clogston, d. 8/22/1969 at 15 in Stewartstown; never married
L. Joan, d. 3/24/1978 at 43 in Pittsburg; married; b. PA
Margaret, d. 3/16/1964 at 78 in W. Stewartstown; widow
Mrs. Herbert, d. 11/20/1928
Mrs. Isaac, d. 6/24/1942 at 80/6/6 in Pittsburg; married
Otis John, d. 5/12/1959 at 42 in Pittsburg; married
Theodore, d. 2/9/1905 at 21
Wallace Michael, d. 9/3/1957 at 0/0/0 in W. Stewartstown

BRUNELLE,
Alfred Clark, d. 11/28/1960 at 44 in Pittsburg; married

BRUNGOT,
infant, d. 6/19/1966 at 36 hrs. in W. Stewartstown
Norman S., Jr., d. 11/12/1985 in Pittsburg

BRYANT,
Cora (Cole), d. 2/5/1952 at 63/8/28 in Pittsburg; widow

BUFFINGTON,
Leon, d. 7/26/1977 at 90 in Franconia; widower; b. NH

BUMFORD,
Edson M., d. 2/5/1987 in Pittsburg
Viola S., d. 9/14/1990 in Stewartstown

BUNNELL,
David, d. 12/10/1938 at 33/9/2 in W. Stewartstown; lobar pneumonia; single
Ernest, d. 12/16/1995 in W. Stewartstown; Nelson Bunnell and Eunice Taylor
Nelson, d. 12/24/1946 at 68/1/13 in Stewartstown; widower

BURGESS,
Mrs. George, d. 1/5/1906 at 24/4/1
Theresa, d. 5/12/1935 at 12/5/28; single

BURNS,
Benjamin, d. 2/11/1921
Benjamin S., d. 1/15/1955 at 59/0/11 in W. Stewartstown; married

BUTEAU,
Andre J., d. 2/19/1993 in Pittsburg; Emile Buteau and Emma Pacquin
Edith E., d. 2/5/2003 in Colebrook; Austin Lord and Mabel Kane

CAMPBELL,
Clayton, d. 10/2/2006 in Colebrook; ----- and Dorothea Frost
Robert E., d. 5/7/1976 at 48 in Pittsburg; married; b. PA

CANTIN,
William C., d. 5/21/1957 at 64 in Pittsburg; married

CARLSON,
Beverly J., d. 3/4/1963 at 26 in W. Stewartstown; married
Herbert C., Jr., d. 4/8/1996 in Hartford, VT; Herbert C. Carlson,
    Sr. and Olive May Conley

CARON,
Anatole, Jr., d. 2/22/1994 in Colebrook; Anatole Caron, Sr. and
    Lucinda Lamy
Constance, d. 3/10/2007 in Colebrook; Hilaire Biron and Pauline
    Couture

CARR,
Charles, d. 3/21/1979 in Littleton; Daniel R. Carr and Jennie M.
    Sweetser
Gayle S., d. 4/5/1989 in Stewartstown

CASS,
Alice, d. 9/23/1979 in Stewartstown; Urban Terrill and Emma
    Dearth
Ernest, d. 11/30/1972 at 87 in W. Stewartstown; married
Laura May, d. 9/2/1946 at 56/3/1 in W. Stewartstown; married

CHALAUX,
infant, d. 4/28/1914; stillborn

CHALOUX,
Celanire, d. 10/3/1990 in Colebrook
Mrs. George, d. 8/12/1917

CHAPPELL,
Doris J., d. 8/19/1995 in North Conway; Frank Prescott and Edith
    Moser
Elizabeth, d. 1/1/1955 at 75 in W. Stewartstown; single
Fred J., d. 12/12/1908

Oscar, d. 1/15/1962 at 75 in W. Stewartstown; single
Rose Bell, d. 2/6/1948 at 67/10/8 in Pittsburg; married

CHASE,
Addison, d. 7/12/1916
Michael Leo, d. 9/19/1965 at 18 in W. Stewartstown; single

CHESTER,
Thomas, d. 12/3/1906 at 82 in Pittsburg

CLARK,
Adelbert, d. 10/28/1930
Annie E., d. 10/9/1978 at 91 in Meredith; widow; b. Canada
William P., d. 6/22/1942 at 57/8/7 in Pittsburg; married

CLERMONT,
Ronald V., d. 8/16/2003 in Lebanon; Noe Clermont and Agnes
    Lepore

CLOGSTON,
Clifton, d. 3/4/2006 in Pittsburg; Clifton Clogston and Evelyn Day
Clifton W., Sr., d. 3/17/1974 at 66 in Pittsburg; married; b. NH
Dorothy, d. 3/13/2006 in Pittsburg; Albert Dalton and Lois Gray
Edmund L., d. 4/2/2003 in Colebrook; Clifton Clogston and
    Evelyn Day
Keith William, d. 4/11/1995 in Colebrook; Clifton Clogston, Sr.
    and Evelyn Day
Paul William, d. 8/15/1985 in Pittsburg

CLOUGH,
Barbara L., d. 6/27/2000 in Lebanon; George Noyes and Edna
    Cluche

COE,
Edith C., Mrs., d. 7/18/1928

COLCORD,
Charles, d. 7/8/2006 in Pittsburg; Clyde Colcord and Elizabeth Dudley
Ernestine R., d. 3/30/1986 in Colebrook

COLE,
Herman C., d. 3/24/1945 at 60/4/12 in W. Stewartstown; single

COLLEY,
Colie C., d. 5/23/1974 at 75 in Colebrook; married; b. VA

COLLINS,
Alice O'Donnell, d. 2/23/1948 at 66/5/6 in Pittsburg; married
Clarissa, d. 5/11/1916

CONCANNON,
William, d. 8/25/1995 in Colebrook; Michael Concannon and Margaret Connolly

CONERY,
Elizabeth Rachel, d. 10/23/1989 in Pittsburg

CONVERSE,
Alice, d. 3/8/1984 in Stewartstown
Harvey H., d. 11/13/1965 at 75 in Pittsburg; married

COONLEY,
Cynthia, d. 12/11/2007 in Pittsburg; Howard Coonley and Leslie May

CORKUM,
May Ella, d. 11/29/1947 at 72/6/28 in Pittsburg; widow

COROR,
Melvina, d. 11/23/1908 at 9/9/5

COURCHENE,
Anatole G., d. 9/1/1999 in Pittsburg; Albert Courchene and Blanche -----

COVELL,
Hilda A., d. 11/23/1986 in Stewartstown
Matthew, d. 7/30/1979 in Hanover; Lesley L. Covell and Ruth Foote
Nora Mayberry, d. 5/12/1961 at 86 in W. Stewartstown; married

COVILL,
Birdie Cody, d. 2/6/1969 at 79 in Lancaster; married
Clyde L., d. 9/9/1989 in Stewartstown
Elaine C., d. 9/4/1980 in Lancaster
Forrest Alfred, d. 1/23/1942 at 40/2/16 in Pittsburg; married
Freda, d. 4/--/1912
Grant, d. 6/22/1962 at 85 in Concord; married
Harland Benjamin, d. 2/28/1947 at 34/5/25 in Pittsburg; single
Josephine Gilbert, d. 9/22/1954 at 42/7/27 in W. Stewartstown; married
Julia D., d. 3/19/1951 at 92/7/3 in Pittsburg; married
Keith, d. 34/5/1954 at 18/8/29 in W. Stewartstown; single
Lafayette, d. 4/12/1954 at 85/2/22 in Pittsburg; widower
Lindsey L., d. 1/4/1999 in Lebanon; Forrest Covill and Hilda Dearth
Margaret C., d. 8/5/1969 at 68 in Lancaster; married
Napoleon, d. 1/11/1964 at 83 in W. Stewartstown; single
Reginald, d. 3/31/1979 in Dover; Grant Covill and Maude Merrill
Roy, d. 6/12/1978 at 82 in Colebrook; widower; b. NH
Shirley, d. 9/19/1974 at 69 in Hanover; married; b. NH
Wilbur David, d. 2/26/1957 at 45/4/4 in W. Stewartstown; married

COVILLE,
Everett, d. 1/7/1975 at 91 in Newburyport, MA; widower; b. NH

CRAWFORD,
Alfred, d. 5/15/1959 at 79 in Pittsburg; married
Ashley, d. 5/7/1954 at 62/10/6 in Pittsburg; single
Caroline, d. 9/1/1988 in Colebrook
Carroll, d. 8/7/1981 in Colebrook
Charles A., d. 10/5/1918
Doris, d. 3/31/1974 at 65 in Colebrook; widow; b. NH
Everett E., d. 12/17/1967 at 81 in W. Stewartstown; divorced
Franklin B., d. 8/22/1911 at 64
George, d. 4/25/1982 in Colebrook
Mary, d. 6/17/1973 at 72 in Lancaster; widow; b. NH
    Myron, d. 2/4/1947 at 80/2/27 in Concord; divorced
Orrie, d. 7/11/1972 at 88 in Pittsburg; married
Raymond, d. 2/18/1965 at 67 in W. Stewartstown; widower
Willie H., d. 8/20/1934 at 68/8/23; widower

CROCKETT,
Lillian Doris, d. 10/30/1997 in Lebanon; George Bentley and
    Anna Horn

CROSBY,
Daniel H., d. 11/15/1923

CROSS,
Addison, d. 1/17/1908 at 67
Harlan, d. 9/2/1917
Harold W., d. 8/27/1969 at 57 in Pittsburg; married
Sarah, d. 5/24/1929

CURRAN,
John, d. 6/22/1920

CURRIER,
Andrew Harold, d. 3/29/1966 at 74 in Newport; married
Caroline, Mrs., d. 5/10/1921
Flora Isabelle, d. 3/11/1973 at 68 in Newton; widow; b. NH
George W., d. 10/12/1916
Gilford Nelson, d. 1/23/1917
John, d. --/--/1914 at 1
Raymond A., d. 3/7/1925

CURTIS,
Madeline J., d. 9/11/1979 in Stewartstown; George Buck and
    Cora Boonson

D'AMBOISE,
Deslie, d. 12/5/2005 in Colebrook; Chester White and Avis Knox

DAILEY,
Franklin F., d. 9/30/1934 at 84/0/4; widower
Mrs. Richard, d. 10/1/1907 at 71

DALTON,
Albert Henry, d. 1/27/1959 at 67 in Pittsburg; married
Lois Martha, d. 6/27/1995 in W. Stewartstown; Patrick Gray and
    Martha Shopple

DANFORTH,
A.K., d. 2/10/1911 at 39
Eugene, d. 6/5/1923
Robert H., d. 5/22/1961 at 73 in Hartford, VT; married
W. E. L. K., d. 6/4/1904 at 59
Willie, d. 4/19/1908 at 0/2
Willie, d. 12/9/1945 at 87/6/12 in W. Stewartstown; widower

DAVIS,
Mildred Gertrude, d. 4/29/1971 at 74 in Colebrook; divorced

Minnie, Mrs., d. 1/24/1929

DAY,
Alfred E., d. 12/17/1982 in Colebrook
Daniel R., d. 3/4/1931
Hallie C., d. 2/6/1966 at 55 in Tilton; widow
Harvey, d. 12/2/1932 at 58/5/5
Holman H., d. 9/1/1942 at 30/3/1 in Pittsburg; married
Howard B., d. 1/5/1951 at 93/9/4 in New Gloucester, ME; married
Irving, d. 11/23/1932 at 60/9/12
Jessie, d. 1/3/1983 in Colebrook
John A., d. 2/18/1911 at 20
Linden Alfred, d. 7/4/1921
Lloyd, d. 8/31/1978 at 80 in Colebrook; married; b. NH
Lyle S., d. 4/7/1953 at 66/9/12 in Pittsburg; widower
Marcus T., d. 2/11/1923
Marshall T., d. 2/6/1923
Martha Ellen, d. 3/3/1958 at 85 in W. Stewartstown; widow
Mary Ann, d. 2/10/1933 at 84/2/24; married
May E., d. 4/7/1924
Nora M., d. 7/14/1933 at 43/3/15; married
Parker Tabor, d. 8/8/1935 at 89/5/23; widower
Wendall W., d. 12/5/1950 at 40/3/8 in Pittsburg; married
Winiford, d. 3/22/1935 at 45/11/15; married

DEARBORN,
Lucy J., d. 8/--/1914 at 67

DEARTH,
Katherine, d. 6/4/1926
Minnie M., d. 2/28/1951 at 56/11/13 in W. Stewartstown; widow

DEBLOIS,
Clara, d. 5/9/1964 at 89 in Pittsburg; widow

DEHL,
Beatrice, d. 2/3/2001 in Lebanon; Charles Beaudette and
    Yvonne Langlois
Emil O., d. 7/27/1975 at 81 in Colebrook; married; b. Germany
Pauline F., d. 9/3/1978 at 76 in W. Stewartstown; widow; b.
    Germany

DEMMONS,
Lonny G., d. 5/11/1990 in Pittsburg

DENMANCHECK,
Mainly, d. 10/8/1918

DESCHENE,
Ada, Mrs., d. 4/13/1931
George O., d. 1/25/1989 in Stewartstown
Geraldine M., d. 9/10/1998 in Pittsburg; George Forbes and Eda
    Harriman

DESROSIERS,
Armand, d. 8/17/1957 at 41 in W. Stewartstown; single
Richard M., d. approx. 7/25/2001 in Pittsburg; Germain
    Desrosiers and Monique Felteau

DICKSON,
Richard Ackley, Sr., d. 1/8/1995 in Lebanon; George Dickson
    and Amanda Ackley

DIMEK,
Charles A., d. 10/30/2003 in Pittsburg; Walter Dimek and
    Barbara Polonski

DOBSON,
Charles T., d. 4/1/1956 at 68 in Pittsburg; married

DODERER,
Ann, d. 3/6/1998 in W. Stewartstown; Hazen Robinson and -----
Arthur E., Sr., d. 4/9/1998 in W. Stewartstown; Karl Doderer and
    Bertha Schier

DOOLAN,
David, d. 5/21/1957 at 39 in Pittsburg; married

DORE,
Helen, d. 10/18/1930

DORMAN,
Benjamin, d. 11/16/1948 at 5/2/20 in W. Stewartstown; single
Thomas, d. 2/10/1962 at 80 in W. Stewartstown; married
Thomas, Sr., d. 9/13/1979 in Lancaster; Walter Dorman and
    Winnie Marsh
Walter, d. 5/20/1926
Winnie Nancy, d. 8/2/1943 at 62/4/20 in Pittsburg; widow

DRISCOLL,
Blanche C., d. 4/18/1950 at 70/10/6 in Pittsburg; widow

DUBRUNE,
Arthur, d. 10/15/1918

DUNLEAVY,
John Martin, d. 12/21/1998 in Plymouth; Martin John Dunleavy
    and Winifred Louise Quimby

DUQUETTE,
Anita, d. 8/19/1925
Nelson, d. 6/9/1959 at 75 in W. Stewartstown; married

DURANLEAU,
Annie A., d. 1/2/1926
Leonard, d. 3/4/1926

DWINELL,
Edwin H., d. 12/14/1970 at 68 in Hanover; married

EATON,
Melvin Robert, d. 6/26/1995 in Pittsburg; Albert E. Eaton and
    Emma Kimball

EMMONS,
Robert B., d. 12/13/2001 in W. Stewartstown; William Emmons
    and Gladys Stout

EVANS,
Ira Leon, d. 11/22/1941 at 57/4/8 in Pittsburg; married

FARLEY,
Elsie, d. 2/2/2004 in Pittsburg; Albert Erxleben and Blanche
    Drake

FARNHAM,
Flora, d. 7/12/1945 at 84/8/13 in Pittsburg; widow

FARNSWORTH,
Harry Dickey, d. 7/6/1958 at 77 in W. Stewartstown; widower
Joshua, d. 11/4/1914 at 69/7
Lucy M., d. 9/8/1937 at 55/9/17 in Colebrook; carcinoma of
    uterus; married
Rebecca, d. 3/19/1911 at 64

FAUST,
Arlene Evelyn, d. 5/13/1996 in Pittsburg; Eugene Williams and
    Margaret Bixby

FELTMATE,
Antoinette K., d. 8/26/2002 in Colebrook; Rudolph Walker and Antoinette Wagner

FERGUSON,
Lois, d. 12/18/1941 at 77/9/0 in Pittsburg; widow

FISH,
Delma Hall, d. 11/18/1998 in Colebrook; Frank Fish and Alice Hall

FISHER,
infant, d. 7/14/1953 at – in W. Stewartstown; stillborn

FISKE,
Harry Bruce, d. 2/16/1970 at 85 in W. Stewartstown; widower

FISSETTE,
Roger Clayton, d. 6/29/1955 at 43/10/8 in Pittsburg; married

FITZGERALD,
Muriel, d. 5/12/1936 at 5/6/11; acute appendicitis

FLANDERS,
Nellie Christine, d. 12/3/1962 at 85 in W. Stewartstown; widow

FOGG,
Katherine Ann, d. 7/6/1993 in Colebrook; James Shallow and Lizzie Day
Leland Mayo, d. 5/20/1998 in Pittsburg; Austin Fogg and Carrie Deyette

FOOTE,
Frederick J., d. 1/21/1986 in Colebrook

Helen Abbe, d. 8/26/1996 in W. Stewartstown; Edward Rathbun and Daisy Abbe
Joanne, d. 5/15/2005 in Lancaster; Forrest Covell and Hilda Dearth

FORET,
John E., d. 11/29/2001 in Colebrook; Gustav Foret and Danica Bosnic

FORTIER,
Mary Ann, d. 1/29/1965 at 40 in W. Stewartstown; married

FOSKETT,
Francine, d. 5/11/2006 in Pittsburg; Frank Rys and Sonia Kuretz

FRAZIER,
Maynard O., Jr., d. 2/18/1984 in Pittsburg

FRENCH,
Alta, d. 9/4/1911 at 10
Azel Holman, d. 5/8/1948 at 52/9/24 in Pittsburg; married
Betsey, d. 7/20/1906 at 76/6/21 in Colebrook
Daphyne W., d. 10/23/1981 in Pittsburg
Hattie Edna, d. 5/22/1944 at 72/4/11 in Pittsburg; married
Julia May, d. 4/11/1995 in Colebrook; Charles Dobson and Minnie Cochran
Leona H., d. 5/9/1950 at 53/5/25 in W. Stewartstown; widow
Lovell, d. 10/23/2006 in Pittsburg; Azel French and Leone Lapoint
Maureen Burke, d. 9/13/1998 in Lebanon; Daniel M. French and Hilary Burke
Melvin Harry, d. 12/23/1949 at 79/7/11 in Pittsburg; widower
Viola Brown, d. 2/11/1970 at 66 in W. Stewartstown; married
Wayland W., d. 1/5/1983 in Colebrook

Wilbur George, d. 5/12/1998 in W. Stewartstown; Melvin French and Hattie Collins

FRIZZELL,
Nathalie Edith, d. 10/1/2001 in Pittsburg; Roy Ernest Whitehill and Laura Mabel Lyons
Peter Jason, d. 8/22/1969 at 16 in Stewartstown; never married
Wilfred C., d. 11/25/1979 in Hartford, VT; Alpheus Frizzell and Catherine Martin

FRYE,
Ervin A., d. 2/2/1993 in Pinellas Park, FL; Royal A. Frye and Nettie B. Allen
James, d. 10/31/1959 at 91 in Pittsburg; divorced

FULLER,
Arnold, d. 2/8/1918
Clark, d. 9/11/1950 at 59/8/25 in Pittsburg; married
Ella Corkum, d. 8/16/1971 at 79 in Colebrook; widow
Frank, d. 11/25/1944 at 75/2/13 in Pittsburg; married
Ronald, d. 8/1/1916

FURGERSON,
Bessie, d. 1/12/2004 in Colebrook; William Heath and Eva Brown
Susan Elsie Kidder, d. 5/16/1959 at 75 in Pittsburg; widow
Wilman, d. 1/22/2005 in W. Stewartstown; Vistor Furgerson and Elsie Kidder

GADWAH,
Bernard H., d. 8/3/1980 in Pittsburg

GALLAGHER,
Eugene J., d. 5/26/2002 in Colebrook; Eugene Gallagher and Agnes Smith
Frank Lyle, d. 3/12/1971 at 73 in Pittsburg; married

GEISSBUHLER,
Bessie, d. 10/13/1978 at 79 in Colebrook; married; b. CT
John, d. 4/16/1982 in Colebrook

GERMAN,
Russell Francis, d. 5/21/1996 in Pittsburg; Morton German and
   Ida Mayes

GEROLAMI,
Thomas J., d. 5/25/1980 in Pittsburg

GIELAR,
Fred S., d. 8/5/2003 in Colebrook; John Gielar and Mary
   Polchlopek

GILBEAU,
Joseph, d. 4/10/1922

GLADDEN,
Lucius F., d. 10/29/1949 at 64/10/21 in Madrid, ME; divorced

GNOXX,
Cleophus, d. 9/18/1923

GOERKE,
Arthur W., d. 9/11/1997 in Colebrook; Jack Goerke and Bertha
   Hayward

GOKEY,
Stanley N., d. 8/11/1998 in Hartford, VT; Henry Gokey and Anne
   Green

GORDON,
Ralph G., d. 3/22/1998 in Boston, MA

GOSLIN,
M., d. 11/19/1916

GOULD,
Leona Pearl, d. 1/28/1982 in Colebrook

GRACE,
Irving Joseph, d. 8/10/2000 in Pittsburg; Orville Grace and Pearl Gadwah

GRANT,
Ruth, d. 11/3/2006 in Colebrook; Harry Huggins and Althea Hurlbert
Scott, d. 8/7/1999 in Lebanon; Leon Grant and Alice Brouette

GRAY,
Eunice E., d. 1/19/2003 in Colebrook; Miles Jeffers and Laura Blodgett
Leora, d. 9/22/1913 at 21/2
Leroy E., d. 2/2/1966 at 75 in W. Stewartstown; married
Martha, d. 12/27/1938 at 78/5/10 in Pittsburg; carcinoma of uterus; widow
Maude Alice, d. 7/19/1958 at 71 in Pittsburg; married
Merrill A., d. 2/2/1938 at 40/7/28 in Hanover; uremia; married
Robert, d. 11/9/2007 in Colebrook; Leroy Gray and Linnie Young
Velma H., d. 7/5/1984 in Colebrook
Venson P., d. 4/29/1931

GREGOIRE,
Maris, d. 1/20/1928

GROSS,
Ida C., d. 5/17/1953 at 90 in Lancaster; widow

GROVER,
Fanny Clark, d. 6/4/1958 at 78 in W. Stewartstown; married
Glenn H., d. 10/28/1965 at 65 in W. Stewartstown; married
William A., d. 5/4/1970 at 90 in W. Stewartstown; widower
William Homer, d. 3/26/1930

GUAY,
infant, d. 7/27/1919

HALL,
infant, d. 7/9/1929
Afton C., d. 5/14/1969 at 82 in W. Stewartstown; divorced
Alberta, d. 6/29/1937 at 51/4/17 in Stewartstown; intestinal
    obstruction; married
Barney Ray, d. 6/28/1973 at 84 in Colebrook; widower; b. NH
Burt, d. 12/13/1947 at 75/8/9 in Pittsburg; widower
Christie R., d. 9/3/1986 in Colebrook
Everett, d. 2/22/1932 at 6/9
Harry, d. 8/9/1946 at 70/1/25 in Pittsburg; married
John G., d. 1/12/1929
Junie Etta, d. 9/11/1940 at 52/4/3 in Pittsburg; married
Kenneth L., d. 9/21/1930
Lucy A., d. 2/22/1979 in Pittsburg; Edward Blodgett and Lucy
    Fellows
Vernon H., d. 9/21/1986 in Colebrook

HANN,
Abbie Jane, d. 7/20/1933 at 29/8/6; married
Austin C., d. 6/8/1998 in Colebrook; Frank Hann and Martha
    Ellingwood
George Henry, d. 4/3/1977 at 76 in Pittsburg; widower; b.
    Canada
Lillian, d. 11/14/1995 in Colebrook; Jubel Wheeler and Lillian
    Luther
Martha Ellingwood, d. 9/9/1963 at 81 in W. Stewartstown; widow

HANSEN,
Henry, d. 10/12/1975 at 79 in Colebrook; widower; b. CT

HARDWICK,
Harry W., d. 11/17/1916

HARPER,
Mark Richard, d. 1/7/1995 in Pittsburg; Richard Harper and Beverly Ricker

HARRIMAN,
Ada Goodwin, d. 6/1/1941 at 77/1/28 in Pittsburg; widow

HARRIS,
Ernest, d. 3/27/1977 at 46 in Lancaster; married; b. NH

HAWES,
Alice Mary, d. 3/5/1940 at 83/10/14 in Pittsburg; widow
Geneva May, d. 3/12/1933 at 46/10/3; married
George H., d. 11/25/1908 at 57/0/16
George William, d. 7/17/1969 at 85 in Pittsburg; widower
John T., d. 3/2/1916
Leonard Andrew, d. 7/17/1956 at 77 in Pittsburg; divorced
Maggie, d. 4/11/1956 at 79 in Pittsburg; widow
Pearl B., d. 11/18/1995 in Lancaster; Hiram Bacon and Nellie Sanborn
Russell Vernon, d. 6/7/1994 in Lebanon; Vernon Hawes and Pearl Bacon
Vernon R., d. 4/28/1987 in Stewartstown

HAWKINS,
William David, d. 11/3/1964 at 0/0/1 in Lancaster

HAYNES,
Alice, Mrs., d. 2/12/1946 at 81/10/29 in Colebrook; widow
Bradley P., d. 8/17/2002 in Colebrook; Stewart Haynes and
 Hazel Danforth
Cheryl L., d. 2/15/1991 in Colebrook
Frank, d. 6/19/1942 at 70/11/5 in W. Stewartstown; single
Fritz H., d. 8/24/1943 at 24/0/2 in Portland, ME; single
George, d. 2/25/1934 at 73/9/22; married
Harry F., d. 3/18/1957 at 66 in W. Stewartstown; married
Hazel Covell, d. 10/23/1959 at 61 in W. Stewartstown; married
Hiram, d. 6/7/1913 at 79
Lester O., d. 8/30/1929
Majoria, d. 8/9/1922
Shirley Elaine, d. 8/14/1946 at 2/11/21 in W. Stewartstown
Stewart H., d. 9/2/1969 at 73 in Colebrook; widower
Terrence, d. 6/12/1983 in Pittsburg

HAZELTINE,
Raymond Cecil, d. 10/16/1945 at 52/8/6 in Pittsburg; married

HEALEY,
Wendell Alvin, d. 2/10/1963 at 53 in Pittsburg; married

HEATH,
infant, d.10/5/1924
Archie Roy, d. 11/13/1958 at 67 in Pittsburg; married
Bert E., d. 10/17/1922
Dan W., d. 7/26/1951 at 78/5/16 in W. Stewartstown; widower
Edward A., d. 9/5/1911 at 0/7
Fred L., d. 4/24/1940 at 71/9/3 in Concord; widower
Hilda C., d. 9/25/1916
Laura, d. 7/18/1974 at 88 in Pittsburg; widow; b. NH
Robert, d. 3/30/2008 in Colebrook; Rufus Heath and Elizabeth
 Davis
William A., d. 9/9/1904 at 47/7/17

HEBERT,
Philias, d. 11/10/1958 at 53 in Riverside; married
Roger, d. 9/14/1966 at 48 in Pittsburg; single

HELINE,
Laura, d. 4/13/1988 in Hanover

HIBBARD,
Elwin G., d. 9/16/1913 at 0/4
George, d. 4/8/2008 in Pittsburg; Ellis Hibbard and Caroline
    Gardner
Harry, d. 9/24/1912
Joel E., d. 9/1/1910 at 73
Laura Robie, d. 12/7/1961 at 77 in Stewartstown; widow
Mary Jane, d. 12/3/1949 at 37/4/9 in Pittsburg; married
Peter O., d. 6/22/1982 in Colebrook
Susie, d. 2/21/1905 at 21/10/22

HICKS,
Marion Day, d. 10/26/1974 at 67 in Colebrook; divorced; b. NH

HIGGINS,
Frederick Keith, d. 8/14/1956 at 32 in Pittsburg; single
Herbert, d. 12/15/1926

HILLIARD,
Ada Lillian, d. 10/18/1971 at 88 in Lancaster; widow
Alma, d. 10/18/1912 at 14
Alma R., Mrs., d. 1/13/1921
Frank M., d. 12/5/1921
George Lee, d. 10/17/1967 at 79 in W. Stewartstown; married
Glenn French, d. 12/23/1995 in W. Stewartstown; Melvin French
    and Harriet Collins
James E., d. 3/10/1923

James L., d. 1/19/1936 at 67/7/20; hydronephrosis plus infection; married
Mary Aldrich, d. 9/1/1959 at 88 in N. Stratford; widow
Mary Jane, d. 12/22/1926
Merton, d. 1/25/1958 at 77 in Hanover; married
Stella A. Hibbard, d. 7/14/1966 at 85 in Greenfield, MA; widow
Wilbur L., d. 3/11/1970 at 73 in W. Stewartstown; married

HODGMAN,
Wyatt Ervin, d. 6/30/1954 at 39 in Pittsburg; married

HOLDEN,
child, d. 11/6/1935 at 0/0/0; stillborn
son, d. 12/14/1936 at 0/0/0; d. delivery
son, d. 2/2/1938 at 0/0/1 in W. Stewartstown; mother injured in auto accident
Cora, d. 5/19/1927
Willie J., Jr., d. 6/4/1931

HOLMES,
son of A. J., d. 6/6/1910
Washington G., d. 1/29/1904 at 55

HOOVER,
Constance L., d. 12/22/1993 in Lebanon; Clifford W. Hoover and Grace F. Fleckner

HORVAT,
Eugene J., d. 8/25/1980 in Hanover

HOUGHTON,
Doris M., d. 1/26/1992 in Colebrook
Lester G., d. 9/5/1985 in Hanover
Roger L., d. 8/24/1985 in Hanover

HOWARD,
stillborn child, d. 8/7/1969 at – in Stewartstown

HOWE,
Bessie R., d. 5/13/1983 in Colebrook
Chester, d. 7/7/1986 in Stewartstown
Lettie Bessie, d. 5/11/1980 in Laconia
Otis, d. 10/5/1986 in Colebrook
Tillie, d. 12/28/1971 at 83 in Whitefield; married

HOWLAND,
Bernard R., d. 9/27/1975 at 58 in Pittsburg; married; b. NH
Floyd, d. 10/13/1977 at 49 in Pittsburg; never married; b. NH
Margaret L., d. 12/16/1974 at 51 in Hanover; married; b. NH
Mercy T., d. 2/11/1952 at 61/9/7 in W. Stewartstown; married
Roscoe Earl, d. 6/23/1975 at 81 in Franconia; widower; b. NH

HUBBARD,
Marjorie L., d. 4/20/1995 in Colebrook; Jeremiah Lunderville and
    Melissa Libby
Winston W., d. 5/21/2002 in Pittsburg; Fred Hubbard and Ellen
    Tozier

HUGGINS,
child, d. 6/3/1941 at ½ hr. in Pittsburg
Ada A., Mrs., d. 4/13/1931
Althea I., d. 2/23/1978 at 72 in Colebrook; married; b. NH
Bessie M., d. 7/21/1918
Celia, d. 7/3/1940 at 63/2/15 in Pittsburg; married
Elnora, d. 10/24/1957 at 81 in W. Stewartstown; widow
Frank Harry, d. 3/26/1955 at 85/4/1 in W. Stewartstown; married
Harry F., d. 3/25/1978 at 75 in Lancaster; widower; b. NH
John C. L., d. 6/14/1915 at 45
Ralph, d. 11/4/1973 at 62 in Colebrook; married; b. NH
Ruth E., d. 6/12/1989 in Colebrook

William A., d. 11/21/1958 at 82 in Colebrook; widower
Wyman S., d. 3/30/1919

HUNTER,
Mable L., d. 6/29/1990 in Lancaster

HUTCHINS,
Ellison K., d. 2/16/2000 in Campton; Howard Hutchins and
    Beatrice Wilkie

INGERSOLL,
infant, d. 4/2/1905
Bert, d. 3/8/1930

JOCK,
Gloria, d. 5/21/1974 at 26 in Colebrook; married; b. NH

JOHNSON,
Almeda M., d. 9/23/1933 at 63/3/2; widow
Arthur E., d. 7/1/1986 in Pittsburg
Carl Arthur, d. 6/3/1993 in Colebrook; Carl Albert Johnson and
    Mary Geary
Charles H., d. 10/1/1922
Charles S., d. 12/5/1937 at 85/1/20 in Pittsburg; chronic
    myocarditis; widower
Christie M., d. 8/8/1988 in Pittsburg
Ellen A., d. 2/9/1949 at 83/1/19 in W. Stewartstown; widow
Embert A., d. 4/19/2003 in Colebrook; William Johnson and
    Margeurite Tirrill
Hattie M., d. 2/22/1950 at 84/1/21 in Pittsburg; widow
Julia, d. 4/27/1936 at 69/5/23; cardiac failure; married
Marguerite E., d. 10/10/1981 in Colebrook
Parker E., d. 5/6/1979 in Hanover; Frank Johnson and Beverly
    Cody

Thomas, d. 5/20/2005 in Pittsburg; Danno Johnson and Mary
 Ann Johnson
William E., d. 12/14/1946 at 82/2/15 in Pittsburg; married
William Embert, d. 3/13/1973 at 74 in W. Stewartstown; married;
 b. MA

JONES,
Howard C., d. 6/2/1985 in Pittsburg

JORDAN,
Susie, Mrs., d. 1/18/1929

JUDD,
Burnham Richard, d. 2/5/1984 in Pittsburg
Flora May, d. 7/26/1932 at 56/6/12
Jennie E., d. 3/5/1907 at 35/11
Madelene A., d. 3/3/2001 in Colebrook; Harry Huggins and
 Althea Hurlbert
Olive Alta, d. 10/27/1971 at 59 in Colebrook; married
Walter Henry, d. 3/31/1940 at 41/6/14 in Pittsburg; married
Willie N., d. 9/27/1944 at 84/9/9 in Pittsburg; widower

JUDGE,
Agnes, d. 10/30/2006 in Colebrook; Archibald Ainsworth and
 Dorothy Stocker
Robert, d. 12/12/2006 in Hart's Location; George Judge and
 Doris -----

KANE,
Edgar Dean, d. 11/10/1980 in Colebrook
Edward, d. 5/19/1964 at 91 in W. Stewartstown; widower
Ethel Dorcas, d. 2/22/2000 in Pittsburg; George E. Knapp and
 Dora May Wheeler
Thomas, d. 11/10/1975 at 68 in Concord; never married; b. NH

KANGAS,
Verno, d. 5/31/1944 at 41 in Pittsburg; married

KEACH,
Amanda B., d. 12/8/1916
Harry Ray, d. 3/16/1952 at 63/10/8 in Farmington, ME; married
James M., d. 9/24/1914 at 75/11
Julia A., d. 12/7/1916

KELSEA,
Edgar H., d. 6/27/1981 in Colebrook

KENDALL,
Allen, d. 7/24/2006 in Colebrook; Stanley Kendall and Ruth
    Woodbury

KENNEY,
Bertha, Mrs., d. 11/7/1907 at 18

KERR,
George, d. 11/18/1922

KEUND,
G. E., d. 10/13/1918

KING,
An John, d. 7/23/1921
Karl E., d. 12/24/2003 in Colebrook; Lester King and Dorothy
    Dicey
Mrs. James, d. 3/11/1932 at 94/2/10

KINGSBURY,
Earl G., d. 5/16/2000 in Lebanon; Fred Kingsbury and Maude
    Thorn

Wayne E., d. 7/14/2001 in Lebanon; Earl Kingsbury and Phyllis Seaver

KNAPP,
Ralph M., d. 11/4/1974 at 60 in Colebrook; married; b. NH
Walter James, d. 8/1/1961 at 28 in Pittsburg; widower

KNIGHT,
Fred Augustus, d. 6/16/1959 at 90 in Pittsburg; married
Gertrude Tabbutt, d. 10/16/1959 at 74 in Pittsburg; widow

KNIGHTS,
Charles A., d. 10/15/1918

KOEHLER,
Charles E., d. 5/23/1978 at 73 in Colebrook; married; b. PA

KOLEV,
Janco, d. 1/4/2007 in Pittsburg; Nikolai Kushev and Ivanka Rusinova

LABRIE,
Steven Robert, d. 12/17/1998 in Pittsburg; Robert A. Labrie and Beverly A. Courchene

LACHANCE,
Andrew, d. 9/23/1939 at 55 in Pittsburg; fractured skull; single
Henry Joseph, d. 9/25/1992 in Hartford, VT; Omer Joseph Lachance and Mary Paquette
Sylvia, d. 8/22/2001 in Colebrook; Norman Robie and Alice Washburn

LAFOE,
Lemuel, d. 12/1/1923
Susan, d. 7/16/1919

LAGASSIE,
Emmerlin, d. 8/13/1905 at 0/5
George A., d. 8/24/1905 at 0/5/11

LAMBERT,
Donald Corliss, d. 8/14/1972 at 75 in Pittsburg; married
George, d. 11/1/2006 in Epsom; George Lambert and Sadie
    Abbott
Laurent, d. 1/7/1991 in Pittsburg

LAMONTAGNE,
Daniel Mario, d. 5/16/1993 in Pittsburg; Robert G. Lamontagne
    and Raymonde Mercier

LAMPMAN,
Clair J., d. 3/20/1988 in Colebrook

LANCTOT,
Aline F., d. 2/12/1983 in Pittsburg
Raymonde, d. 9/11/1989 in Littleton

LAND,
W. J., d. 10/17/1918

LANDRY,
Helen, d. 10/24/1999 in Colebrook; David Zinick and Fanny
    Solomon
Wilfred, d. 10/9/1918

LANE,
Nye W., d. 5/5/1997 in Colebrook; James Lane and Sybil
    Gatchell

LANGLOIS,
Alton Fred, d. 9/15/1940 at 51/0/16 in Pittsburg; married

LANK,
Robert, d. 7/4/2005 in Colebrook; Walter Lank and Ann Follis

LANSCOTT,
Lawrence, d. 7/21/1925

LAPEARLE,
infant, d. 2/--/1917

LAPELLE,
Philip, d. 4/15/1914 at 3

LAPERLE,
infant, d. 5/10/1919
Pauline, d. 12/13/1928

LAPOINT,
Richard, d. 6/10/1978 at 58 in Stratford; divorced; b. NH

LAPOINTE,
Edith, d. 12/10/1981 in W. Stewartstown
Ernest Henry, d. 2/11/1964 at 72 in Milford; married

LAROCHELLE,
J. Hubert, d. 11/9/1962 at 53 in Pittsburg; married

LATENDRESSE,
Claude, d. 9/15/1987 in Pittsburg

LATUCKY,
Shauna Margaret, d. 3/29/1995 in Lebanon; James Mitchell and Margaret Stevenson

LAUGHTON,
Herbert J., d. 9/13/1969 at 16 in W. Stewartstown; never married
Nella, d. 1/10/1977 at 47 in W. Stewartstown; divorced; b. NH

LAURIE,
Harriet J., d. 11/8/2003 in W. Stewartstown; Ulysses Gardner
    and Arlene Boyd
Wesley, d. 8/14/2007 in Lebanon; Forrest Laurie and Frances
    Lamb

LAVALEY,
Nathan, d. 5/17/1944 at 67/2/1 in Pittsburg; widower

LAVELLETTE,
Mrs. Elmire E., d. 6/9/1931

LAWRENCE,
Louis, d. 12/29/1906 at 0/3/20

LEARY,
Lila M., d. 5/28/1976 at 67 in Pittsburg; married; b. MA

LEAVITT,
Claude W., d. 8/25/1907 at 26/3/12
Elizabeth MacKay, d. 2/8/1997 in Colebrook; George MacKay
    and Mazie Rhodes

LECLARE,
Edith, d. 11/1/1922

LEFERLE,
Anna, d. 8/12/1909 at 0/1/1

LEIGH,
Lester Covill, d. 8/3/1997 in Pittsburg; Lester Robert Leigh and Virginia Mae Covill

LEPPANEN,
Rosemarie, d. 9/11/2001 in Lebanon; Ralph Wilson and Eleanor Bierwith

LESTAGE,
Fredony, d. 12/19/1963 at 61 in Concord; single

LEVESQUE,
Nelson Henry, d. 7/21/1960 at 19 in Pittsburg; single
Theophile, d. 3/3/1942 at 27/5/10 in W. Stewartstown; married

LEVILLETTE,
William J., d. 12/14/1922

LIEBMAN,
Charles, d. 5/2/1976 at 80 in Fort Myers, FL; married; b. CT

LINCOLN,
James, d. 9/21/2007 in Colebrook; Charles Lincoln and Ruth McDonald
Ruth, d. 2/16/2007 in Hooksett; John Shackleton and Alice Hawes

LOCKE,
Guy E., d. 8/25/1964 at 60 in Pittsburg; married

LORD,
infant, d. 4/5/1919
Alfred R., d. 3/9/1945 at 19/11/0 in Germany; single
Allen C., d. 4/5/1953 at 78/8/3 in Pittsburg; divorced
Austin Philip, d. 11/21/1961 at 54 in Clarksville; married

Charles H., d. 5/3/1978 at 86 in Pittsburg; married; b. Canada
Charlotte E., d. 10/10/1941 at 77/1/8 in Pittsburg; married
Earl W., d. 6/8/1967 at 50 in Pittsburg; divorced
Edith E., d. 11/4/1953 at 75/5/18 in Pittsburg; married
Ella M., d. 12/17/1979 in Stewartstown; Andrew Currier and Martha Shoppe
Henry Charles, d. 3/20/1961 at 72 in W. Stewartstown; married
Henry Scott, d. 11/11/1943 at 92/5/22 in Pittsburg; widower
Kate, d. 12/19/1987 in Colebrook
Leslie George, d. 8/19/1997 in Colebrook; Lester Lord and Helen Cahill
Lester H., d. 1/9/1983 in Pittsburg
Mabel, d. 1/16/1978 at 75 in Colebrook; widow; b. NH
Mary C., d. 6/3/1932 at 76/11/5
Otis H., d. 3/27/1916
William E., d. 1/26/2003 in W. Stewartstown; William Lord and Edith Gray
William Henry, d. 10/4/1965 at 91 in W. Stewartstown; widower

LOYND,
John Walter, d. 10/31/1982 in Pittsburg

LUCHON,
John F., d. 10/20/1918

LUPINSKI,
Barbara, d. 1/10/2007 in Lebanon; Francis Lupinski and Tesse Uzarski

LUTHER,
son of John, d. 6/28/1912
Jessie M., d. 5/4/1919
John A., d. 4/16/1939 at 66/0/14 in Pittsburg; acute indigestion; widower
Sidney, d. 12/7/1955 at 85 in W. Stewartstown; widower

William G., d. 7/23/1912

LUTZ,
Harold J., d. 4/24/1988 in Pittsburg

LYFORD,
Kate, d. 11/4/1928
Sylvester, d. 2/24/1923

MAHONEY,
Damien, d. 1/8/2005 in Pittsburg; Thomas Mahoney and Helen Farrell

MAHURIN,
Ida Coty, d. 8/24/1956 at 85 in Colebrook; widow

MAILLET,
Harold E., d. 7/9/1957 at 63 in Lancaster; married

MANDIGO,
Arthur A., Rev., d. 1/10/1943 at 60/10/25 in Pittsburg; married

MANK,
Martha Eleanor, d. 9/9/1989 in Hanover

MARCHAND,
Richard J., d. 5/24/1975 at 23 in Pittsburg; never married; b. NH

MAREOW,
Margaret, d. 10/10/1916

MARQUIS,
Edith, d. 7/21/1998 in Colebrook; Adrien Maurais and Marie Anna Paquette

Leon P., d. 3/19/1997 in Lebanon; George Marquis and Amanda Fortin

MARSH,
Bruce Allen, d. 5/15/1952 at 0/0/22 in W. Stewartstown
Clara, d. 4/5/1915 at 63
Elwin J., d. 11/24/1951 at 73/6/18 in Pittsburg; widower
Ethel Jean, d. 12/22/1943 at 0/4/2 in Pittsburg; single
George A., d. 10/11/1939 at 50/1/19 in Pittsburg; bronchial pneumonia; single
Mable G., d. 1/5/1981 in Colebrook
Pauline, d. 6/6/1976 at 54 in Lancaster; married; b. NH
Robert J., d. 2/7/1967 at 80 in Lancaster; divorced
Samuel Leroy, d. 1/25/1960 at 68 in N. Stratford; married
Wilfred John, d. 5/21/1957 at 42 in Pittsburg; single

MASTERS,
infant, d. 9/30/1923
daughter, d. 4/23/1944 at 0/0/0 in W. Stewartstown
Ambrose S., d. 1/9/1996 in Stewartstown; William Masters and Cecile Draper
Bruce Elliott, d. 5/28/1969 at 6 in Pittsburg; never married
Florence F., d. 1/5/1961 at 54 in W. Stewartstown; married
Leland R., d. 4/27/1997 in Colebrook; William Masters and Celia Draper
Maude, d. 5/27/1983 in Pittsburg
Peter Corey, d. 11/20/1999 in Pittsburg; Russell Masters and Verna Hall
Russell E., d. 9/28/1990 in Colebrook
Vena Harriman, d. 12/5/1956 at 66 in Pittsburg; married
Vena McKeage, d. 7/24/1970 at 65 in W. Stewartstown; widow
Weldon, d. 12/28/1968 at 72 in Hanover; married
William, d. 9/26/1922
William Allen, d. 11/4/1915 at 21

MATKOVICH,
John, d. 11/12/1918

MATTON,
Gene, d. 11/2/1963 at 25 in Pittsburg; married

MAYBERRY,
Willie, d. 8/22/1941 at 57/3/9 in Pittsburg; single

McCANNON,
William, d. 10/2/2005 in Colebrook; Joseph McCannon and
 Darlene Williams

McCOMISKEY,
Tammy Sue, d. 12/28/1966 at --; stillborn; b. W. Stewartstown
Walter G., d. 8/31/1987 in Pittsburg

McCUTCHEON,
William, d. 3/3/1922

McKEAGE,
George W., d. 5/15/1963 at 65 in Oakland, ME; single
Iris, d. 10/4/1918
Ivo, Jr., d. 8/18/1930
Ivo R., d. 2/18/1960 at 62 in Pittsburg; married
James G., d. 4/30/1924
Lewis, d. 1/6/1933 at 30/1/24; single
Robert, d. 5/20/1947 at 77/7/25 in Colebrook; divorced
William H., d. 7/28/1936 at 77/1/11; mitral regurgitation; widower

McLAUGHLIN,
infant, d. 6/21/1917

McLEOD,
Byron S., d. 6/11/1971 at 87 in Concord; single

McQUEENEY,
Sean F., d. 12/10/2000 in Colebrook; Francis McQueeney and
 Dorothy Lavallee

MELKONIAN,
Sam, d. 6/10/1984 in Pittsburg

MERRILL,
Caroline A., d. 1/25/1911 at 84
Cecil, d. 1/25/1908 at 0/2
Charles, d. 4/6/1936 at 72/7/4; broncho pneumonia; divorced
David P., d. 8/25/1922
Fay Charles, d. 5/31/1966 at 70 in W. Stewartstown; divorced
Margaret Sarah, d. 2/20/1959 at 56 in Pittsburg; married
Monica, d. 12/14/1988 in Colebrook
Richard Earl, d. 1/17/1955 at 0/0/8 in W. Stewartstown
Ruth Ida, d. 12/27/1977 at 56 in Lebanon, CT; married; b. NH
Willie Gerald, d. 2/15/1966 at 65 in Pittsburg; widower

MEUNIER,
Francis X. M., d. 8/14/1962 at 53 in Pittsburg; married

MILLER,
Eva Bulmer, d. 4/5/1971 at 80 in Colebrook; widow

MILLS,
Ora, d. 4/5/1932 at 47/4/14

MITCHELL,
Donald, Jr., d. 11/20/2008 in Pittsburg; Donald Mitchell, Sr. and
 Cornelia Ahearne

MOORE,
daughter, d. 10/10/1960 at 25 min. in W. Stewartstown

MORRISON,
Everett A., d. 11/3/1972 at 68 in Pittsburg; married

MORSE,
Shawn R., d. 10/6/2001 in Concord; Doug Morse and Wendy Berkoski

MOUSSEAU,
infant, d. 1/23/1917
Anna, d. 10/28/1939 at 67/10/17 in Pittsburg; pernicious anemia; married
Atlee B., d. 9/30/1971 at 80 in Pittsburg; widower
Katherine, d. 10/11/2004 in Nashua; Karl Smith and Alice Keyser
Keane Arlene, d. 12/27/1995 in Pittsburg; Atlee Mousseau and Monica Rene Covell
Pierre Alex, d. 4/29/1946 at 90/10/28 in Colebrook; widower

MURPHY,
Edward, d. 12/3/1941 at 51/4/2 in Pittsburg; married

NORTHCOTT,
Oliver, d. 9/6/2005 in Lebanon; Henry Northcott and Mary Freake

NOYES,
George Allen, d. 12/1/1944 at 46/9/12 in Pittsburg; married
Howard, d. 1/15/1981 in Colebrook
Ira A., d. 8/29/1950 at 65/4/4 in Pittsburg; married
Lawrence R., d. 5/1/1999 in Colebrook; George Noyes and Lela Brockney

NUTTING,
Bert, d. 5/2/1944 at 78/0/15 in Concord; single
Willie J., d. 10/22/1940 at 78/2/28 in W. Stewartstown; widower

O'BRIEN,
Camilla Emilie, d. 12/9/1997 in Pittsburg

O'HARE,
Alice May, d. 10/1/1965 at 83 in Pittsburg; widow

O'NEIL,
Wayne V., d. 3/--/1951 at 25/10/22 in N. Stratford; married

OAKES,
Charles, d. 5/2/1954 at 77 in Manchester; married

ORMSBEE,
Nina, d. 7/17/1957 at 67 in Hanover; divorced
Willard O., d. 1/25/1944 at 28/3/27 in Salt Lick Loop, OH;
   married

OSGOOD,
Minnie, d. 5/3/1941 at 77/5/2 in Berlin; divorced
William, d. 10/27/1938 at 66/7/8 in Pittsburg; acute indigestion;
   married

OWEAND,
Odlong, d. 9/5/1906 at 1/6 in Hereford, PQ

OWEN,
Connie Ruth, d. 10/1/1965 at 8 hrs. in W. Stewartstown
Edwin Ralph, d. 3/10/1962 at 10 hrs. in W. Stewartstown

PAGE,
Frederick Seaward, d. 6/24/1993 in Pittsburg; William F. Page
   and Bertha E. Seaward

PAPINEAU,
Harriet F., d. 3/30/2000 in W. Stewartstown; Reuben Fuller and Florence Bunnell

PAPUCKA,
Anthony, d. 10/16/1943 at 58/5/0 in Pittsburg; single

PAQUETTE,
Jean Baptiste, d. 12/10/1941 at 85/6/0 in Pittsburg; widower
Rene, d. 12/14/1991 in Pittsburg

PARISEAU,
David, d. 2/5/1995 in Colebrook; Theodore Pariseau and Denise Laperle

PARKER,
Geraldine N., d. 2/2/2002 in Pittsburg; Clyde Curtis and Madeline Buck
Harley Luther, Sr., d. 5/29/1998 in Lancaster; Edwin Parker and Ida Libby

PARKHURST,
Earle, d. 5/10/1927

PARKS,
Charles H., d. 11/9/1930
Iva Belle Blodgett, d. 7/7/1957 at 94 in Pittsburg; widow

PARSONS,
Hattie, Mrs., d. 10/10/1907 at 23/7

PAUSHA,
Joseph J., d. 11/26/1989 in Pittsburg

PEARSON,
Ernest Franklin, d. 6/26/1959 at 76 in Franklin; married

PEARSONS,
Samuel E., d. 4/16/1957 at 73 in Concord; married
Zella L., d. 12/24/1911 at 0/11

PELLERIN,
Leonard Arthur, d. 7/22/1979 in Hartford, VT; Arthur Pellerin and Nora Menard

PELOQUIN,
Raymond M., d. 5/24/1975 at 24 in Pittsburg; married; b. NH

PEPEIN,
infant child of Joe, d. 9/20/1915; stillborn

PERAULT,
Joseph Francis, d. 9/6/1944 at 65/11/21 in Pittsburg; widower

PERKINS,
Philip Arnold, d. 12/26/1989 in Pittsburg

PERRON,
Brandon J., d. 8/30/1989 in Colebrook
Peter E., d. 6/28/1980 in Pittsburg

PERRY,
Charles L., d. 3/27/1907 at 58
Jamon, d. 11/12/1926
William C., d. 10/27/1953 at 89 in W. Peru, ME; widower

PERSON,
Marion, d. 10/30/1968 at 86 in Boscawen; widow

PHILBROOK,
Harriet M., d. 4/9/1941 at 53/11/20 in Stewartstown; widow
Leone P., d. 9/30/1976 at 58 in Hanover; married; b. NH

PHILLIPS,
Gladys Lea, d. 10/25/1957 at 66 in W. Stewartstown; widow
Homer, d. 10/16/1938 at 44/5/0 in W. Stewartstown; lobar pneumonia; married

PICKERING,
Saima E., d. 12/27/1999 in Colebrook; Lauri Nisinen and Hilda Manninen

PIERCE,
Brenda Jean, d. 8/24/1973 at 13 in Colebrook; single; b. NH

PIGEON,
Ernest, d. 8/17/1951 at 70/8 in Pittsburg; married

PIPER,
Priscilla Irlene, d. 2/21/1994 in Colebrook; Carl Tewksbury and Dorothy Whitney

POND,
Bremer, d. 9/2/1959 at 75 in Hanover; single

PONZEK,
Edward J., d. 4/23/1981 in Colebrook

PORTER,
Clyde H., d. 11/9/1997 in Pittsburg; Clyde O. Porter and Jean C. Gallant

POTTER,
Emma Cordelia, d. 3/2/1948 at 75/2/29 in W. Stewartstown; married
Lavona, d. 5/29/1949 at 31/4/24 in Colebrook; married

PREHEMO,
Carlene, d. 1/11/1994 in Colebrook; Henry Rodrique and Regena Hicks
Gale, d. 19/1987 in Colebrook

PRESCOTT,
Edith, d. 5/9/1953 at 58 in Hanover; married
Frank Elwood, d. 2/13/1954 at 72 in W. Stewartstown; widower

PUTNAM,
Rita S., d. 1/4/1982 in Pittsburg

QUIMBY,
Almeda N., d. 12/20/1961 at 61 in Stratford; divorced
Nancy, d. 7/17/1924

RANCLOES,
Francis George, d. 12/7/1966 at 70 in Pittsburg; married
Lottie Young, d. 7/14/1971 at 78 in Colebrook; widow
Thomas, d. 3/30/1992 in W. Stewartstown

RAY,
Lewis C., d. 12/22/1974 at 43 in Colebrook; married; b. WV

RAYMOND,
Jacqueline, d. 9/23/1953 at 0/0/1 in W. Stewartstown

REED,
Emily E., d. 12/23/1908 at 65

REYNOLDS,
Carl R., d. 7/9/1950 at 57/9/22 in Windsor; divorced
Dolena Anne M., d. 6/4/1946 at 70/7/29 in Pittsburg; married
Frederick L., d. 1/1/1947 at 67/10/3 in Falmouth, ME; married
Hortense M., d. 1/9/1980 in Hanover
Maynard W., d. 6/16/1947 at 64/5/15 in Pittsburg; married

RICH,
Carrie F., d. 7/5/1938 at 45/11/23 in Guildhall, VT; suicidal drowning; married

RICHARDS,
Bond Charles, d. 7/9/1957 at 66 in W. Stewartstown; single
Eliza, d. 2/1/1927
Fred, d. 9/1/1936 at 66/5/4; apoplexy; married
Sophia, d. 1/11/1913 at 74

RIDEOUT,
Mary E., d. 8/26/1908 at 0/3

RILEY,
John H., Sr., d. 5/27/1997 in Manchester; Joseph Riley and Angie Welch

ROBBINS,
Carolyn, d. 7/2/2007 in Colebrook; Herbert Walker and Mary Pratt
Charles, d. 3/30/2004 in Colebrook; Charles Robbins and Annie Brunette
Ray Edward, d. 1/10/1938 at 0/10/3 in Pittsburg; leaking of cerebrospinal fluid

ROBIE,
son, d. 8/1/1956 at 0/0/0 in W. Stewartstown
Alice M., d. 10/2/1978 at 97 in W. Stewartstown; widow; b. NH

Charles W., d. 4/20/1916
Ezra, d. 7/2/1968 at 70 in N. Stratford; widower
Gerald Marvin, d. 7/18/1945 at 42/8/16 in Pittsburg; married
Lena Wilhamina, d. 4/6/1954 at 55/7/28 in N. Stratford; widow
Moses S., d. 8/6/1953 at 46 in Hartford, VT; divorced
Mrs. Joseph, d. 4/9/1920
Norman, d. 9/12/1964 at 92 in Pittsburg; married
Norman I., d. 12/19/1925
Wilma J., d. 4/3/1991 in Concord

ROBILLARD,
Francis, d. 4/1/1993 in Nashua; Joseph Robillard and Louise Wright

ROBINSON,
Eric J., d. 7/25/2000 in Colebrook; Julian Robinson and Elsey Gibbons
Evelyn M., d. 5/20/2002 in Lebanon; Joseph Belion and Orise Beddard
Francine, d. 8/10/1953 at 0/0/3 in W. Stewartstown
Gerard, d. 8/8/1953 at 0/0/1 in W. Stewartstown

ROBY,
Addie, d. 10/7/1905 at 52
Emma A., d. 3/6/1910 at 59
Gloria Beverly, d. 2/1/1933 at 4/3/27; single
Hial, d. 6/16/1972 at 71 in Jefferson; widower
Ida, d. 8/13/1914
Mabelle Davis, d. 1/26/1934 at --; married

RODRIQUE,
Henry, d. 2/17/2007 in Colebrook; Joseph Rodrique and Mary Roy
Shirley May, d. 8/7/1956 at 0/3/16 in Lancaster

ROGERS,
Gloria, d. 10/9/1979 in Columbia; Samuel J. Washburn and Edith Brown

ROIX,
Phebe, d. 9/13/2004 in Colebrook; John Adams and Cordie Cox

ROUSSEAU,
infant child of Louis, d. 9/21/1915

ROWELL,
James R., d. 4/3/1931
Peggy Lee, d. 3/30/1976 at 14 hrs. in Concord; b. NH
Viola, d. 5/27/1936 at 16/6/15; acute nephritis; single

ROY,
Carol, d. 3/28/2005 in Colebrook; Joseph O'Brien and Eugenia Gardner
Vincent E., d. 11/28/1980 in Hanover
Wilbrod, d. 10/17/1994 in Stewartstown; Henri Roy and Georgine Plante

ROYAL,
Alyne, d. 1/2/2005 in Colebrook; Edward Sylvester and Mary Rita Groves

SANBOURN,
Rebecca, Mrs., d. 10/2/1921

SARAZIN,
Aime J., d. 7/25/1989 in Pittsburg

SARGENT,
Frank, d. 6/10/1914 at 65
Lester O., d. 6/19/1983 in Colebrook

SAVAGEAU,
Paul, d. 9/20/1986 in Pittsburg

SAWYER,
Carma F., d. 7/9/1991 in Colebrook

SCHOFF,
infant of Mr. and Mrs., d. 1/16/1905
Edwin A., d. 10/25/1917
Hattie Amelia, d. 1/9/1953 at 79/11/8 in W. Stewartstown; widow
Hiram B., d. 1/31/1905 at 82
Lizzie A., d. 6/20/1975 at 87 in Stewartstown; widow; b. NH
Lord Raymond, d. 8/27/1905 at 0/8/9
Loren, d. 5/2/1907 at 0/4/9
Perley R., d. 6/6/1948 at 67/3/26 in Pittsburg; married
Winnifred B., d. 4/28/1965 at 65 in Biddeford, ME; married

SCHOPPEE,
Herman H., d. 4/8/1951 at 71/3/11 in Colebrook; divorced

SCHROEDER,
Charles, d. 10/11/1918

SCOTT,
infant child of Rod, d. 8/18/1915
Annie, d. 11/9/1941 at 73/11/17 in Pittsburg; widow
Arthur, d. 3/7/1961 at 66 in Pittsburg; married
Austin Henry, d. 9/5/1968 at 78 in W. Stewartstown; married
Charles E., d. 5/21/1904 at 71/10/21
Edward, d. 12/7/1930
Emma Stover, d. 6/1/1965 at 61 in W. Stewartstown; married
Fred Thomas, d. 3/30/1970 at 77 in Pittsburg; married
George Carroll, d. 4/14/1954 at 58/2/20 in Pittsburg; widower
Gilbert, d. 1/25/1942 at 76/3/3 in Pittsburg; married

Harry F., d. 4/20/1987 in Stewartstown
Iva Ethel, d. 11/27/1996 in Colebrook; Harvey Day and Martha
    Shallow
Lena, d. 3/26/1992 in W. Stewartstown
Mary Ellen, d. 10/1/1965 at 82 in Pittsburg; widow
Nellie Rae, d. 3/5/1983 in Colebrook
Rachel Cairns, d. 8/13/1960 at 91 in Pittsburg; widow
Roderick, d. 1/28/1926
Sarah, d. 11/7/1904 at 74
Simeon, d. 1/3/1923
Victor Cairns, d. 12/24/1959 at 62 in Pittsburg; single
Willard, d. 12/10/1987 in Pittsburg

SHAFER,
Lorraine J., d. 1/6/1998 in Berlin, VT; George Stanhope and
    Fannie Corey

SHALLOW,
James, d. 10/5/1942 at 64/2/4 in Pittsburg; married
Lizzie Day, d. 2/12/1966 at 79 in W. Stewartstown; widow
Phillip C., d. 3/17/2003 in Colebrook; Clyde Shallow and
    Catherine Riley

SHANNON,
Vern, d. 7/28/2005 in Colebrook; Otis Shannon and Sylvia
    Strawn

SHATNEY,
infant son of Mr. and Mrs. D., d. 9/11/1905 at 0/3
Anita, d. 4/17/1985 in Colebrook
Avis M., d. 11/25/1975 at 76 in Hanover; widow; b. NH

SHIELDS,
John M., d. 5/16/1982 in Pittsburg

SMALL,
Harvey, d. 10/17/1918

SMITH,
Donald M., d. 10/4/1981 in Pittsburg
John, d. 4/8/1918
John D., d. 2/27/1904 at 73
Myrtie, d. 4/30/1954 at 84 in W. Stewartstown; widow
Patricia June, d. 2/6/1997 in Colebrook; Atlee Burpee Mousseau
    and Fern Marrian Covill
Peter, d. 10/2/1918
William A., d. 11/16/1910 at 71

SPRAGUE,
Helen, d. 5/23/2008 in W. Stewartstown; Louis Pfanstiebl and
    Nellie James

STANDARD,
Clarence, d. 11/5/1937 at 35/3/19 in Pittsburg; angina pectoris;
    married

STANLEY,
Theresa M., d. 5/26/1985 in Pittsburg

STANTON,
Addie M., d. 3/24/1937 at 61/10/29 in Stewartstown; aortic
    stenosis; married
John Clark, d. 12/9/1941 at 77/5/9 in W. Stewartstown; widower

STEBBINS,
Richard M., Sr., d. 1/22/1990 in Pittsburg

STEVENS,
Harry, d. 5/19/1961 at 73 in W. Stewartstown; widower

STILES,
Blair W., d. 10/7/1989 in Pittsburg
Wallace Guy, d. 2/21/1983 in Manchester

STODDARD,
Doris Maker, d. 8/8/1967 at 67 in W. Stewartstown; married
Oral Erwin, d. 11/23/1972 at 76 in W. Stewartstown; widower

STOLL,
James Rodney, d. 1/31/1978 at 32 in Pittsburg; married; b. CT

STONE,
Grace Phyliss, d. 4/16/1993 in Pittsburg; Alfred Kershaw and
    Ethel Wayhill
Wilfred, d. 7/22/1971 at 71 in Pittsburg; married

STOVER,
infant, d. 3/27/1929

STRAW,
Irene, d. 1/28/2005 in W. Stewartstown; Frank Hann and Martha
    Ellingwood
Merton Vaughn, d. 3/18/1989 in Colebrook

STURGIS,
Ethel S., d. 1/8/1980 in Lancaster

SUMBERY,
Samuel L., d. 10/20/1904 at 66/10

SWAIN,
Henry G., d. 9/3/1947 at 82/0/5 in W. Stewartstown; widower

SWEENEY,
John Vincent, Jr., d. 3/13/1993 in Pittsburg; John Vincent
    Sweeney, Sr. and Margaret McGrath
Julius, d. 9/12/1991 in Pittsburg

SWEET,
Helen Williams, d. 6/28/1967 at 54 in Pittsburg; married

TABOR,
Nina W., d. 11/23/1985 in Colebrook
Parker Wilson, d. 10/30/1949 at 65/2/29 in Pittsburg; married
Richard A., d. 4/18/1909 at 61
Sarah J., d. 4/10/1933 at 80/7/20; widow

TAYLOR,
Julia, d. 6/7/1922

TERRILL,
Addison, d. 2/14/1910 at 65
Artie, d. 10/28/1950 at 53/3/21 in Concord; single
Henry, d. 9/25/1917
Lillian A., d. 2/3/1961 at 71 in Laconia; single
Lillian Cilley, d. 11/8/1964 at 55 in Colebrook; divorced
Pearley Albertm, d. 3/5/1967 at 75 in Manchester; married
Whitcomb, d. 2/7/1910 at 60

THIBAULT,
Exilia, d. 3/4/1927
Mrs. Veleda, d. 3/15/1931

THIBEAULT,
Claude J., d. 8/4/1963 at 9 hrs. in W. Stewartstown
Elvina, d. 2/6/1937 at 30/7/22 in Pittsburg; pulmonary
    tuberculosis; single

Herminise C., d. 4/22/1939 at 65/4/16 in Pittsburg; apoplexy; widow
Joseph F., d. 8/3/1980 in Colebrook
May F., d. 3/24/1982 in Colebrook
Raymond, d. 8/8/2005 in Lebanon; Joseph Thibeault and Rose Ida Marquis
Rose-Ida, d. 1/26/1991 in Colebrook

THOMAS,
William Robert, d. 9/3/1969 at 72 in Pittsburg; married

THOMPSON,
Eva Huggins, d. 1/22/1958 at 84 in W. Stewartstown; married
Joseph, d. 12/16/1904 at 72

TILLOTSON,
Elizabeth, d. 5/7/1909 at 7

TIRRELL,
Harvey, d. 6/8/1915

TOWLE,
infant, d. 1/26/1955 at 0/0/0 in W. Stewartstown
Charles William, d. 1/28/1956 at 92/1/3 in Colebrook; widower
Edward A., d. 3/30/1944 at 53/0/3 in Berlin; married
Frederick King, d. 6/22/1928
Luke, d. 4/1/1949 at 82/2/5 in W. Stewartstown; married
Maria, d. 5/31/1950 at 87/8/4 in Concord; widow
Thomas, d. 6/17/1956 at 51 in Colebrook; married

TOWNE,
George, d. 12/11/1915 at 51

TREMBLAY,
Ernest, d. 9/4/2005 in Colebrook; Ernest Tremblay and Yvonne Gentes

TRESHINSKY,
Edward, d. 5/31/1980 in Pittsburg

TURNER,
Frances, d. 3/14/2005 in Colebrook; Charles Fletcher and Doris Peters
George Washington, d. 9/24/1954 at 60 in W. Stewartstown; married
Nellie A., d. 1/16/1958 at 62 in W. Stewartstown; widow

TWOMBLY,
Sherman E., d. 9/27/2003 in Colebrook; Willis Twombly and Rachel Seavey

URAN,
Frank, d. 12/8/1974 at 54 in Colebrook; married; b. NH

VALHOS,
Arthur, d. 2/3/2003 in Colebrook; Nicholas Valhos and Vascilacho Scopetti

vonDOHRMANN,
Elizabeth, d. 9/19/2004 in Colebrook; Frederick Taeger and Kathleen Byrne

WALDRON,
Lucy, d. 7/20/1942 at 69/3/12 in Pittsburg; married

WARE,
Leon Edward, d. 7/24/2001 in Pittsburg; Arthur J. Ware and Jessica McGuiness

WASHBURN,
Alice Ruene, d. 11/28/1986 in Pittsburg
Edith M., d. 9/8/1984 in Stewartstown
Eunice, d. 10/9/1979 in Columbia; Harry Fiske and Blanche Hall
Joseph A., d. 2/26/1911 at 55
Kenneth Roger, d. 11/3/1992 in Lebanon
Reuben Gould, d. 10/2/1995 in Pittsburg; Samuel Washburn and
    Edith Brown
Samuel, d. 1/13/1930
Thomas G., d. 2/27/1935 at 63/5/13; married
William Henry, d. 1/12/1957 at 39 in Pittsburg; married
Willis Edward, d. 1/21/1998 in Colebrook; Samuel Washburn and
    Edith Brown

WATERHOUSE,
Gary E., d. 9/8/1968 at 36 in Pittsburg; married

WEBSTER,
Barbara R., d. 1/1/1986 in Colebrook

WESCOTT,
Beatrice, d. 7/21/1981 in Colebrook

WHEELER,
twins, d. 7/23/1919
Bessie, d. 12/28/1906 at 26 in Pittsburg
Clarence, d. 3/20/1932 at 73/3/4
Claudia, d. 10/11/1987 in Quebec, Canada
Donald, d. 3/28/1976 at 36 in Pittsburg; married; b. NH
Doris F., d. 1/5/1950 at 37/1/26 in Pittsburg; married
Elwin, d. 3/28/1947 at 72/6/22 in Pittsburg; single
Frank, d. 9/22/1923
Jubel, d. 6/23/1946 at 74/0/11 in W. Stewartstown; widower
Lillian, d. 5/19/1926

Linden, d. 7/24/1990 in Stewartstown
Mildred, d. 4/2/1920
Raymond, d. 12/4/1973 at 65 in Lancaster; widower; b. NH
Walter, d. 9/24/1988 in Stewartstown

WHITE,
Avis, d. 2/8/1980 in Colebrook

WHITTEN,
Wesley, d. 4/14/2005 in Colebrook; Willis Whitten and Rena
    Woodward

WIBBELT,
William F., d. 9/23/2003 in Lebanon; William Wibbelt and Anna
    Thoren

WILKINSON,
Ann Lamb, d. 4/11/1995 in Lancaster; David Brodie Smith and
    Ann Mason Lamb
William Lee, d. 10/3/1986 in Colebrook

WILLIS,
Ivan, d. 9/3/1939 at 79/11/27 in W. Stewartstown;
    arteriosclerosis; widower
Leslie Joseph, d. 2/23/1959 at 50 in Pittsburg; married
Lillian, Mrs., d. 12/21/1921
Meltiah S., d. 12/16/1906 at 68/3 in Pittsburg

WILSON,
Pauline, d. 11/11/2005 in Colebrook; John Williams and Regis
    Keith

WOOD,
George L., d. 10/18/1947 at 63/0/12 in W. Stewartstown; married
Sadie Owen, d. 10/11/1959 at 70 in Lancaster; widow

WOODWARD,
Ellen E., d. 5/19/1954 at 84 in Concord; widow

WRIGHT,
Flora Wilson, d. 1/25/1955 at 84/9/12 in W. Stewartstown; widow
Jennie, d. 7/29/1954 at 86 in W. Stewartstown; widow
Robert, d. 10/24/1938 at 75/5/22 in Pittsburg; carcinoma of stomach; married
Samuel H., d. 1/13/1964 at 67 in W. Stewartstown; married

YOUNG,
Alice Lucinda, d. 5/2/1993 in Pittsburg; Bert Hall and Alberta Haynes
Alma, d. 11/6/1989 in Stewartstown
Clayton Farnsworth, d. 12/31/1966 at 62 in W. Stewartstown; married
Everett B., d. 4/5/1938 at 60/0/20 in Pittsburg; acute dilatation of heart; married
Florence, d. 6/2/1930
Hazen Noah, d. 3/21/1967 at 74 in W. Stewartstown; widower
Helen M., d. 11/13/2002 in Lebanon; Jesse Young and Florence Whitney
Hilda, d. 11/1/1975 at 48 in Pittsburg; widow; b. NH
Hollis Homer, d. 9/6/1970 at 79 in Colebrook; married
Holman H., d. 5/2/1992 in Boston, MA; Hollis H. Young and Melvina Young
Ivan, d. 1/16/2008 in Colebrook; Stanley Young and Alma Gardner
Ivan Dalbert, d. 10/3/1957 at 79 in Pittsburg; widower
Jesse W., d. 4/17/1945 at 62/10/22 in W. Stewartstown; widower
Leon B., d. 8/16/1974 at 82 in W. Stewartstown; never married
Linnie, d. 11/27/1954 at 76/9/15 in Pittsburg; married
Melvina Isabell, d. 3/24/1971 at 69 in Pittsburg; widow
Muriel Labaree, d. 8/6/1964 at 65 in Pittsburg; married

Phillip L., d. 1/23/2001 in Colebrook; Ivan Young and Linnie Hawes
Richard, d. 12/13/1920
Roy J., d. 5/7/1935 at 58/7/20; widower
Stanley F., d. 8/12/1979 in Colebrook; Ivan Young and Melinda Hawes
Stewart, d. 12/8/1966 at 94 in Hanover; married
William Joshua, d. 11/24/1958 at 44 in W. Stewartstown; married
Woodrow W., d. 1/29/1916

UNKNOWN,
male, d. ca. 2/27/1940 in Pittsburg

Other Heritage Books by Richard P. Roberts:

Alton, New Hampshire Vital Records, 1890–1997

Barnstead, New Hampshire Vital Records, 1887–2000

Barrington, New Hampshire Vital Records

Dover, New Hampshire Death Records, 1887–1937

Gilmanton, New Hampshire Vital Records, 1887–2001

Marriage Records of Dover, New Hampshire, 1835–1909

Marriage Records of Dover, New Hampshire, 1910–1937

Milton, New Hampshire Vital Records, 1888–1999

Moultonborough, New Hampshire Vital Records

New Castle, New Hampshire Vital Records, 1891–1997

New Hampshire Name Changes, 1768–1923

New Hampshire Name Changes, 1923–1947

Ossipee, New Hampshire Vital Records, 1887–2001

Rochester, New Hampshire Death Records, 1887–1951

Vital Records of Durham, New Hampshire, 1887–2002

Vital Records of Effingham and Freedom, New Hampshire, 1888–2001

Vital Records of Farmington, New Hampshire, 1887–1938

Vital Records of Lyme and Dorchester, New Hampshire, 1887–2004

Vital Records of New Durham and Middleton, New Hampshire, 1887–1998

Vital Records of North Berwick, Maine, 1892–2002

Vital Records of Orford and Piermont, New Hampshire, 1887–2004

Vital Records of Pittsburg, New Hampshire, 1904–2008

Vital Records of Tamworth and Albany, New Hampshire, 1887–2003

Vital Records of Tuftonboro and Brookfield, New Hampshire, 1888–2005

Vital Records of Wakefield, New Hampshire, 1887–1998

Vital Records of Warren, New Hampshire, 1887–2005

Wolfeboro, New Hampshire Vital Records, 1887–1999

www.ingramcontent.com/pod-product-compliance
Lightning Source LLC
Chambersburg PA
CBHW060118170426
43198CB00010B/938